Social Interaction and Teacher Cogn

Studies in Social Interaction
Series Editors: Steve Walsh, Paul Seedhouse and Christopher Jenks

Presenting data from a range of social contexts including education, the media, the workplace, and professional development, the *Studies in Social Interaction* series uncovers, among other things, the ways in which tasks are accomplished, identities formed and communities established. Each volume in the series places social interaction at the centre of discussion and presents a clear overview of the work which has been done in a particular context. Books in the series provide examples of how data can be approached and used to uncover social-interaction themes and issues, and explore how research in social interaction can feed into a better understanding of professional practices and develop new research agendas. Through stimulating tasks and accompanying commentaries, readers are engaged and challenged to reflect on particular themes and relate the discussion to their own context.

Series Editors
Steve Walsh is Professor of Applied Linguistics at Newcastle University

Paul Seedhouse is Professor of Educational and Applied Linguistics at Newcastle University

Christopher Jenks is Assistant Professor of English and Intensive English/TESOL Coordinator at the University of South Dakota

Titles available in the series:
Social Interaction in Second Language Chat Rooms   Christopher Jenks
Social Interaction and L2 Classroom Discourse   Olcay Sert

Visit the Studies in Social Interaction website at
http://www.euppublishing.com/series/ssint

Social Interaction and Teacher Cognition

Li Li

EDINBURGH
University Press

Edinburgh University Press is one of the leading university presses in the UK. We publish academic books and journals in our selected subject areas across the humanities and social sciences, combining cutting-edge scholarship with high editorial and production values to produce academic works of lasting importance. For more information visit our website: edinburghuniversitypress.com

© Li Li, 2017

Edinburgh University Press Ltd
The Tun – Holyrood Road
12(2f) Jackson's Entry
Edinburgh EH8 8PJ

Typeset in 10/12 Minion by
Servis Filmsetting Ltd, Stockport, Cheshire,
and printed and bound in Great Britain by
CPI Group (UK) Ltd, Croydon CR0 4YY

A CIP record for this book is available from the British Library

ISBN 978-0-7486-7574-6 (hardback)
ISBN 978-0-7486-7575-3 (paperback)
ISBN 978-0-7486-7576-0 (webready pdf)
ISBN 978-0-7486-7578-4 (epub)

The right of Li Li to be identified as the author of this work has been asserted in accordance with the Copyright, Designs and Patents Act 1988, and the Copyright and Related Rights Regulations 2003 (SI No. 2498).

CONTENTS

List of Abbreviations	vii
Acknowledgements	viii
Introduction	1
Dynamics of EFL Classrooms	5
Structure of the Book	8

Part A: Survey

1 Language Teacher Cognition: An Overview — 13
- The Importance of Teacher Cognition — 13
- The Development of Language Teacher Cognition — 15
- Key Concepts — 20
- Three Theoretical Perspectives — 30
- Summary — 32

2 Approaches to the Study of Teacher Cognition — 34
- Introduction — 34
- Research Approaches — 34
- Methodological Issues — 48
- Summary — 50

3 Teacher Cognition and Interaction — 52
- Introduction — 52
- Cognition and Conversation — 52
- Data Sources and Analysis — 60
- Summary — 70

Part B: Analysis

4 Learning to Teach and Pre-service Teacher Cognition — 75
- Pre-service Teacher Cognition — 75
- Teacher Knowledge and Knowing — 76
- Developing Content Knowledge — 78

	Developing Pedagogical Knowledge	85
	Developing Self as a Teacher	97
	Summary	103
5	Developing Expertise and In-service Teacher Cognition	104
	Introduction	104
	Expert Versus Novice	104
	Distributed and Multiple Expertise	106
	Summary	133
6	Interactive Decision-making and Teacher Cognition	135
	Introduction	135
	Interactive Decision-making	136
	Unpacking Interactive Decisions	137
	Summary	156

Part C: Applications

7	Understanding Pedagogy	161
	Introduction	161
	Understanding Teaching and Learning	162
	Understanding Pedagogical Knowledge and Teaching Methods	163
	Understanding Instructional Practice	166
	Understanding Interactive Decision-making	172
	Summary	174
8	Language Teacher Education	176
	Part 1: Understanding Teacher Learning through Teacher Cognition	177
	Part 2: Implications of Teacher Cognition on Teacher Learning	183
	A Collaborative Dialogic Reflective Practice (CDRP)	187
	Future Directions	190
	Final Remarks	194

Appendix: Transcription Conventions	196
References	198
Index	218

LIST OF ABBREVIATIONS

BAK	beliefs, assumptions and knowledge
BALLI	Beliefs about Language Learning Inventory
CA	conversation analysis
CALL	computer-assisted language learning
CDRP	collaborative dialogic reflective practice
CELTA	Certificate in Teaching English Language to Adults
CIC	classroom interactional competence
CLT	communicative language teaching
DP	discursive psychology
EFL	English as a Foreign Language
ESL	English as a Second Language
IDRF	Initiation-Dialogic space-Response-Feedback
ITRF	Initiation-Thinking space-Response-Feedback
IRF	Initiation-Response-Feedback
LPCs	lesson planning conferences
LOTE	Languages Other than English
L2	second language
SCT	sequence-closing third
SLA	second language acquisition
SLTE	second language teacher education
TBLT	task-based language teaching
TESL	Teaching English as a Second Language
TESOL	Teaching English to Speakers of Other Languages

ACKNOWLEDGEMENTS

The following figures are reproduced with permissions.

Figure 1.1 Clark and Peterson's model of teachers' thought process and action (1986: 257). From Wittrock, *Handbook of research on teaching*, 3E. © 1986 Gale, a part of Cengage Learning, Inc. Reproduced by permission. www.cengage.com/permissions

Figure 1.2 Elements and processes in language teacher cognition (Borg 2006: 283) © Simon Borg (2006), *Teacher cognition and language education: research and practice*, Continuum Publishing, by permission of Bloomsbury Publishing Plc.

INTRODUCTION

(Y=Yuan; S=Student)

```
1   Y    ((clapping his hands))Ok!
2        (5.0)
3        can some group give some information of how er (.)
4        English Christmas(.) and er (.)what is your discussion
5        if possible (2.0)
6        NAME what about you?
7        (10.0)
8   S    en (.) [((3 unintelligent))
9   Y           [Sorry? I can't hear you, louder please... they
10       all have a very what?=
11  S    =a delicious food=
12  Y    =oh delicious dinner right? £yes yes I am sure£ (2.0)
13       on Christmas Eve, or er on Christmas Day?=
14  S    =Christmas eve=
15  Y    =on Christmas Eve? possible...what else? thank you.
```

This is an English classroom in a Chinese secondary school, where a teacher is teaching a lesson on 'how English people celebrate Christmas'. Examine the extract, what can you learn about this teacher's beliefs/thinking about language teaching?

> From this extract, I can clearly tell Yuan's intention to create space for students' contributions to the dialogue. The use of rather long pauses at lines 5, 7 and 12 indicates the intention to allow students space to formulate a response and possibly rehearse it before speaking. This is particularly important for EFL classrooms where students have fewer opportunities to practice oral English, and when there is, students usually feel embarrassed to speak publicly (Li 2011). The value of learner contribution may also have a discursive explanation when we look at the way Yuan's questions were positioning the learners through the analysis of conversation analysis (CA) construct, an adjacency pair. At lines 3-4, the first pair part invites some information about English Christmas as the expected second part. Yet, before an appropriate second part was delivered,

Yuan produces another first pair part, which positions the responders rather differently, this time as a reporter of the group topics rather than an informant of 'how English people celebrate Christmas'. The teacher's questions here can be interpreted as a genuine request or 'pre-announcement' (Terasaki, 2005). After a rather long silence, Yuan nominates a speaker, who responds with a second pair part to Yuan's second first pair part – she mentions 'food' (line 11), as what the group discussed. After another long (2 s) pause at line 12, Yuan again changes the positioning of the respondents in a new first pair part, this time projecting as conditionally relevant a second pair part containing information of 'when' to have this 'delicious food' to help the student offer greater precision in her response, which she does in line 14. Closer examination of the student's responses suggests that she tries to limit the chance of making mistakes by providing minimum input (line 11). Yuan follows up with further questions to expand contribution opportunities. It is possible that this strategy succeeds in generating more student talk. This extract displays Yuan's understanding about teaching and the role of learners: learning takes place in interaction and students should actively contribute to the class. Yuan provides students with opportunities to engage in a conversation and this is evidenced throughout the extract by different interactional strategies employed. For example, he seeks clarification in line 9 to ensure that the whole class is able to understand this contribution and to maintain the flow of the interaction, provides an embedded correction by rephrasing it as 'delicious dinner' (line 12) and uses indirect feedback to avoid possible tension (line 15). Yuan also positions himself differently, as an organizer (line 3) and a converser (lines 9, 13) whereas his authoritative role is minimal.

A number of other things can be observed from this extract, but here I'd like to specifically emphasise the value of interaction in understanding teacher cognition. Over the past decade, there has been a surge of interest in language teacher cognition, as evidenced by special issues of *Language Teaching Research* (2010), System (2011), *The Modern Language Journal* (2015) along with more than 600 publications since the 1990s to date. This level of interest confirms that the field has changed from a relatively new and undeveloped area into an important and well-researched field of inquiry, which promotes understandings of classroom instruction, pedagogical effectiveness and teacher development. To date, discussions have appeared in the literature on the degree of 'match' between learners' and teachers' beliefs (e.g. Peacock 1999; Cohen and Fass 2001); on beliefs about subject matters (for example grammar and grammar teaching; literacy) (e.g. Andrews 2003, 2006, 2007; Svalberg and Askham 2014); on changes in teachers' beliefs (e.g. Peacock 2001; Mattheoudakis 2007); on the influence of beliefs on teachers' classroom behaviour and the convergence of practice from beliefs (e.g. Breen et al. 2001; see Basturkmen 2012 for a review); and on the influence of beliefs on both pre-service and in-service teacher education programmes (Busch 2010).

Much of this research has focused on the mental state of teachers using data collection methods such as questionnaires, interviews, metaphor analysis and verbal comments. Very few have considered classroom interaction in the investigation of teacher cognition. This book highlights the importance of social interaction, recognising its value as a lens through which teacher cognition can be studied. It sets out to examine language teachers' knowing, thinking, conceptualising, stance-taking and doing through interactions in various settings. This is what I would like to call cognition-in-interaction, which refers to the ways in which teachers construct knowledge, understandings and propositions when they engage in interaction. The process emphasises cognition as being socially constructed in specific contexts. Throughout the book, the position adopted is that interaction should, and indeed does, play a central role in understanding teacher cognition. The following points are central to the argument of this book:

1. Cognition is socially constructed, a consequence or outcome of interaction with others. Cognition is displayed and developed in situ.
2. Talk is a medium of action, which is locally and situationally organised (te Molder and Potter 2005).
3. Teaching is a series of interactional events (Ellis 1998), while teachers are active, thinking decision-makers who play a central role in shaping these events (Li and Walsh 2011).
4. The second language classroom is a dynamic and complex series of interrelated contexts, in which interaction is seen as being central to teaching and learning (Walsh 2006).

There are at least three reasons for studying teacher cognition through social interaction. First, by studying interaction we can gain insights into how teachers' decision-making and social actions occur. Rather than trying to peer into teachers' heads as they teach, we can access their decisions, their cognitions by focusing on their actions and interactions. Second, a study of interaction casts light on how cognition is developed in situ; that is, the ways in which sequences of interaction display teachers' moment-by-moment thinking and decision-making. Third, the study of interaction shows how contexts emerge and provides some evidence as to the ways in which contexts both shape and are shaped by teachers' knowledge, behaviour and understanding (Li and Walsh 2011). This book aims to bring interaction to the centre of the study of teacher cognition, whereby talk is a practical, social activity located in practice and, more importantly, talk is seen as a medium of action. The book is intended to extend and clarify issues to do with the nature and role of cognitive entities in interaction and analysis in the context of teacher learning and development. The kinds of questions relevant to researchers in teacher cognition this book asks revolve around the nature of the cognitive entities in professional practices. Questions include:

1. How does teacher cognition figure in the analysis of interaction? How does interaction research shed light on the nature of teacher cognition?
2. How is 'cognition' described, understood and oriented to by teachers in the course of interaction?

3. What are the implications of such work on teacher education, effective pedagogy and teacher learning overall? Alternatively, what value can interactional analysis add to the current and dominant cognitive perspective of teacher cognition in teacher education, effective pedagogy and teacher learning?

Social interaction, as a lens for studying cognition, includes the acts, actions or practices of individuals and refers to any behaviour (talk) that tries to affect or take account of each other's subjective experiences or intentions in educational settings, such as student–teacher interaction in classrooms, and teacher–teacher interaction in lesson planning sessions. In this book, detailed transcriptions of verbal and non-verbal behaviours are made and subjected to a fine-grained analysis, using the principles and theoretical underpinnings of CA. That is, teacher cognition is studied using CA principles, focusing on how understanding, knowing, thinking, conceptualising, stance-taking and similar psychological processes are displayed in talk. The rationale for using CA principles is to uncover the ways in which intersubjectivity (or joint meaning-making) is organised by the participants themselves, rather than to approach the data from an extraneous viewpoint. That is, the focus is placed on how participants display for one another their understanding of the situation they are in. In such talk-in-interaction, speakers display in their sequentially 'next' turn as an understanding of what the 'prior' turn was about and how they are positioned and oriented to it (Hutchby and Wooffitt 2008). Data therefore are not approached with a predetermined set of features but treated in a rather open manner; as Seedhouse (2004) argues, CA provides an emic analysis of social action in classrooms from an ethnomethodological perspective, allowing 'data to speak for themselves'.

Another contribution of the book is to present fine-grained, 'up-close' descriptions of English as a Foreign Language (EFL) teachers in their professional contexts. Research in language teacher cognition has been mainly conducted in contexts where English is used as a first language (L1) or a second language (ESL). Ben-Peretz (2011) in her review of teacher knowledge from 1988 to 2009 points out that much of the research in teacher knowledge in general education is based on Western cultures and calls for research conducted in other cultures to provide 'a different view of teacher knowledge' (2011: 9). The same observation is made by Breen et al. (2001), Borg (2003b), Li and Walsh (2011) and Li (2012). These researchers emphasise the importance of understanding TESOL (Teaching English to Speakers of Other Languages) classrooms by focusing on L2 settings and non-native English teachers.

Thus, this book mainly locates itself in an EFL context, where language teacher cognition research is still a relatively young domain of inquiry (Borg 2006). There are two reasons for focusing on an EFL context. First, in order to understand teaching and learning EFL and contribute to the understanding of effective pedagogy, it is important to gain insights into how teachers understand, perceive, think and behave in their professional contexts. A classroom can be viewed as a controlled learning environment, a social and cultural space, a school of autonomy, and an ideology of foreign language learning (Tudor 2001), and these visions of classrooms are reflected in and shaped by teachers' understanding and knowledge of language teaching and learning. The EFL context is a unique learning environment where language is learnt both for linguistic and functional reasons. Students' principal point of contact with the target language is in the formal instructed environment – classrooms. For this reason, this context should be studied in some detail. Second, there are very few studies of non-native speaking (NNS) EFL teachers: the lack of attention to this group may not only result in a failure to understand current practice in TESOL, but also in a failure to understand and develop EFL teachers from those countries (Li and Walsh 2011: 40). The large number of NNS language teachers around the world 'face different challenges than those teachers whose subject matter is their own first language' (Bailey et al. 2001: 111) and a book focusing on EFL teachers can contribute to a greater understanding of foreign language teacher cognition research and stimulate continued research in this field.

DYNAMICS OF EFL CLASSROOMS

The prerequisite in understanding EFL teachers is to understand the professional context in which they work. In an ESL context, students are immigrants or visitors or language students preparing for further study. Usually, students do not share a native language or a common culture and have extensive daily exposure to English-speaking culture, whereas in an EFL context English is not the dominant language. Students usually share the same language and culture and they have very few opportunities to use English. Learning English may not have any obvious practical benefit, other than for pursuing further academic study.

Some of the more distinctive features of EFL contexts are now presented under three headings: language classrooms, contexts in pedagogy, and key characteristics of language teachers and learners.

LANGUAGE CLASSROOMS

Tudor (2001) talks about visions of the classroom and suggests that differing perspectives on the nature of the classroom can arise depending on what 'learning a language' entails and what approaches are used. Therefore meanings of 'classroom' are heavily influenced by the expectations of the different parties that are involved, such as parents, school leaders, policy-makers, teachers, learners and the society. Van Lier (1988) makes this point as follows:

> The classroom is not a world unto itself. The participants (teachers and learners) arrive at the event with certain ideas as to what is a 'proper' lesson, and in *their actions and interaction* they will strive to implement these ideas. In addition the society at large and the institution the classroom is part of have certain expectations and demands which exert influence on the way the classroom turns out. (1988: 179, my emphasis)

It is worth noting the influence of teacher and learners on the nature and culture of the classroom. Both learners and teachers have their beliefs about the learning environment and their ideology of the classroom contributes to their actions and interactions in this environment. The point being made here is that their ideology of the classroom is displayed through *their action and interaction*. Clearly, there is a relationship between action, interaction, and teachers' and learners' beliefs. With regard to language classrooms, it is also important to note the strong influence of society and the institution on the nature of the classroom. In many EFL contexts English is not considered as a tool but as a subject by society at large and the institution. From this observation, we can conclude that there are broadly two types of EFL classroom: the first, the most traditional and arguably the most widespread, treats English as a subject and focuses mainly on its linguistic forms; the second, conversely, treats English as a skill with a focus on communication.

In a typical form-focused classroom, learning a language is restricted to a mastery of its structural rules and vocabulary. One of the weaknesses of this approach is that it pays very little attention to context in the process of understanding and using the language. In classrooms where communication is the main focus on the other hand, context is key to understanding how language should be used. So we can say that while both types of classroom focus on language, they present very different perspectives on what language is and how it should be learnt (see Seedhouse et al. 2010).

In sum, it is clear that EFL contexts are very different from ESL classrooms, where language is both the central objective of the lesson and the tool for achieving it (Willis 1992). And more importantly, learners see the relevance of the language they learn in real-life situations where there are opportunities for them to use and apply the language.

Despite the fact that language is the primary focus of the EFL classroom, the classroom is also a social context which is jointly constructed by learners and the teacher. As Walsh (2006) argues, any ESL lesson (including EFL) can be viewed as 'a dynamic and complex series of interrelated contexts, in which interaction is central to teaching and learning' (2006: 62). Like Seedhouse (2004), Walsh highlights the fact that classrooms are made up of a series of locally produced contexts, co-constructed by teachers and learners, a position which contrasts strongly with the view of the classroom as a single, static context. That is, even a form-focused lesson, should not be viewed as a single context. Series of micro-contexts are constructed with the development of the lesson, when both learners and the teacher contribute to the flow and direction of that development.

CONTEXTS IN PEDAGOGY

Kennedy and Kennedy point out that teacher attitudes should not be seen as something static but as something that interacts with 'the social norms and the perceived behavioural control which is specific to a particular context' (1996: 359). Similarly, Tudor suggests that '(T)eachers are active participants in the creation of classroom realities, and they act in the light of their own beliefs, attitudes, and perceptions of the *relevant teaching situation*' (2001: 17, my emphasis). In this way, it is important to note that a teaching situation, or rather context, influences what teachers do in classrooms in a variety of ways. 'Context' is a complex phenomenon, with different perspectives defining it differently. It is useful to acknowledge here that any classroom, as an institutional context, comprises at least two sets of components: 'pragmatic and mental', or 'macro and micro'.

A pragmatic context could include a wide range of factors such as the class size, teaching materials and resources, testing and teacher training. Class size is a huge issue in pedagogical considerations. The kind of activities and tasks that a teacher can do with a class of ten students is very different from what can be done with a class of forty, fifty, even 100. In most EFL contexts, class size varies from forty to 100 (e.g. Shamim 1996a, cited in Tudor 2001; Li 2008), which limits the kinds of communicative activity that language teachers can offer. There is also great variety in terms of the range of practical conditions in which teaching and learning is conducted. Some EFL contexts provide their students with facilities and resources for authentic English exposure, such as computers and computer-assisted language learning (CALL) resources, newly published ELT books and materials, a progressive curriculum and so on, while others rely solely on teachers as the knowledge source. Then there are other factors such as a teacher's status and training. Not all EFL teachers have received ELT training before they become a teacher and many of them learn to become a teacher while teaching. Another important factor which influences teaching and learning, especially a teacher's approach to pedagogy, is testing. It is a common assumption that teachers adapt their teaching methodology and content to reflect the demands of assessment in many EFL contexts. In the literature of teacher cognition, the influence of tests or the washback effect has been widely recognised as one of the contextual factors which accounts for the divergence between teachers' beliefs and practices (Kern 1995; Li 2013).

The 'mental' component of context refers to the beliefs, values, assumptions, norms and perceptions that both teachers and learners bring to the practical context of teaching and learning. These values, beliefs and expectations influence the pedagogical decisions teachers make, and the interactions which take place in classrooms. Tudor (2001) talks about teaching methodology as both a theoretical principle and a pedagogical reality. It is these contexts that account for the methodology as pedagogical reality. What we see in teachers' articulation and classroom practices are the products shaped by these contexts. Therefore, both practical and mental contexts need to be considered in investigating teacher cognition.

Situated in a Chinese context, Li (2013) divides contexts into macro and micro; the former concern language policy, curriculum, tests, language status, teachers' and learners' characteristics, learning styles, materials and textbooks, while the latter are defined by moment-to-moment interactions in classrooms. The macro-context can be seen as being similar to the pragmatic element of context identified by Tudor (2001). However, distinctions need to be made between micro-context and mental context. Mental context is part of the negotiation at the micro-context. That is to say, values, beliefs are developed and shaped in the micro-context. Li argues that the macro-context guides overarching pedagogy and instructional activities but the moment-to-moment variables shape what a teacher does in a particular lesson (2013: 186). Therefore, in order to understand the complexity of teachers' beliefs about teaching and learning, it is important to understand the complexities of both macro- and micro-contexts and how they interact.

KEY CHARACTERISTICS OF LANGUAGE TEACHERS

The key characteristics of language teachers are closely defined by the professional contexts in which they work. Typically, the following are relevant:

1. The nature of the subject matter. Foreign language teaching is the only subject where effective instruction requires the teacher to use a medium the students do not yet fully understand. This brings a language issue for the language teachers, as they have to spend more time preparing lessons because they have to think carefully about how to explain things in a foreign language.
2. The interaction patterns necessary to provide instruction. Effective foreign language instruction requires classroom organisation such as group work and pair work which is desirable but not necessary for effective instruction in other subjects.
3. The challenge for teachers to increase their knowledge of the subject, both linguistic and cultural. It is difficult for foreign language teachers to increase their subject knowledge as they teach communication skills not facts. Therefore, increasing subject knowledge might be feasible for other subjects through books; it is not for language teachers unless they are exposed to the language environment. Such opportunities are rare.
4. The role of language teachers: The teacher is viewed as the primary source of the language input in the classroom, especially where speaking and listening are concerned. Language teachers represent a different culture and language other than the native culture and language.

In sum, EFL teachers are different from mainstream subject teachers in the way that they are not only defined by the professional contexts but also by the nature of the subject in the contexts. These features of EFL teachers inevitably influence their thinking, understanding, decision-making and teaching.

STRUCTURE OF THE BOOK

There are three parts and eight chapters in this book.

PART A: SURVEY

Part A is a survey of the field of teacher cognition. This part comprises three chapters, focusing on the development of language teacher cognition research, approaches to the investigation of teacher cognition and the use of interaction to study language teacher cognition. Chapter 1 reviews the construct and development of teacher cognition and situates language teacher cognition research broadly in mainstream teacher education. The concept is explored from different theoretical perspectives: a cognitive-based perspective, an interactionist perspective and a discursive psychology (DP) perspective. Chapter 2 summarises and critiques the mainstream methodological approaches to the study of language teacher cognition.

In Chapter 3, an alternative approach is presented, based on a discursive psychological perspective to the study of teacher cognition. Rather than viewing cognition as a static trait which remains constant in different contexts, DP views cognition as something which is negotiated through interaction with others. Cognition is viewed as a phenomenon which is displayed publicly rather than something which remains in the private realm of the mind. Thus, rather than attempting to make sense of what people know (in their heads), DP deals with publicly observable cognition and interprets the construct from the participant's point of view rather than from an observer's perspective. DP traditionally uses discourse analysis in the investigation of psychological matters and motives, such as attitudes, knowing, remembering and believing, and discourse is treated as the primary action for human action, understanding and intersubjectivity (Potter 2012a). In recent years the principles of CA have been adopted in DP (Hutchby and Wooffitt 2008). The fine-grained, 'up-close' analysis offered by CA provides in-depth understanding of what people 'think in action'. This chapter demonstrates the relationship between interaction and what teachers think, know, believe and do in professional contexts, and illustrates how cognition is displayed in social interaction. It makes a strong case for looking at cognition through interaction and illustrates how teachers' knowledge, understandings and beliefs are understood in natural talk.

PART B: ANALYSIS

The second part of the book offers an analysis of teacher cognition from a discursive psychological perspective. There are three chapters in this section and each of them focuses on one aspect of teacher cognition. Chapter 4 considers student teachers' knowledge and belief development as they undertake a programme of teacher education. Using detailed transcripts of group discussion, micro-teaching and practicum, and pre-service teachers' reflections on becoming a teacher, this chapter provides insights into pre-service teachers' thinking, decision-making, knowledge and beliefs about language teaching and learning, and about being a language teacher. Chapter 5 explores the construct of expertise by comparing novice and expert teachers in terms of their cognitions. This chapter uses detailed transcripts of social interaction in teachers' professional activities, for example, teaching, lesson preparation and self-reflection to discuss how cognition is distributed in interaction and the fluidity of expertise. Chapter 6 concerns critical moments in teaching and explores how teachers make their interactive decisions (Tsui 2003), or online decision-making (Walsh 2006, 2011), by looking at classroom data and self-reflection. Teachers, as active decision-makers, are constantly making choices to maintain students' interest and engagement (Richards 1998a). By analysing teachers' unanticipated decisions, this chapter intends to provide insights into the nature of pedagogical decision-making.

PART C: APPLICATIONS

Part C consists of two chapters focusing on the application of research in teacher cognition. Chapter 7 discusses the practical implications of researching teacher cognition for understanding teaching and learning, pedagogical knowledge and teaching methods. Suggestions are made regarding how individual teachers develop pedagogy by analysing what they know, do and believe in their professional contexts, in relation to instructional practice and interactive decision-making. Chapter 8 discusses the implications of teacher cognition in teacher education and professional development. Suggestions are made regarding how to enhance teacher learning and development in EFL contexts.

PART A: SURVEY

1

LANGUAGE TEACHER COGNITION: AN OVERVIEW

Teacher cognition is a central concern in the mainstream of educational development, and research on teacher cognition has been of interest for decades (for a review see for example Pajares 1992). However, language teacher cognition has been studied mainly in the last twenty years (see for example Borg 2006; Barnard and Burns 2012). Research on language teacher cognition has focused on two particular curricular areas: grammar and literacy instruction (see Borg 2003a), although in recent years research interest in teacher cognition has evidenced a movement into other areas, for example intercultural competence (Llurda and Lasagabaster 2010; Young and Sachdev 2011) and technology integration (e.g. Brannan and Bleistein 2012; Li 2014). In this chapter, as a first step towards investigating teacher cognition through the lens of social interaction, I outline the importance of teacher cognition, review the development of language teacher cognition and explore the construct from different theoretical perspectives. I will not attempt to provide a comprehensive review of the literature on language teacher cognition, but highlight some important issues which will be discussed in-depth in the book.

THE IMPORTANCE OF TEACHER COGNITION

Studying teacher cognition is important in understanding teachers' perceptions and decisions, teaching and learning, the dynamics of the classroom, effective pedagogy and teacher learning.

Research suggests that teacher cognition directly affects both teacher perceptions and judgements of teaching and learning interactions in the classroom, which result in different behaviour in classrooms (Clark and Peterson 1986; Clark and Yinger 1987; Borg 2006; Li and Walsh 2011). More accurately, teacher cognition heavily influences the way teachers plan their lessons, the decisions they make in the teaching process and what kind of learning they promote in the classroom (Pajares 1992; Li 2012). Breen et al. (2001: 471) argue that teachers' articulated understanding in relation to their classroom work can complement observational studies by enabling research to 'go beyond description towards the understanding and explanation of teacher action'. There is certainly a link between teachers' understanding about their pedagogical considerations and their instructional decisions in the classroom (Borg 2003b; Mangubhai et al. 2004). In this respect, Pajares argues that 'beliefs are far more influential than knowledge in determining how individuals organize and define tasks and problems and are stronger predictors of behaviour' (1992: 311). Davis endorses this view and remarks 'that people's beliefs are instrumental in influencing their behaviour is a truism; people act on the basis of perceptions and their "definition of the situation" (2003: 207). He goes on to illustrate an example of a person who 'believes' a mouse hiding under the table will 'act' as though there is a mouse under the table, regardless of whether the belief is or is not correct (ibid.).

Equally, researching what teachers understand and how they act in teaching can provide a window to understanding what teaching and learning is from teachers' perspectives, and how they develop their pedagogical considerations in lesson planning, teaching and evaluating students. This is important on two levels: first, we are able to explore what constitutes teaching and learning from teachers' points of view; second, we are able to gain possible insights into how the various elements which make up teaching and learning work and interact, for example material choice, task design, interactional patterns and assessment.

Researching teacher cognition is crucial to understanding the dynamics of the classroom. Teacher cognition can reflect the ways an evolving identity 'self-as-teacher' is interpreted, as well as how what is understood can be put into classroom practice (Clark and Peterson 1986; Bullough et al. 1992). Relationships between the teacher and learners, and between learners, are an important feature of teaching and learning. The dynamics of classrooms reflects visions of the classrooms. A classroom can be considered as a socio-cultural space where both the teacher and learners follow social values and norms, or a controlled learning environment where subject knowledge shapes this relationship. In recent developments in educational research, a classroom is also viewed as a school of autonomy where both the teacher and students have responsibility and power to construct the kind of teaching and learning they believe in. A foreign language classroom is also an ideology of foreign language learning where participants negotiate what language is and how it is learnt. To understand the dynamics of the classroom therefore constitutes a major part of understanding pedagogy.

As early as the 1970s, Fenstermacher (1979) highlighted the importance of studying teacher cognition in research on teacher effectiveness. That is, by revealing the process of decision-making, a better understanding of teaching and learning can be achieved, therefore improving educational effectiveness (Brophy and Good 1986). The effectiveness of pedagogy can also be understood as appropriate methodology. Breen et al. (2001) have emphasised that researching teacher cognition may lead to frameworks for language pedagogy emerging directly from classroom work on a range of different teaching situations that would generate grounded alternatives to the 'accepted wisdom' of language teaching methodology. Researching teacher cognition therefore can contribute to the development of practical pedagogical principles which are context-bound. This is especially relevant to the context where an innovation is expected within the teachers' principles and practice, for example from the adoption of a new technique or textbook to the implementation of technology or a new curriculum. Studying teacher cognition has significance in two ways: first, it provides insider knowledge about the plausibility of such innovation and potential barriers and possible conditions; second, strategies or guidelines or pedagogies developed by teachers within that particular situation can facilitate such innovation and speed up its adoption. The underlying assumption is that teacher cognitions are essential 'factors shaping teachers' decisions about what knowledge is relevant, what teaching routines are appropriate, what goals should be accomplished, and what are the important features of the social context of the classroom' (Speer 2005: 365).

Studying teacher cognition also has significant implications for teacher learning. Breen et al. (2001) suggest that research on teacher cognition has been taken by researchers in the field of second language teacher education (SLTE) as a source of experientially-based professional 'know-how' that may serve as a focus both for initial teacher education and for reflection in ongoing teacher development (Richards and Lockhart 1994; Freeman and Richards 1996). In teacher education, Horwitz (1985) proposes that teachers' preconceived beliefs may interfere with prospective teachers' understandings and receptivity to the information and techniques presented in a teacher education programme. There is also evidence from the literature that teachers' thinking is part of their professional development to improve their effectiveness in the classroom (Nespor 1987; Weinstein 1989).

THE DEVELOPMENT OF LANGUAGE TEACHER COGNITION

Since the development of cognitive psychology and ethnographic techniques in the late 1970s and early 1980s, there has been a growing emphasis on teachers' thought processes. More accurately, a shift was made from teaching effectiveness, concerned primarily with teachers' classroom behaviour, students' classroom behaviour and student achievement, to teachers' mental lives, in the recognition of the influence of thinking on behaviour. This also corresponded to a general change in many disciplines from product (behaviour) to process (thinking). Thus, understanding teachers and teaching requires insights into the thinking process and the cognitive basis of decision-making rather than purely describing behaviours. Clark and Yinger outlined the importance of understanding the thinking processes of teachers: 'how teachers gather, organize, interpret, and evaluate information is expected to lead to understandings of the uniquely human processes that guide and determine teacher behaviour' (1987: 1). This development of teaching can be viewed as the starting point of research in teacher cognition. According to Clark and Peterson (1986), teacher thinking research primarily constitutes three important aspects: teacher planning (pre-active and post-active thoughts), teachers' interactive thoughts and decisions, and teachers' theories and beliefs. Much research since then has focused on the first two domains of teacher cognition: teachers' planning and interactive thoughts and decision-making (see also Clark and Peterson 1986; Borg 2003b). However, the study of teachers' beliefs and theories began to attract more and more attention from the mid-1980s and emerged as an important and distinct area. In terms of research on language teacher cognition, although early research into language teachers' beliefs and attitudes can be traced back to the early 1970s in the field of reading and reading instructions(Duffy and Metheny (1979) was perhaps one of the earliest studies addressing language teachers' beliefs), it is not until the 1990s that research 'picked up momentum' and continued to develop as an important area (Borg 2003b: 83).

In the development of language teacher cognition, there are three frameworks meriting detailed discussion.

TEACHER THOUGHT PROCESS

Clark and Peterson's (1986) model of teacher thought process is perhaps the earliest framework tapping into the nature of teacher cognition and providing an agenda in researching this area. The model of teacher thought and action depicts two domains that are importantly involved in the process of teaching, namely teachers' thought processes, and teachers' actions and their observable effects (see Figure 1.1). Differences between the two domains lie in whether they are 'observable' and what research paradigmatic approach they represent. Teachers' thought processes are unobservable whereas teachers' actions and their observable effects constitute observable phenomena. Therefore, 'the phenomena involved in the teacher action domain are more easily measured and more easily subjected to empirical research methods than are the phenomena involved in the teacher thought domain' (Clark and Peterson 1986: 257).

In Clark and Peterson's model of teachers' thought process (Figure 1.1) there are three main elements, namely teachers' planning (pre-active and post-active thoughts), teachers' interactive thoughts and decisions, and teachers' theories and

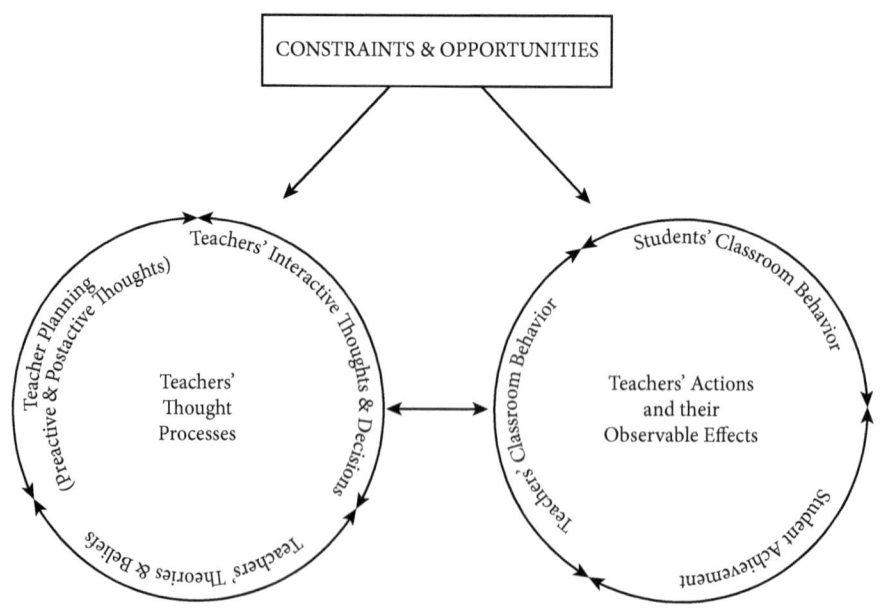

Source: From Wittrock (1986)

Figure 1.1   Clark and Peterson's model of teachers' thought process and action (1986: 257).

beliefs. According to this model, teaching is an 'improvisational performance' (Richards 1998b: 74; Li 2013). Research has shown a clear distinction between teachers' planning and teachers' interactive thoughts and decisions; in other words, the differences between what teachers think/plan to do and what teachers actually do when they are interacting with students in class (e.g. Bailey 1996). However, little research has focused on studying the difference/distinction between pre-active and post-active thoughts and decisions because the teaching process is cyclical and the pre-active and post-active thoughts affect each other, and therefore the distinction is 'blurred' (Clark and Peterson 1986: 258). Teaching is a series of interactive decisions, so when teachers teach they interact with their lesson plans, materials at hand, activities and students' responses, and they make adjustments accordingly, based on their understanding of effective teaching. The process of making adjustments forms part of teachers' decision-making while teaching and provides bases for immediate post-active and the future pre-active thoughts. Put simply, decision-making is an outcome of teachers' interaction with their students in classrooms (Li 2013).

The third category, teachers' theories and beliefs, which represents the rich knowledge that teachers have, affects their planning and their interactive thoughts and decisions. Equally, teachers' planning, interactive thoughts and decisions might respectively affect the development of teachers' thoughts and beliefs. Therefore, the relationship between these domains is a reciprocal one as indicated by the double-headed arrows in Figure 1.1. Clark and Peterson describe the relationship thus: 'teachers' actions are largely caused by teachers' thought processes, which then in turn affect teachers' actions' (1986: 258).

BAK (BELIEFS, ASSUMPTIONS AND KNOWLEDGE)

Woods (1996) develops a multidimensional cycle of planning and decision-making within teaching. He further proposes a model to signify the evolving system of beliefs, assumptions and knowledge (BAK) that recursively informs/is informed by the context of teaching:

> the BAK was part of the perceiving and organizing of the decisions. When a decision was considered, it was considered in the context of BAK, and when it was remembered later it was also remembered in the context of BAK.
> (Woods 1996: 247)

Like schemata, he argues that 'BAK (Belief, Assumption and Knowledge) networks are structured in the sense that knowledge, assumptions and beliefs can be posited in terms of interrelated propositions, in which certain propositions presuppose others' (ibid.: 196). Woods claimed that hypotheses about teachers' BAK were based on the elicitation of themes and hypothesising propositions about those themes; the relationships among them are based on the teachers' verbalisations. Thus, the notion of BAK includes not just elements of teachers' beliefs but also relationships between these elements. Woods' work has advanced the field in several aspects but the major contributions lie in the relationship between knowledge and belief, the nature of belief and the approach to the study of it. Unlike others, Woods reduces the distinction between knowledge and beliefs rather than highlighting it, as he puts it 'in order to take appropriate action, people need to understand; and to understand they need knowledge about the world and specifically about the situation they are in' (ibid.: 59). He clarifies that some themes in his BAK, those involving considerations of institutional constraints, for example, are clear expressions of teachers' knowledge of the teaching situation rather than their beliefs or assumption about language, learning and teaching. However, it is also evident that such knowledge is intimately connected to the teacher's beliefs and assumptions. Woods also clearly recognises the nature of BAK – that these elements do not exist as individual entities but combine into patterns in particular situations, a position which reflects contemporary thinking of teacher cognition.

TEACHER COGNITION

Arguing that the field of language teacher cognition lacks a programmatic research agenda conceived within an overall unifying framework, Borg (2006) proposes a framework of teacher cognition, how it develops and the interwoven and interactive relationships between cognition and teacher learning, as well as their classroom practices. Borg (2003b: 81) terms teacher cognition the 'unobservable cognitive dimension of teaching – what teachers know, believe, and think'.

Figure 1.2 presents a schematic conceptualisation of cognition and its relationships with important factors in teachers' lives, including their schooling experience, their professional development, their classroom teaching and the specific contexts they are in. The key ideas about teacher cognition presented in this diagram are summarised as follows:

- Teachers' experiences as learners (both in schooling and professional activities) inform and develop their cognitions, which also affect their classroom practices, while being shaped by the contextual factors. It is important to take account of the role of personal experience in the development of preconceptions about education. This is in line with research on personal practical knowledge.
- Context and 'learning' experience (including professional development) are important factors that shape teachers' beliefs. It recognises classroom practice as part of context, which includes what happens around and inside the classroom. Classroom practice thus is defined by the interaction of teacher cognition and contextual factors, which in turn consciously or unconsciously shape the cognition. Borg concludes, 'teacher cognitions and practices are mutually informing, with contextual factors playing an important role in mediating the extent to which teachers are able to implement instruction congruent with their cognitions' (ibid.: 284).
- The concept of teacher cognition is used as a collective term for various psychological constructs, including beliefs, knowledge, theories, attitudes, images, assumptions, metaphors, conceptions and perspectives, principles, thinking and decision-making. Compared to earlier work in teacher cognition,

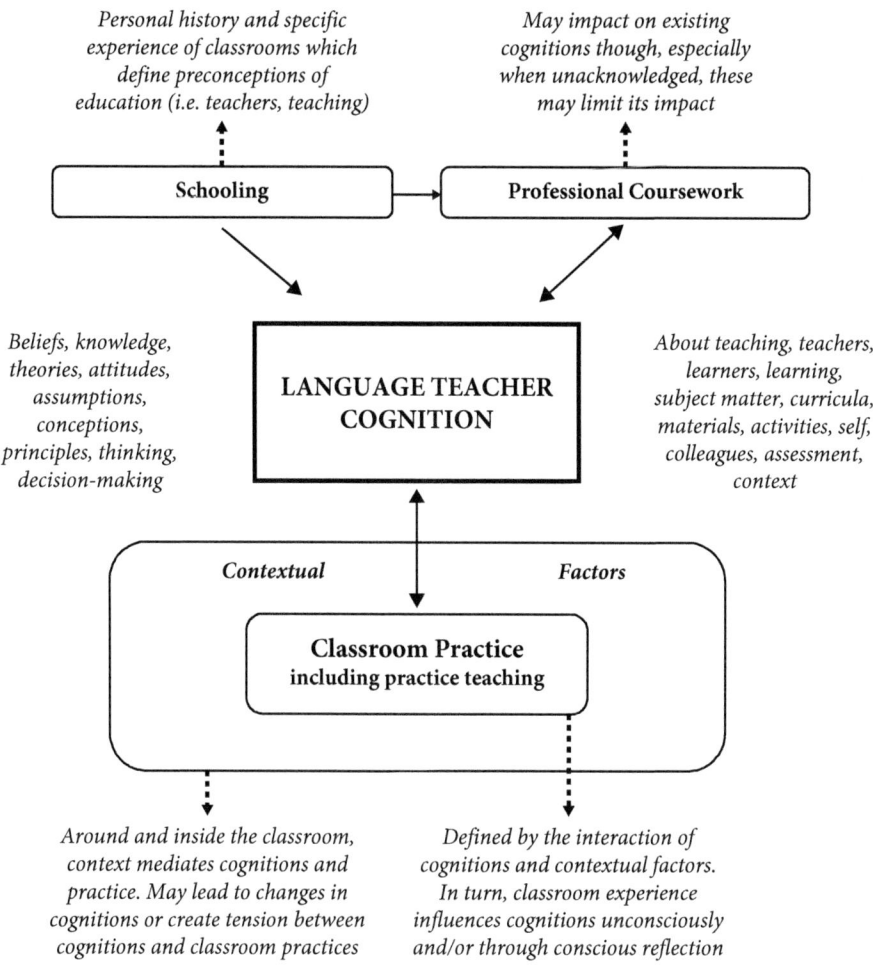

Figure 1.2 Elements and processes in language teacher cognition.

adding decision-making is an important development since decision-making in pre-teaching, while-teaching and post-teaching are key elements of teacher cognition.
- This conceptualisation identifies the different components of teacher cognition: teaching, teachers, learning, students, subject matter, curricula, materials, instructional activities and the teacher self, colleagues, assessment and context.

This diagram suggests two important things for studying teacher cognition: teacher (professional) learning and contextual factors. Much research focuses on these two areas to explore how teacher cognition can enhance teacher learning and the role of contextual factors in causing discrepancies, divergences or tensions between teacher cognition and classroom practice. Borg suggests that 'although professional preparation does shape trainees' cognitions, programmes which ignore trainee teachers' prior beliefs may be less effective at influencing these' (2006: 284). Many researchers thus explore ways to correct or influence pre-service teachers' cognition on the basis of an assumption that pre-service teachers have misconception or wrong cognition before they start the teacher education.

KEY CONCEPTS

Empirical research has focused on the examination or investigation of different aspects of teacher cognition, among which teacher knowledge, interactive decisions, beliefs and teachers' professional learning have emerged as the most researched and most important areas. These are now discussed below.

TEACHER LEARNING

Teacher learning is a complex system rather than an event, made complex by the situations in which the teacher works, the student, the educational system, the curriculum and school culture. Thus, in order to understand teacher learning, local (cultural) knowledge, problems, routines and context all must be taken into consideration. Various learning theories have been used to investigate teacher learning, for example socio-cultural theory (Vygotsky 1978), community of practice (Wenger 1998), Kolb's experiential learning (1984), reflection-in-action (Schön 1983) and reflective practice. From a socio-cultural perspective, learning is 'inherently situated in a social, interactional, cultural, institutional and historical context' (Wertsch 1991: 85; Cole and Wertsch 1996). As Vygotsky suggests, higher human mental functions such as learning and thinking are social in their nature. He emphasises that '(E)ven where we turn to mental (e.g. internal) processes, their nature remains quasisocial. In their private sphere, human beings retain the function of social interactions' (1981: 164). Teacher learning from a socio-cultural perspective thus is an interactive process, where knowledge and understanding develop through collaboration with others. Cognition is socially mediated or influenced by others in social interaction; it is socially shared cognition. Teachers' knowledge and beliefs are shaped by various features of the socio-cultural and educational contexts, and teacher learning is a process of meaning negotiation with these contexts, such as socio-educational ethos (Kennedy and Kennedy 1998), the institutional culture (Holliday 1994) and teacher education (Richards and Pennington 1998). Communities of practice on the other hand further reveal the social nature of teacher learning and the need for teachers to participate in a professional community and reflect with peers who share a similar concern or passion and aim to learn how to do better through interaction (Wenger 2009). At the heart of teacher learning is about belonging to the community, becoming a member, and practising in the community. Learning is experience (Wenger 1998: 5). For teachers, becoming a teacher, developing teacher identity and a sense of belonging, teaching and being recognised by the community is learning. Learning is not restricted to the classroom, but is enhanced through the process of teachers participating in the community.

Experiential learning (Kolb 1984) emphasises the importance of reflection and experimentation. Teacher learning should not only take place in teacher training but in the teaching context where teachers can reflect upon their actions and thinking, and experiment with new ideas. Reflection thus is a key element in teacher learning. Reflection is a mental processing that one engages to fulfil a purpose or to achieve some anticipated outcome, which is clearly seen as a learning opportunity (Moon 2005: 1).

For both Dewey and Schön, reflection begins and happens in working practice. Dewey (1933) stressed the importance of each individual's lived experience as a starting point for learning. The development of thinking, in particular reflective thinking, is at the core of a Dewey's philosophy. Schön (1983) developed the notions of *reflection-in-action* and *reflection-on-action*. Learning opportunities thus are created through conscious reflection on the decisions that teachers make during and after the action. For example, a teacher could reflect critically after a class whether activities were successful, materials were appropriate or student participation was sufficient. Equally, a teacher could reflect during the action when they plan and teach to evaluate and adjust their plan.

Teacher learning is much more centred in teacher education or preparation, and professional development. Teacher education programmes generally operate under the assumption that teachers need a discrete amount of knowledge, either subject or pedagogy. Learning to teach is a process of learning theories in one context, practising in another and applying in a third one. So 'the true locus of teacher learning lay in on-the-job initiation into the practices of teaching and not in the processes of professional teacher education' (Freeman and Johnson 1998: 399). Freeman and Johnson (1998) summarised four types of research on teacher learning, including the role of prior knowledge and beliefs in learning to teach, the ways in which such teaching knowledge develops over time, the role of context in teacher learning, and the role of teacher education as a form of intervention in these areas in particular in changing teachers' beliefs about content and leaners. Teacher learning takes place in various forms and ways as outlined above. One way to help teachers to learn is to create a space for them to engage in collaborative reflection through examining their practice and beliefs, which I will discuss further in a later chapter.

TEACHER KNOWLEDGE

Research has shifted from teacher thinking to teacher knowledge in recognition of teacher knowledge as one important aspect of teacher's professional life, and as 'part of a revolution in how educators think about classroom practice' (Connelly et al. 1997: 666). Connelly et al. (1997) emphasise that teacher knowledge and knowing affects every aspect of the teaching act and suggest that studying the construction and expression of teacher knowledge is one important means of improving education through research. Teacher knowledge has been a research interest in teacher education since the early 1980s (e.g. Clark and Peterson 1986; Ben-Peretz 2011). The scope of research into teacher knowledge also expanded from content subject knowledge and pedagogical concerns to teachers' personal, practical knowledge which derived from their own experience. The concept of practical knowledge is knowledge 'broadly based on (teachers') experiences in classrooms and schools and is directed toward the handling of problems that arise in their work' (Elbaz 1981: 67). For Elbaz, teachers' practical knowledge 'encompasses first-hand experience of students' learning styles, interests, needs, strengths and difficulties, and a repertoire of instructional techniques and classroom management skills' (1983: 5). Elbaz conceptualises teachers' practical knowledge using four categories: the content, orientations, structure and cognitive style. Practical knowledge includes knowledge the teacher has about themselves, learners, the context and the subject matter, which is acquired through different orientations and structures. Five orientations were identified by Elbaz, namely situational, theoretical, personal, social and experiential. The structure of practical knowledge includes practical principles, rules of practice and image. In her words, '(T)he rule of practice may be followed methodically while the principle is used reflectively,' and the image guides action in an intuitive way (Elbaz 1981: 49–50). Through enacting the various images, teachers develop their cognitive style.

Building on Elbaz's work on teachers' knowledge (1981, 1983), Connelly and Clandinin introduced the personal dimension of teachers' practical knowledge, which is 'experiential, embodied, and reconstructed out of the narratives of a user's life' (1985: 183). For Connelly and Clandinin, a teacher's personal practical knowledge is found in the teacher's practice. It is, for any teacher, a particular way of 'reconstructing the past and the intentions of the future to deal with the exigencies of a present situation' (1988: 25). In contrast to the cognitive view of teacher knowledge, Connelly and Clandinin's work emphasises the 'personal' and 'experiential' aspect of the knowledge construction of individual teachers and this perspective represents a more situational form of knowledge than formal professional knowledge (Munby et al. 2001: 881). To achieve understanding of personal practical knowledge, teachers' professional and personal history or experiences must be taken into consideration 'through interpretations of observed practices over time' and 'through reconstructions of the teachers' narratives of experiences' (Clandinin 1985: 363). Connelly and Clandinin (1995) theorise that 'professional knowledge landscapes' allow researchers to talk about 'space, place, and time', because the professional knowledge landscape is seen as composed of relationships among people, places and things – both at the intellectual and moral level. They also advocate the research methodology of 'narrative inquiry' to investigate teachers' personal practical knowledge and much work in this area since has followed the path of Connelly and Clandinin's construction of professional knowledge landscape and narrative inquiry (e.g. Tsui 2007; Xu and Connelly 2009).

Teachers' practical knowledge has been interpreted differently in various studies but perhaps Clandinin and Connelly's set of concepts is helpful in defining and understanding its nature – a set of specific concepts, including 'image', 'rules', 'maxims', 'principles', 'personal philosophy', 'metaphor', 'cycles' and 'rhythms', and 'narrative unity' clearly suggests the personal elements. In particular, they argue that the 'image' can be seen as central to understanding teachers' lives (Clandinin and Connelly 1986;

Connelly et al. 1997). Indeed, recent studies emphasise the importance of the professional images teachers construct through the lens of personal experience in learning and teaching (e.g. Tsui 2007). In exploring an immigrant Chinese language teacher's personal practical knowledge, Sun (2012) made the observation that cultural heritage has a strong influence on shaping the teacher's personal practical knowledge and their teaching practice. He also echoed Clandinin et al. (2009) regarding the intertwined relationship between personal practical knowledge and identity.

In the field of second language (L2) education, interest in teacher knowledge started to emerge in the1990s. Golombek (1998) classified language teachers' knowledge into four categories – knowledge of self, knowledge of subject matter, knowledge of instruction, and knowledge of contexts – which are similar to Elbaz's categories. It is important to note that these categories can overlap. In fact, in some studies, practical knowledge is also considered interchangeable with other concepts, such as 'beliefs'. For example in Wyatt, 'formal knowledge (e.g. course and modules) was accommodated into Sarah's (the teacher) practical knowledge as she engaged in designing, teaching and evaluating increasingly richer and more sophisticated communicative tasks' (2009: 18). He concludes that 'in-service teacher education outside English-speaking Western ELT can make a difference with regards to PK growth in CLT' (ibid.: 20), hence the need to consider the impact of formal instruction on the teacher's practical knowledge development. This is also reported in Morton and Gray's (2010) study that student teachers' practical knowledge is developed through joint meaning construction in lesson planning sessions with their tutor. In such a discursive practice, joint lesson planning is used as a channel for student teachers to accumulate their practical knowledge – to some degree, it is similar to students' own learning experiences and background knowledge.

It is clear that although it is personal practical knowledge that individual teachers accumulate in their experience, cultural norms and formal education have a stronger impact than one might expect. Research so far into teachers' practical knowledge has been largely based on Elbaz's framework (1981, 1983) and acknowledges that practical knowledge is personal, contextual, experiential, tacit and subject specific. Research also sheds light on the nature of practical knowledge as an open and developing concept, which is 'evolving, changing and growing' (Johnson and Golombek 2002: 8). In a longitudinal study, Ruohotie-Lyhty (2011) explored eleven newly qualified teachers' personal practical knowledge through teacher discourse, and suggested that teachers' perception and conceptualisation of their environment was important in the development of their professional knowledge. Tsang (2004) investigated practical knowledge growth of three student teachers in Hong Kong and came to the conclusion that student teachers did not always refer to their personal practical knowledge in their interactive decisions, yet personal practical knowledge did play a part in informing post-active decisions, which in turn improves future lesson planning.

INTERACTIVE DECISIONS

The metaphor of teacher-as-decision-maker (Nunan 1992) reflects how teachers conceptualise their work and the kind of decision-making underpinning teaching (Tsang

2004). Teachers make many interactive decisions, decisions made 'in the moment by moment progression of a lesson and in the context of competing pressures such as time, the attention span of the learners, curricular demands, exam pressures and so on' (Walsh 2006: 48). Such interactive decision-making constitutes a major part of teachers' classroom behaviour, especially when unexpected classroom events emerge. Walsh (2006) suggests that teachers vary in their ability to create learning opportunities and make good interactive decisions. Making good interactive decisions, then, is an important consideration of teachers' classroom practice and a recognition that teachers are active thinkers who constantly make decisions in the process of teaching rather than following the plan rigidly. Shavelson and Stern's (1981) review also proposed a model of interactive decision-making based on the assumption that teaching consists of well-established routines. Teachers make interactive decisions in order to adjust their plans, behaviours and materials based on student reaction and behaviour. This model highlights the role of student behaviours in interactive decisions, but recent research also challenges this model as many other factors might influence the interactive choices teachers make (Borg 2006). Tsang indicates that '(W)hat teachers think and believe shapes the way they understand teaching and the priorities they give to different dimensions of teaching' (2004: 164).

A classroom always consists of a series of unanticipated events, which requires teachers to make interactive decisions (Tsui 2005), and less is known about how teachers draw upon – but not act upon – their theories in teaching. This issue is further explored in Chapter 6.

BELIEFS

Teachers' belief is probably the most frequently used term in the literature to refer to teacher cognition. It is a central construct in every discipline that deals with human behaviour and learning (Fishbein and Ajzen 1975; Ajzen 1988) and the best indicator of the decisions individuals make (Nisbett and Ross 1980; Bandura 1986). Despite the vast research into teachers' beliefs, the diversity of different labels for the same concept has resulted in 'definitional confusion and inconsistency' (Eisenhart et al. 1988) or a 'messy construct' with different interpretations and meanings (Nespor 1987; Pajares 1992). Pajares presents a dauntingly long list of interchangeable terms for 'beliefs', including attitudes, values, judgements, axioms, opinions, ideology, perceptions, conceptions, implicit theories, explicit theories, personal theories, to name but a few (see Pajares 1992: 309). Because of the differences within these terms and the potential confusion it may cause by using them interchangeably, Pajares (1992) suggests that researchers should define clearly what the term means and clarify what is to be investigated.

So a starting point of researching this area would be to explore the concept itself. Nisbett and Ross suggest a definition of beliefs as 'reasonably explicit "propositions" about the characteristics of objects and object classes' (1980: 28). Sigel defines beliefs as 'mental constructions of experience – often condensed and integrated into schemata or concepts' (1985: 351). Harvey construes beliefs as, 'a set of conceptual representations which signify to its holder a reality or given state of affairs of sufficient validity, truth or trustworthiness to warrant reliance upon it as a guide to personal thought and action' (1986: 660). Eisenhart et al. define beliefs as 'an attitude consistently applied to an activity' (1988: 54), while Calderhead terms them 'suppositions, commitments and ideologies' (1996: 715) which can be interchangeable with terms such as 'attitudes', 'judgments', 'opinions', 'ideologies', 'perceptions', 'conceptions', 'conceptual system', 'preconceptions', 'dispositions', 'implicit theories', 'personal theories' and 'perspectives'. Richardson defines beliefs as 'psychologically held understandings, premises, or propositions about the world that are felt to be true' (1996: 103). M. Borg summarises the common features of the definition of beliefs and concludes that 'a belief is a proposition which may be consciously or unconsciously held, is evaluative in that it is accepted as true by the individual, and is therefore imbued with emotive commitment; further, it serves as a guide to thought and behaviour' (2001: 186). She further states that when considering teachers' beliefs, they usually refer to teachers' pedagogical beliefs.

All these definitions and different labels for the same term emphasise that there is no consensus. This said, a general definition for beliefs might be inappropriate (Törner 2002), as Wilson and Cooney rightly pointed out that 'concern over a precise definition of belief pales in importance compared with the issue of understanding the nature of teachers' thinking and what provides for foundation for teacher change' (2002: 145). However, others believe that there are certain characteristics that beliefs entail by drawing from reviews of teachers' beliefs and thinking, as well as the role of attitudes and beliefs in learning (e.g. Clark and Peterson 1986; Richardson 1996). For example, Bryan (2003) summarises beliefs as psychological constructions that:

(a) include understandings, assumptions, images, or propositions that are felt to be true (Richardson, 1996); (b) drive a person's actions and support decisions and judgements (Pajares, 1992); (c) have highly variable and uncertain linkages to personal, episodic, and emotional experiences (Nespor, 1987); and (d) although undeniably related to knowledge, differ from knowledge in that beliefs do not require a condition of truth (Richardson, 1996). (2003: 837)

Although there is no consensual meaning for beliefs, few would argue that the biggest confusion lies in the distinction between knowledge and beliefs, because beliefs came about as a result of research evidence that teacher knowledge cannot fully explain the nature of teacher instruction (Ball et al. 2001), and the interactive decisions teachers make in teaching. Indeed, according to Pajares (1992), one factor accounting for the messiness of the construct was the desire of the researchers in distinguishing beliefs from knowledge.

Beliefs or knowledge?
Shulman (1986) and Richardson (1996) debate the differences between beliefs and knowledge, but it is difficult to pinpoint where knowledge ends and a belief starts. Abelson (1979) identifies four features of beliefs – 'existential presumption, affective and evaluative loading, and episodic structure' – which basically explains beliefs as a personal rather than a universal influential factor which guides and explains

individual's behaviour (cited in Pajares 1992: 309). Some researchers, however, consider these two as a group of fuzzy intertwined concepts. Woods (1996) is not the only one who conflates the distinction between beliefs and knowledge. Grossman et al. suggest that the distinction between beliefs and knowledge about the subject matter is 'blurry at best' (1989: 31). Richards and Lockhart also emphasise the interrelatedness between belief and knowledge, claiming 'what teachers do is a reflection of what they know and believe, and teacher knowledge and "teacher thinking" provided the underlying framework or schema which guides the teacher's classroom actions' (1994: 29). Similarly, Verloop et al. state the impossibility of setting a clear boundary between knowledge and beliefs as they claim 'in the mind of the teacher, components of knowledge, beliefs, conceptions, and intuitions are inextricably intertwined' (2001: 446). Pajares (1992), by reviewing research done in distinguishing belief from knowledge, points out the difficulty of studying teachers' beliefs again due to the problem of definition when beliefs come to its relationship with knowledge. Although, he argues, beliefs are more influential than knowledge when people come to their decisions, he states that these two elements are actually intertwined: 'beliefs underlie both declarative and procedural knowledge' (1992: 312–13). He further clarifies that 'belief is based on evaluation and judgement; knowledge is based on objective fact' (ibid.: 313). For example, teachers have information or knowledge about communicative language teaching (CLT) methods and the perspective of relevance and appropriateness of CLT in their context. The unique evaluative and affective nature of beliefs is used by researchers to distinguish beliefs from knowledge in research (Speer 2005).

Origins of teachers' beliefs
Teachers' beliefs about learning may be based on their training, their teaching experience, or may go back to their own experience as language learners (Freeman 1992). Horwitz (1985), Johnson (1994) and Mok (1994) find that prospective foreign language teachers have many preconceived ideas about how languages are learned and how they should be taught, and the beliefs they hold are greatly influenced by their previous learning experiences. Indeed, much research has reported that student teachers' beliefs originate from their experiences of learning a second language, particularly in secondary school or formal classrooms (Horwitz 1985; Peacock 1999). Williams and Burden (1997: 56) argue that such beliefs are 'culturally bound', formed in early life before a student reaches college (Weinstein 1989), and are resistant to change (Farrell 1999). Where teachers' beliefs originate and how they develop are well-researched areas, yet present a complex picture and an ongoing debate.

Dimensions of beliefs
Research findings often take the form of categorisations and classifications of beliefs, and there are various types of beliefs depending on their source and nature (see Borg 2006). Categorisation and classification can differ. Some researchers seek relatively comprehensive classification as they believe all aspects of teaching and learning are interrelated and intertwined (e.g. Li 2008, 2012). Others have chosen to centre their focus on a single category or a small set of categories. Nevertheless, they all attempt

to characterise the belief one might hold about a particular issue or aspect in language learning and teaching. Richards and Lockhart (1994) declare that teachers' belief systems consist of both subjective and objective dimensions, including language, learning, teaching and the curriculum. Similarly, Calderhead (1995) has identified five concepts in studying teachers' beliefs: teaching, learning and learners, subject matter, professional development and the teacher.

English has different meanings to different people, and, therefore, it is instructive to examine the underlying beliefs teachers hold about English and how this may influence attitudes towards English teaching and classroom practice. Richards et al. (1992) reveal that English language teachers in Hong Kong whose first language is Chinese thought English had more grammar rules than Chinese, though they did not think English had such a large vocabulary. This might explain why so many Chinese English language teachers consider grammar important and emphasise grammar teaching in their classroom practice. Therefore, how teachers define English language, their understanding of the importance of learning a language and the difficulties learners may face feasibly could all reflect what a teacher believes English language is.

In the literature, what teachers believe about teaching and learning is identified as the most important factor influencing their understanding about classroom pedagogy. Plomp et al. (1996) define learning as a process in which four components interact: the teacher, the student, curriculum content and goals, instructional materials and infrastructure. Therefore, in a language classroom, teachers' beliefs can be inferred from an understanding of teacher and learner roles in classrooms, the definition of learning, the perceived 'best way' to learn and the qualities of 'best' students. For example, Brick summarises Chinese understanding of learning as a process which 'involves mastering a body of knowledge that is presented by a teacher in chunks small enough to be relatively easily digested' (1991: 154). Under this view of learning, both teachers and learners are concerned with the end product of learning, that is learners are expected, at an appropriate time, to be able to reproduce knowledge in the same form as it was presented to them.

Nespor (1987) and Richards et al. (2001) point out understanding teachers' beliefs can be realised by understanding how teachers define their work. When observing L2 classrooms, it is not surprising to find different teachers adopting different teaching methodologies. Johnson (1992a) explains how ESL teachers with different dominant theoretical orientations provide strikingly different literacy instruction for non-native speakers of English. Richards introduced the concept of *teacher maxims* which contain goals, values and beliefs held about the content, the process of teaching and their understanding of context in which their work suits and the roles they play, which was termed as '*culture of teaching*' (1996: 284). These values, beliefs or goals serve as the background to their decision-making and their behaviour in classrooms.

In L2 teaching, the teacher's role in a classroom, the teaching methods, the materials the teacher has adopted, the approach to managing the classroom, their understanding of effective teaching and their interpretation of being a good language teacher may reflect teachers' beliefs of teaching. Richards et al. (1992) found Chinese L2 teachers interpret their roles in the classroom as providing useful learning experiences, offering a model of correct language use, answering learners' questions, and correcting learners' errors. They believe their main role as an English teacher is to help students discover effective approaches to learning, to pass on knowledge and skills to their pupils, and to adopt teaching approaches to match their students' needs.

Beliefs and practice
One important strand of research in teachers' beliefs has focused on the relationship between beliefs and the classroom (e.g. Cundale 2001). In the substantial body of literature on teachers' beliefs, beliefs and practices are often described as either stated or enacted (cf. 'professed' and 'attributed'; Speer 2005). Over the past thirty years, research has suggested that teachers' beliefs heavily influence their pedagogical practice (for example, Ng and Farrell 2003; Mangubhai et al. 2004), their instructional decisions in the classroom (Tillema 2000), and acceptance and uptake of new approaches, techniques and activities (Donaghue, 2003). For example, Ng and Farrell (2003) found evidence that what teachers say and do in their classrooms is governed by their beliefs, while Williams and Burden (1997: 57) note, 'teachers' deep-rooted beliefs about how languages are learned will pervade their classroom actions more than a particular methodology they are told to adopt or course book they follow'. Similarly, Richards and Lockhart (1994) state that teachers' classroom practices are heavily guided and influenced by teachers' knowledge and beliefs, for example when planning lessons and giving instructions as well as when interacting with children. Woods (1991: 4) points out the relationship between teachers' beliefs systems and their decision-making. He claims that decisions and beliefs differ dramatically between teachers, but, for each teacher, there is strong evidence that the decisions made in planning and carrying out the course are internally consistent, and consistent with deeper underlying assumptions and beliefs about language, learning and teaching. On the other hand, Woods suggests that the issue of the relationship between beliefs and action has not been discussed in the same way as that between knowledge and action (2003: 207), and there is considerable disagreement as to the precise relationship between stated/professed and enacted/attributed beliefs (e.g. Basturkmen et al. 2004; Orafi and Borg 2009).

There are different perspectives with regards to these discrepancies, inconsistencies or mismatches. First, there is the highly complex relationship between beliefs and practice (Li 2013). Teachers' beliefs are a complex interactive system, which covers a range of dimensions, such as learners, curriculum, teaching and learning, professional development and self. These are intertwined with each other and cannot be considered separately from classroom practice (Li 2008). In addressing the relationships between teacher's beliefs and practices, Speer argues that methods and research designs might cause the inconsistency of teachers' beliefs and actions: 'it is certainly plausible that teachers might state beliefs and behave in a manner inconsistent with those beliefs. There are, however, other potential explanations for these findings tied to methods and research designs that warrant consideration' (2005: 368). In Speer's view, lack of shared understanding between the researcher and the investigated teachers might cause inconsistency as the findings represent the researcher's view rather than the teachers'.

The contextual factor so far is still the most widely recognised factor accounting for the discrepancy between teacher cognition and classroom practice. Shavelson and Stern's (1981) review also was the first to highlight the influence of contextual factors on teachers' behaviours. Students (e.g. their learning styles, preferences and linguistic levels) are often recognised as one of the most important contextual factors which influence what teachers do in classrooms. Other similar influential factors include wider school environments and the immediate classroom, and school culture and its norms and recognised values (Davis 2003). Sato and Kleinsasser revealed in a Japanese context that teachers' beliefs were closely tied to context, or to the school's (technical) culture – its norms and values. Norms, which teachers described as 'managing students and various task assignments' and 'keeping pace with other teachers', guided not only what they taught but how they taught (Sato and Kleinsasser 2004: 811). These understandings helped develop teachers' beliefs about teaching 'the same way for the common test and to maintain classroom management' (ibid.). This research evidence suggests that language teachers' behaviour is certainly linked very closely to their social, cultural and institutional context (Burns and Knox 2005; Li 2008). Contextual factors put strains on teachers, resulting in their 'inability to apply the new ideas within the existing parameters of syllabus, examinations, and other practical constraints' (Lamb 1995: 75). There are also other influential factors, for example years of teaching experience (Tsui 2003; Gatbonton 2008) and the teacher's level of thought processes and reflections. Basturkmen (2012) reviewed mainly doctoral research into the correspondence between language teachers' stated beliefs and practices to conclude that contextual factors bear on the correspondence of teachers' stated beliefs and practice, for example situational constraints, schools and classrooms. However, she concludes that methodological choices of the research do not have any influence on the research findings in the degree of correspondence between beliefs and practices.

In considering the relationship between teachers' beliefs and practice, one important review worth mentioning is Shavelson and Stern's (1981) work on teachers' pedagogical thoughts, judgements and decisions. This review advances our thinking in the interrelationship between teacher cognition and classroom practice. It not only confirms that teacher cognition shapes teachers' behaviour but furthermore suggests that classroom events will in turn influence the subsequent decisions a teacher may make, as they remark: 'a decision will, in all likelihood, be changed somewhat by the consequent behaviour of the teacher' (1981: 460). Simply put, teacher cognition and behaviour have 'symbiotic relationships' (Foss and Kleinsasser 1996: 441). Thus, Clark and Peterson argue the necessity for considering both thought and action together in the research on teacher cognition because '(T)eacher behaviour is substantially influenced and even determined by [the] teachers' thought process' (1986: 255) and they further argue that 'the process of teaching will be fully understood only when these two domains are brought together and examined in relation to one another' (ibid.: 258).

THREE THEORETICAL PERSPECTIVES

Despite the rapid development of teacher cognition research in the last decade, Borg (2003b) contends that teacher cognition in language education is still relatively undeveloped, fragmented and lacking any coherent guiding agenda or framework. Similarly, Li (2013) has pointed out that empirical research, especially taking different theoretical perspectives and methodological considerations, is lacking. There are three theoretical perspectives of the study of teacher cognition: the cognitive, the interactionist and the discursive psychological. In a review of the literature, very few studies define the theoretical perspective of the construct (but see Speer 2008; Li 2013). However, I argue that the importance of the theoretical in researching teacher cognition cannot be overlooked, as the theoretical underpinnings not only define the nature of the construct but direct the kind of research methodology one should adopt.

COGNITIVE PERSPECTIVE

The majority of existing research on teacher cognition takes a cognitive perspective, which views beliefs and psychological constructs as fixed assumptions or prepositions held by teachers. In this tradition, beliefs are considered as a person's static traits that remain constant across situations. Research following this tradition defines cognitions as propositions, assumptions, perspectives, concepts and so on, held by teachers consciously or unconsciously, and research tends to focus on the realm of reality inside teachers' heads. Most research in teacher cognition follows this traditional thinking and tends to elicit what teachers think about and perceive one or many aspects of their professional lives. It is problematic as it might not be appropriate to view cognitions from a single theoretical stance because a cognitive-based perspective ignores the contexts and interactive nature of teachers' daily work in classrooms. Although research has to some degree acknowledged the influence of context on teachers' beliefs and practice, it tends to operate at a macro-level, focusing on issues such as curriculum, testing, educational policy and school cultures (e.g. Sato and Kleinsasser 2004). While such studies are clearly of value, they may not always provide adequate insights into what happens at the micro-level, when teachers are engaged in specific practices. Even when focus is placed on both beliefs and practice, research within this framework tends to focus on mismatch, discrepancy, the inconsistency of teachers' beliefs and classroom practices. Research tends to describe what teachers know and believe and functions for 'using those as frameworks for examining systematicity in participants' actions in the classrooms' (Speer 2005: 376).

INTERACTIONIST PERSPECTIVE

The interactionist perspective questions the implicit premise that beliefs may serve as an explanatory principle for teacher actions. According to Skott (2001), the motives of the teachers' actions should not be seen as predetermined by his or her school subject priorities, rather they must be understood as entities that may be transformed or even emerge in and as a result of his or her interactions with students'. This perspective challenges the sole determinant role of beliefs in shaping classroom practices. Thus, in the interactionist view it is inappropriate to focus on inconsistency or discrepancy between beliefs and practice, as beliefs are the products of social interaction. Teachers' interaction with students and tasks therefore might exert a stronger influence on teachers' behaviour in the classroom, which might not match what they claim to believe. The inconsistency, as Skott (2001) explains, 'is an observer's perspective that does not do justice to the complexity of the teacher's tasks'. From this perspective, belief research should be conducted with the idea that teachers' and students' activities do make sense, and the focus should be placed on the understanding of teachers' beliefs and actions as a unified one. Therefore, research in this tradition focuses on the emergence of beliefs in interaction and places high value on the actual practice of the teacher. Argyris and Schön (1974) suggest that people's beliefs should be inferred from the ways in which they act rather than from what they say they believe. This view has been taken on by an interactionist perspective of beliefs, and classroom interaction data are used to understand how teachers attempt to relate sensibly to a multitude of different and possibly subjectively incompatible aspects of the situations at hand. Compared to the cognitive perspective of teacher cognition, the interactionist perspective opens a space for researchers to reconsider the dominant premise that beliefs are and should be the main influence on the classroom, although the classroom practices may be mediated by external or internal constraints. It certainly advances our thinking about the relationship between teachers' beliefs and practice and the impact of beliefs on practices. The key position of this perspective is that beliefs are fluid and they emerge as a result of teacher–student interactions.

DISCURSIVE PSYCHOLOGICAL PERSPECTIVE

Another theoretical perspective comes from the 'discursive' branch of psychology. To quote te Molder and Potter (2005: 19), DP, first coined by Edwards and Potter (1992), is the 'perspective that has addressed cognition in the context of interaction most systematically in a psychological context'. It 'reflects upon descriptions, explanations and justifications given in the course of a talk or a written report' (Gellert 2001: 35). In DP, 'the subject matter of psychology has to take account of discourses, significations, subjectivities and positionings, for it is in these that psychological phenomena actually exist' (Harré and Gillett 1994: 22). DP challenges the view of mainstream psychology that language or talk is a channel to the externalising of underlying thoughts and a passive and neutral means of communication; rather, it treats language as a central activity in social life and 'it is a vehicle through which our sense of the world, and indeed psychological concepts themselves (such as memory, attitude, or cognition) are actively constructed' (Hutchby and Wooffitt 2008: 6). Therefore, this perspective focuses on the ways in which beliefs and knowledge 'emerge' from discourses and are 'accomplished' locally, and is more interested in 'how issues like knowing are dealt with by the participants *themselves*' (Barwell, 2003: 203, emphasis in the original). It studies how these psychological concepts are deployed in, oriented to and managed in the language (talk or text) by people. It looks at the different sorts of things that are said, how they are said, to what purpose and to what effect in interaction, following the tradition of CA (Hutchby and Wooffitt 2008). te Molder and Potter (2005: 3) summarise that both CA and DP emphasise that:

- Talk is a medium of action.
- Talk is locally and situationally organised.
- The point of view of the interactant is basic to understanding talk-in-interaction.
- The primary analytic approach is the empirical study of natural interaction.

DP focuses on the psychological motives, attitudes and morals that underpin conversations and interactions (Edwards and Potter 1992), and it uses materials from real-world situations, where people act and interact in particular settings – in families, in workplaces, in schools and so on (Potter 2012a). As stated earlier, cognition-in-interaction is a special kind of psychological reality – not the one defined by the mental state or process, but by the participants orienting practically in an ongoing interaction following the rules for turn-taking. From a discursive psychological perspective, cognitions are publicly displayed in natural utterances which are shaped by the understanding of the prior turns, and which shape the development of the next turn. For this reason, DP adopts discourse analysis (especially CA in recent developments). This perspective has led the study of teacher cognition to very different approaches and the focus has shifted from the mental construct of participants to the displayed positions and understandings of the participants. In particular, it places emphasis on action and natural talk and views beliefs as locally constructed and publically displayed understandings, for example by analysing student–teacher interactions in classrooms as well as interviews with teachers about their beliefs (Morton 2012). The findings represent the discursive practices of teachers of those particular moments rather than their overarching beliefs, and the focus is on the participants' points of view through the analysis of 'publicly displayed' discourse. In a word, from a DP perspective beliefs are not static but are socially constructed; thus, the focus is not placed on the deliberate separation of beliefs from practice. DP is critiqued by Speer (2005), who argues that there is the possibility that it fails to achieve shared understandings as the findings/analysis are shaped by researchers' understandings of particular terms, which may or may not be shared by the participants. However, the merit of CA lies in uncovering the tacit reasoning procedures underlying the production and interpretation of talk in organised sequences of interaction (Hutchby and Wooffitt 2008). Simply put, CA allows the data to speak for the phenomenon and how participants orient to each other.

SUMMARY

This chapter has reviewed relevant work on teacher cognition with respect to its development, significance dimensions and theoretical perspectives. Considering the concept itself in both general education and language teaching research, there is a widely shared opinion that teacher cognition plays a central role in understanding teaching and learning, classroom dynamics and pedagogy, as well as developing teachers. Based on the analysis of related literature, the following features concerning teachers' beliefs have been recognised.

First, much of the research has been conducted within the cognitive perspective of cognition, emphasising the mental state of the teacher, although contextual influences are recognised. This work has significance in bringing teacher cognition to the centre of pedagogy and has some significant virtues, yet it does not provide for the focused investigation of teacher cognition-in-interaction, given the importance of interaction in teachers' professional lives. Thus, much research is needed to take either an interactionist or a discursive psychological perspective to investigate the concept. Second, there are no standard beliefs teachers should hold about teaching or learning, and, therefore, it is not necessary to try to change beliefs to the 'right ones'. However, it is meaningful to help teachers to be reflective and self-conscious of their beliefs for the benefit of personal professional development as well as for developing their pedagogical awareness and practice. In Chapter 2, approaches to investigating teacher cognition are reviewed and critiqued.

2
APPROACHES TO THE STUDY OF TEACHER COGNITION

INTRODUCTION

Research in teacher cognition has been characterised by a proliferation of concepts and terminology (see Chapter 1). Problems of terminology are not merely what Clandinin and Connelly (1987: 488) refer to as 'simply different words naming the same thing', but have more to do with the complexity of the nature of the construct and the difficulties of investigating it. Understandings of teacher cognition are closely linked to the method of investigation; as with much educational research, findings are closely linked to the research methods and instruments used (see also Li and Walsh 2011). Nevertheless, methodological issues or considerations in researching teacher cognition have rarely been explored, with only very limited discussion to date.

Among the limited studies, Borg (2006) presents four categories of data collection methods – self-report instruments, verbal commentary, observation, and reflective writing – and provides a detailed review of empirical studies following those methods. Borg (2012) compared research methods adopted in twenty-five articles published in 2011 on the focus of the study, context and participants, the research stance, data collection and analysis. Both publications contribute to our understanding of the current research agenda and are a sound starting point to help researchers in teacher cognition to consider different data collection methods. This said, typically for work in this area, neither of them addresses methodological issues. Thus, in this chapter, I review methodological approaches to the study of language teacher cognition, considering both methodological approaches and research methods.

RESEARCH APPROACHES

Investigating cognition can be very difficult since personal theories may be subconscious so that teachers might be unable to articulate them. In reviewing the literature very few studies consider research strategy or methodology, but there is a related inquiry: learners' beliefs about second language acquisition (SLA). There are two interesting works on approaches to learners' beliefs about SLA which could shed light on the investigation of teachers' beliefs. Kalaja (2003) groups research about SLA beliefs into two approaches. The first, and the dominant one, referred to as 'mainstream', is to complete an inventory of different beliefs by indicating the strength of agreement or disagreement; for example, BALLI (Beliefs about Language Learning Inventory) developed by Horwitz (1985, 1987). Another popular strategy is to use interviews and focus group discussions (Wenden 1986, 1987), which is categorized as 'alternative' (Kalaja 2003).

Barcelos (2000, 2003) proposes three main approaches to the study of learner beliefs according to what beliefs mean, research methodology used, and other factors associated with beliefs, namely nominative, metacognitive and contextual. According to Barcelos (2003), the normative approach considers beliefs as synonyms for preconceived notions, myths or misconceptions (Horwitz 1987: 126). The methodology associated with such an approach normally is Likert-type questionnaires. The metacognitive approach defines beliefs as metacognitive knowledge and most of the studies applied the framework on metacognitive knowledge (Wenden 1987, 1998, 1999, 2001). The type of data collected within this approach consists of verbal accounts through semi-structured interviews and self-reports. The contextual approach emphasised the close relationship between beliefs and context, and the aim of such an approach is to gain a better understanding of beliefs in specific contexts. Various data can be collected and diverse analysis is used (see Barcelos (2003) for more details). Both Kalaja and Barcelos' work offer interesting perspectives on the investigation of beliefs from the learners' stance.

My own view on current studies about teacher cognition however differs from theirs. Whereas their approaches draw heavily upon evidence of SLA and learning, for teacher cognition there are more layers contributing to the construct: for example, teaching and professionalism, being a teacher, educational effectiveness and the dynamics of classrooms. More importantly, different theoretical positions will result in different methodological approaches. Taking into consideration the different theoretical perspectives of understanding (language) teacher cognition I outlined in Chapter 1, I would like to propose three main methodological approaches in researching teacher cognition: cognitive, contextual and discourse. While it is not always easy to establish a clear link between a particular theoretical perspective and a methodological approach, typically researchers adopting a cognitive perspective have used both cognitive and contextual approaches, while those studies using a discourse approach are framed within an interactionist perspective. In what follows, I will consider the research methodologies utilised in the literature and point to the need to consider the use of CA within the perspective of DP.

COGNITIVE APPROACH

The cognitive approach is closely linked to a cognitive perspective on beliefs, viewing the construct as fixed, prior-defined assumptions held by the teacher. The underlying assumption is that teachers hold propositions, assumptions, perceptions and conceptions of language learning and teaching, which guide their management of classroom teaching techniques. The nature of beliefs thus is stable, fixed, can be described or elicited by self-report instruments. This approach also indicates that beliefs or assumptions held by the teacher might be contradictory, therefore the motive of the research might be associated with illuminating the misconceptions. Cross-sectional research or tests are probably the most distinctive research methods associated with this approach. Cross-sectional research often adopts Likert-scale questionnaires, like BALLI (Horwitz 1985), the Beliefs Inventory (Johnson 1992a), or a scenario-based questionnaire (e.g. Borg 2006), or tests to investigate teachers' knowledge (e.g. Andrews 1999, 2003; Andrews and McNeil 2005). Although semi-structured interviews are often used as well, and studies are qualitative in nature, the primary focus of such research is still on cognitive knowledge.

Cross-sectional research
Cross-sectional surveys have been a strong feature of research on language teacher cognition, in which self-completion questionnaires and structured interviews are very common. The self-report questionnaire is considered a useful and appropriate tool by researchers in teacher cognition research for three reasons: (1) it is a widely used and useful instrument for collecting survey information, providing structured, often numerical data, and is comparatively straightforward to analyse (Wilson and McLean 1994); (2) it supplies standardised answers with little scope for the data to be affected by 'interpersonal factors' (Denscombe 1998); and (3) it encourages pre-coded answers, and 'the knowledge needed is controlled by the questions, therefore, it affords a good deal of precision and clarity' (McDonough and McDonough 1997: 171). The closed questions are useful in that they can 'generate frequencies of response amenable to statistical treatment and analysis; and meanwhile they also enable comparisons to be made across groups in the sample' (Oppenheim 1992: 115). Among the many questionnaires, Horwitz's (1985) BALLI and Lightbown's and Spada's (1993) are widely used.

The BALLI was designed to 'assess teacher opinions on a variety of issues and controversies related to language learning' (Horwitz 1985: 334), and was piloted with 150 first-year foreign language students. This 34-tier self-report questionnaire includes five areas of foreign language learning: difficulty of language learning, foreign language aptitude, the nature of language learning, learning and communication strategies, and motivation and expectations. Horwitz used this scale to raise the student teachers' awareness of beliefs on a one-semester teaching methodology, although no findings of her cohort were reported. Due to its initiating significance, BALLI has gained popularity in this research area varying from small- to large-scale, and in different contexts, including measuring learners' beliefs (e.g. Chawhan and Oliver 2000).

In researching teacher cognition, BALLI has been considered a reliable tool to elicit teachers' beliefs, in particular in comparative studies across cultures. Yang (2000), for example, conducted a survey of sixty-eight primary English teachers in Taiwan on their beliefs about language teaching and learning, and further compared his findings with Horwitz (1985) and Kern (1995). All of the studies drew the conclusions that it is easier for children than adults to learn a foreign language and that it is important to listen and repeat a lot and to practice in the language lab.

BALLI was also used in a longitudinal study by Peacock (2001), who conducted a three-year study on 146 pre-service ESL teachers' beliefs about L2 learning using modified questionnaires (BALLI), in combination with other data collection tools. In reporting findings from BALLI, Peacock noted that very little change took place to the student teachers' beliefs about language learning over the three-year TESL methodology training course. Also, pre-service teachers' beliefs were different from those of experienced teachers in terms of grammar, vocabulary and the role of intelligence in learning a language.

Despite its popularity, BALLI has been challenged, especially in researching learners' beliefs, for example Kuntz (1996) has raised several issues concerning the instrument's validity. However, Nikitina and Furuoka re-examined Horwitz's BALLI instruments in the Malaysian context and concluded that 'Horwitz's instrument can be considered to be a suitable tool for conducting research on language learning beliefs in [a] different socio-linguistic stetting' (2006: 217) and to 'endorse the applicability of BALLI as a research tool for assessing learners' beliefs and evaluating a unique environment of the language classroom' (ibid.: 218).

Lightbown's and Spada's (1993) Likert scale is another popular tool adopted by researchers to elicit teachers' beliefs. This instrument contains twelve items, for which Lightbown and Spada also provided a benchmark informed by language learning theory with which to measure and compare teachers' and students' thinking. Davis conducted a survey on teachers' and students' beliefs regarding aspects of language learning in a Chinese-English translation programme in Macao, PRC, by using this questionnaire. The study found that teachers and students shared the same beliefs about language learning resting upon 'a common theoretical base comprised of an admixture of *behaviourism, innatism* and *interactionism*' (2003: 217). The study reported that 'language is learned mainly through imitation; students with high IQs are good language learners; when students are allowed to interact freely (for example, in pair or group work), they learn each other's mistakes' (ibid.: 216). The emphasis of the importance of imitation, intelligence and corrective feedback reflected the teachers' beliefs about language learning. Davis also demonstrated how teachers' beliefs performed a dual function: on the one hand teachers saw themselves as performing 'an extension of a parental role in education', while on the other they regarded themselves as powerful educators, who can 'make a significant difference in their students' language competence at any age' (ibid.: 218).

Brown and McGannon (1998) used Lightbown's and Spada's (1993) questionnaire to explore the beliefs about L2 learning of trainee teachers at Monash University. They surveyed thirty-five trainee teachers of Languages Other than English (LOTE) and TESL to test how strong Lorti's 'apprenticeship of observation' was on their beliefs. The questionnaire was administered twice in three weeks so that belief changes could be tracked before and after the teaching practicum. Differences were found between trainer and trainees and there were few changes, in particular in the area of error correction. They conclude that both trainer and trainees need to be aware of the influence of 'apprenticeship of observation' and suggested that trainers should provide trainees with opportunities for 'guided reflection'.

MacDonald et al. (2001) also used Lightbown's and Spada's scale to investigate the beliefs of student teachers who were studying at undergraduate and postgraduate level to become teachers of English to Speakers of Other Languages (TESOL). The main objective of this research was to examine the extent to which a research and theory course influenced key beliefs held by students during their period of study in a UK university. They concluded that certain changes in key beliefs in student teachers' attitude and beliefs towards language learning did take place during programmes.

Apart from BALLI and Lightbown and Spada (1993), other questionnaires have been developed to investigate teachers' beliefs in different socio-cultural contexts and in specific domains, for example in grammar (e.g. Andrews 2003; Borg and Burns 2008) and technology uptake (e.g. Li 2008). Among these studies, two merit a discussion in terms of design and also the scale of participants: Borg and Burns (2008) and Li (2008). Both studies combined quantitative and qualitative data, although Li adopted a mixed method design while Borg and Burns had both closed and open-ended sections in their questionnaire.

Borg and Burns (2008) designed and administered a questionnaire to investigate teachers' beliefs about integrating grammar in adult TESOL classrooms and their reported practices. The questionnaire contained fifteen statements (five point Likert scale) covering a range of key issues in grammar teaching, such as the role of explicit teaching and explicit knowledge, the position of grammar in instructional sequences, the role of the teacher, the importance of practice, deductive and inductive learning, comparisons between teaching children and adults, and the integration of grammar with other skills. The questionnaire also had an open-ended question section which aimed to elicit the extent to which teachers felt such integration took place in work and provide an illustration of this. According to Borg and Burns, the open-ended questions' section was 'the source of the most insightful data in this study' (2008: 460). This questionnaire then was administered to 176 language teachers from eighteen countries and they found that teachers are generally favourably disposed to some elements of explicit grammar work. They concluded:

> Overall, the portrait of grammar teaching which emerges here from teachers' responses to the 15 statements is one characterized by regular phases of explicit work, a desire to encourage students to discover rules (without discounting the use of direct explanation), and regular opportunities for grammar practice. (Ibid.: 477)

The grammar work, as Borg and Burns point out, should not occur in isolation but in relation to skills-oriented work.

Li (2008) designed a questionnaire to investigate EFL teachers' beliefs about technology use in Chinese secondary classrooms. This questionnaire was used in combination with focus group interviews, and was administered to 450 teachers. The questionnaire contained sections of knowledge, perception, attitudes and action, which is guided by what teachers know, believe and do. This large-scale survey revealed that teachers have strong beliefs about the potential of technology and presented positive attitudes towards its integration. However, in their reported practice, teachers did not depict a similarly positive picture. School support and professional development exert a strong influence on their decision-making, but, more importantly, their pedagogical beliefs affect whether and how they use technology in teaching English.

Most of the studies using questionnaires have provided a general picture of the kinds of beliefs teachers may have. They have mainly described or classified beliefs in both content and pedagogical areas, and have made assumptions as to how beliefs could influence teachers' instructional practices, without considering the actual classroom practice. These studies have limited themselves to establishing or gaining insights into the complexity of classroom practice. In other words, this kind of approach only reveals a segment of teachers' beliefs: stated/espoused beliefs. Studies using cognitive approaches can produce clear and precise pictures through well-designed questionnaires involving a large number of respondents; however, they are limited in the sense of getting a whole picture of what teachers think and believe, as the questionnaire items are developed by researchers themselves and teachers are restricted by the choices. Furthermore, there is a risk of misunderstanding about the beliefs inventory.

Some of the research to date is qualitative in nature and uses a range of data elicitation methods to explore teachers' beliefs and perceptions, for example interviews, written logs and repertory grids.[1] Despite the qualitative nature of the research, most studies are still based on the underlying assumptions about the nature of the cognitions as mental states or mental lives of teachers. Even talking about practices is treated as a channel to gain access to the underlying reality (i.e. their 'mental' lives). For example, Borg (2006) points out that interviews reflect the assumption that cognitions can be articulated by teachers and that they can provide an account of the cognitive processes in their practice. Wyatt argues that the use of interviews could allow the researchers to access the participating teachers' 'thoughts, feelings and beliefs' (2009: 20). This kind of data collection method is therefore used widely by researchers in the investigation of teacher cognition.

Breen (1991) used written logs (similar to diaries or journals) to examine sixty-three experienced ESL teachers on the beliefs about language learning during their undertaking of a Master's degree at Lancaster University by asking them to teach their native language to L1 students of the same course, and he concluded that behaviour was based on a 'personal conceptualization of the teaching-learning process' (1991: 215). Many of them revealed in the teaching session that 'language is a system' which included grammar and vocabulary (ibid.: 230).

Similarly, Chan (1999) investigated twenty one-year full-time Postgraduate Diploma in Education (PGDE) (secondary course) student teachers' beliefs using semi-structured interviews. She concluded that the student teachers' beliefs were deep-rooted in their growing environment and culture, and rooted beliefs were hard to change because the legacies of the past successfully linked to the present environment. Chan pointed out that the beliefs of the student teachers reflected two distinctive types of views on teaching and learning: the ideal and the real. The ideal type reflected the progressive views on teaching and learning when teachers acted as facilitators to help learners to develop in an 'ideal' and supportive environment, while the reality type, on the contrary, reflected the present and real learning environment which was characterised by large class sizes, the cramming involved in teaching schedules, the overemphasised importance of examinations. Chan argued that the ideal type could be the stimulus for student teachers to learn but also for a confrontation with 'reality', which was suggested in the specific educational context, examinations' influence on teaching and learning.

Interviews have offered a different perspective of teacher cognition, especially in recognition of the influence of context. However, interviews provide a summary of what was said by participants, rather than how it was said. What is not revealed from an ordinary interview (especially when thematic content analysis is used) is information about emphasis, intonation, delays, hesitation and feelings. The transcript is usually cleaned up and there is a danger of not recording what was actually said in the way in which it was said.

Tests
Tests are normally used to measure teachers' factual knowledge (e.g. linguistic knowledge). There is evidence of using tests in the study of UK teacher trainees' knowledge about language, but there is very little research using tests in foreign language contexts (but see Andrews 1999, 2003; Andrews and McNeil 2005). Tests are very limited in researching teacher cognition as they mainly measure teachers' linguistic knowledge of a specific area, for example error correction, grammar rules etc. There are two obvious weaknesses in using tests: first, they can produce an inaccurate picture of what teachers know about the language as it is almost impossible to test how much knowledge a teacher might have about the language they teach; second, linguistic knowledge constitutes only a very small part of teachers' knowledge. Borg also points out the challenging issue of getting in-service teachers' participation in such tests as they 'may represent a threat to one's self-esteem and the prospect of embarrassment can be a powerful disincentive' (2006: 182). He suggests that tests need to be used very sensitively in the study of what teachers know about language.

Mixed methods
To date, much of the research on teachers' beliefs (and learners' beliefs) has relied on self-reported data. The difficulty of eliciting teachers' beliefs through reported data also hides the fact that they may wish to produce certain beliefs rather than state their own; for example, they might wish to produce a particular image of themselves. Lee and Yarger (1996) have suggested a comprehensive investigation of teacher education to include multiple modes of inquiry or triangulation to capture complexities (see also Foss and Kleinsasser 1996, 2001). Similarly, Gatbonton (1999) suggests a combination of qualitative and quantitative methods may be profitable. Clearly, given the value in using both quantitative and qualitative methods to investigate beliefs, there is a tendency to move in the direction of multiple methods. Johnson (1992a), for example, used a Multidimensional TESL Theoretical Orientation Profile, consisting of an Ideal Instructional Protocol, a Lesson Plan Analysis Task, and a Beliefs Inventory, to determine the extent to which thirty ESL teachers possessed theoretical beliefs about L2 learning and teaching which reflect the methodological divisions of skill-based, rule-based and function-based approaches toward L2 teaching. The results suggest that the majority of these teachers possess clearly defined theoretical beliefs which consistently reflect one particular methodological approach. This

Beliefs Inventory, consisting of fifteen items, was then used in different contexts in the investigation of teachers' beliefs. Johnson chose three secondary-level ESL teachers identified as having different theoretical orientations to determine the extent to which ESL teachers' instructional practices are consistent with their theoretical beliefs through transcribed classroom observations. The results revealed that literacy instruction for non-native speakers of English was consistent with each teacher's theoretical orientation. Although Johnson's focus was on the relationship between belief and practice, it was one of the earliest which combined questionnaires and other instruments in an investigation of teachers' beliefs. Since then, more studies have experimented with other ways of investigating beliefs and have employed other data collection techniques together with questionnaires.

CONTEXTUAL APPROACH

In recognition of the influence of contextual factors on teachers' beliefs, the contextual approach has become more popular in contemporary research. A number of research studies explore language learning beliefs by employing a contextual approach (Allen 1996). As Kramsch (2003) has claimed, research employing contextual approaches uses ethnography, narratives and metaphors. Case studies are also used. Bernat and Gvozdenko (2005) conclude that case studies are qualitative in nature and contribute to an interpretive paradigm. They further point out that research using a contextual approach not only fits in with different theoretical frameworks (for example, phenomenographical or neo-Vygotskian socio-cultural) (e.g. Alanen 2003), but also adopts different methods of data collection including ethnographic classroom observations, diaries, discourse analysis and naturalistic interviews (see Bernat and Gvozdenko 2005 for further discussion).

The case study
The case study has presented itself as an appropriate strategy to address the complexity of teacher cognition and the influential factors of the context. Although only a very few studies clearly label themselves as case studies (e.g. Li and Walsh 2011), more studies have adopted this approach.

In most case studies more than one method is used and focus is gradually shifted from articulated beliefs to the understanding of what teachers believe and how they practice in their contexts (although in some cases they are a single case study, meaning that they only use one type of data collection method). Breen et al. (2001) uncovered teachers' principles and classroom practice of eighteen experienced ESL teachers to adults and children in Australia from observed lessons, subsequent interviews and elicitation procedures. The findings revealed principles that were common to the majority of the teachers that guided their work, such as 'taking account of individual differences between students and/or the specific characteristics of individual students' (2001: 489) and 'enabling their students to best remember and recall what is taught' (ibid.: 491). Furthermore, the findings showed that a single principle held by the individual teacher may be realised in action through several distinct practices, which coincided with Ernest's (1989) study about two mathematics teachers: having similar knowledge but teaching in different ways. Conversely, 'a single practice may be an expression of more than one principle' (Breen et al. 2001: 495).

Richards et al. (2001: 41) propose that 'changes in teachers' practice are the result of changes in teachers' beliefs', and the change is 'multidimensional and is triggered both by personal factors as well as by the professional contexts in which teachers work'. They distributed a questionnaire to 112 ESL teachers to investigate their beliefs about language teaching and learning. The most commonly reported core belief centred on the role of grammar in language teaching and the related issue of how grammar should be taught. The participants either addressed the importance of grammar for communication, comprehension and clear expression, or described grammar as the foundation of English language learning, or the need for grammar in the early stages of language learning. The second largest category of beliefs emerging from this study was about learners, that they ought to be independent, self-directed and responsible for their own learning. The importance of the learning strategy and autonomous language learning were also addressed. The third most common key belief the teachers held was the importance of language skills, especially reading instruction. The participants also reported the characteristics of being a good teacher in the dimensions of teacher–student relationships and teacher roles. Considering the purposes of learning a language, most participants agreed that language learning is for communication and should be pragmatic and student-centred.

Andrews (2003) surveyed 170 secondary English teachers in Hong Kong and interviewed and observed seventeen teachers to examine their beliefs about subject matter, specifically about grammar and pedagogy. The study revealed that 'the individual experience of teaching their subject in a particular context influenced their beliefs and their pedagogical practice' (2003: 372). Context and experience have been noticed as important factors which shape teachers' beliefs (Lee and Yarger 1996; Sato and Kleinsasser 2004), as in Andrews' (2003) study data showed clearly how teachers were influenced by the contexts in which they worked. It is also noted that teachers' beliefs and practices are influenced 'not only by the macro-culture of society (and such factors as the syllabus, the textbooks, the examination system, the expectations of parents, and student characteristics), but also by the micro-culture of their particular institution' (ibid.: 372). This study also reported the links between 'guided principles' and practices – a principle is reflected in different practices, and one practice results from different principles (Breen et al. 2001).

Sato and Kleinsasser (2004) investigated the beliefs, practices and interactions of nineteen teachers in a Japanese high-school English department using interviews, observations and teachers' documents. The study revealed that the teachers' beliefs were closely tied to context, or the school's (technical) culture – its norms and values. Such norms, such as 'managing students and various task assignments took precedence over teaching, and communication and collaboration consisted of keeping pace with other teachers and getting through the day', guided not only what they taught, but how they taught (2004: 811). These understandings helped develop teachers' beliefs about teaching 'the same way for the common test and to maintain classroom management' (ibid.). The study noted how 'the school's (technical) culture influences to a greater extent an individual's beliefs, practices and interactions than an individual's beliefs, practices and interactions influence a school's (technical) culture' (ibid.: 814).

Farrell and Lim (2005) investigated and compared the beliefs with actual classroom practices of two experienced English teachers with regards to grammar teaching in a primary school in Singapore, using interviews, observation and students' written work. In both cases, they found that strong beliefs were held about the importance of grammar regarding writing, and also for both speech and listening comprehension. The teachers also believed in the importance of providing grammar drills. Although classroom instruction was generally guided by their beliefs in both teachers' classrooms, divergence of their stated beliefs and classroom practices was also witnessed. The factors which accounted for the divergence included teachers' reverence for traditional grammar instruction and time issues, as 'the demand on their time came not only from the syllabus demands and the school administration, but also from the parents' (2005: 10). However, the mismatch between the espoused beliefs of a teacher and beliefs-in-action might bring about what Willams and Burden (1997: 54) describe as 'confused and confusing messages' to students.

Li and Walsh (2011) compared the beliefs and classroom practices of a novice and an experienced teacher, using interviews and classroom interaction. Li and Walsh (2011) is perhaps one of the very few studies which clearly suggests a case study strategy. Their study suggests that teachers' beliefs and their classroom practices exist in a complex and complicated relationship, a 'symbiotic relationship': beliefs are both shaped by and shape ensuing interactions. They illustrate their points by commenting on how beliefs and practices influence each other in both teachers' cases.

> Li Fang's stated beliefs of the primacy of vocabulary appeared to strongly influence her teaching and the ways in which she interacted with her students, focusing, for example, on knowing the meaning, pronunciation and form of new words. Likewise, her practice of going over new words took up quite a big chunk of her lesson and suggests that she attaches importance to this activity. Similarly, we can see how Da Xin's beliefs about the primacy of 'oral communication skills' is reflected in his attempted 'conversations' with his students and his 'control' in clearly demonstrated IRF patterns. His extensive use of IRF may reveal something about Da Xin's beliefs about learning; a suggestion, perhaps, that for him IRF is central to learning. (2011: 53)

In particular, they argue the case for using multiple methods to investigate teachers' beliefs, in their case an interview in combination with classroom data, which I will return to in the next section.

Li's study is another which clearly defines its research strategy: '(T)his study adopted a qualitative case-study approach' (2012: 38). Li (2012) also provides reasoning on the appropriateness of the case study in researching teacher cognition. She wrote:

> Case study encourages exploration of a contemporary phenomenon within its real-life context (Yin, 2009), and it is consistent with participative and

socio-cultural views of learning, the current context; it encourages exploration of multiple perspectives using different researching tools, such as interview, observation and diary; it is exploratory, starting with a broad focus and then narrowing in light of data which this study intends to do to understand individual's experience. Overall, case study suggests itself as the best method as it benefits from 'providing a rich and vivid description of events with the analysis of them' (Hitchcock and Hughes, 1995, p. 317). (Ibid.: 38)

Further, she links the choice of methods and research strategy to the nature of beliefs by referring to Pajares who argues that 'beliefs cannot be directly observed or measured but must be inferred from what people say, intend, and do – fundamental prerequisites that educational researchers have seldom followed' (1992: 314). Indeed, Pajares has pointed out the importance of using teachers' articulated comments and teaching behaviours:

teachers' verbal expressions, predispositions to action, and teaching behaviours must all be included in assessments of beliefs (my emphasis). Not to do so calls into question the validity of the findings and the value of the study. (Ibid.: 327)

From this quote, we can thus see the importance of examining beliefs through the lens of action. Another important advantage of case studies not thoroughly exploited previously is their potential for comparing teachers' practice through classroom observation to their stated beliefs. Beliefs, understanding and knowledge are associated with non-verbal behaviour and according to Cohen et al. (2000: 188) observation studies are superior to experiments and surveys when this kind of data is being collected. Classroom observation, together with interviews, seem to be the ideal tools for exploring and understanding beliefs at both theoretical and practical levels. The merit of a case study strategy lies in the capacity to provide further understandings of a group or culture. A case study strategy does not necessarily allow generalisations to be made, but it does provide detailed descriptions which can contribute to our understandings of a language teacher and corresponding belief system.

Alternative techniques
Other techniques to elicit teachers' beliefs have been advocated, such as visualisation activity – an activity to create mental images and pictures for certain purposes, the repertory grid technique, stimulated recall, and metaphor analysis.

DISCOURSE APPROACHES

Although cognitive or contextual approaches are predominant in teacher cognition research, still some researchers have utilised other approaches, which are largely influenced by interactionist perspectives and discursive psychological views of cognition. They place emphasis on interaction, and research methodologies largely fall within the branch of ethnomethodology, including interactional analysis and CA. So, rather than using language to gain access to a hidden mental realm, or to ascertain the reliability or truth of participants' descriptions or accounts, in Potter and Hepburn's words, a social constructionist perspective focuses on:

> a world of descriptions, claims, reports, allegations and assertions as parts of human practices, and it works to keep these as the central topic of research rather than trying to move beyond them to the objects or events that seem to be the topic of such discourse. (Potter and Hepburn 2008: 275)

And from the interactionist perspective, cognition is considered as a unified concept. I shall discuss the methodologies derived from these perspectives next.

In researching language learning beliefs, Kalaja supports the use of discourse analysis, and criticises questionnaire and content analysis of learners' statements; she notices that questionnaires 'only measure beliefs in theory and not on actual occasions of talk or writing' and that the analysis of interviews shows that 'the data are read selectively and analysed in broad categories' (1995: 197). Kalaja therefore proposes using naturalistic discourse data in researching learners' beliefs. The starting point for utilising classroom observation is that beliefs should be inferred from the ways in which teachers act (Argyris and Schön 1974) as well as from what they say they believe. Similarly, Richards and Lockhart consider that teachers' knowledge and beliefs 'provide the underlying framework or schema which guides teachers' classroom practice' (1994: 29). From their perspective, teachers' actions reflect their knowledge and beliefs, that is that by observing 'what they do and say' in the classrooms, 'what's in their heads' can be accessed. This view has resonance with a claim of difference between espoused theory (theory claimed by a participant) and theory in action (what is done in the classroom), so it is necessary to look not only at what they claim but also at what they do in practice.

There are a few studies on teacher cognition investigating the concept through the lens of classroom interaction (e.g. Li and Walsh 2011; Li 2012), adopting a broadly discourse analytic perspective. Perhaps the earliest and most well-known proponents of discourse analysis are Sinclair and Coulthard (1975), whose observation that most classroom discourse follows an initiation–response–feedback/evaluation (IR(F/E)) structure is still highly relevant to the study of classroom discourse today. For every move made by a student, teachers typically make two; for example:

```
I (Initiation) T: what's the past tense of go?
R (Response) S: went
F/E (Feedback/Evaluation) T: went, excellent.
```

Studies adopting a discourse analytic or interactionist view compare what teachers say with their classroom interaction (what they do). Li (2012) used classroom interaction data to illustrate the kind of activity and teaching focus her teachers had in their practices. By considering both teachers' articulated beliefs together with their interactions with students, this study demonstrated the development trajectory of her participants over a one-year TESOL course. In her study, Liang, one teacher, practiced as a grammar-oriented teacher and acted as a knowledge provider (see Extract 2.1). Very little student contribution was observed and when it was, it was very limited to the vocabulary level and the focus was on accuracy.

Extract 2.1[2]

```
1   T    last week we learned simple past tense simple past
2        future tense in speaking English now let's make a
3        review you use past tense to describe something
4        happened in the past and simple past future tense
5        to describe something WAS going to happen ok?=
6   SS   =yes.
7   T    next we will do a warm up activity practising use
8        the simple past tense now here a report written by
9        Jason and here what this man everyday what he does
10       so now what you need to do is rewrite this report
11       what she what he did last Wednesday (.) ok?
```

Without interactional data, the above observation of Liang focusing on 'drilling' would not be easily justified. The interactional analysis here was used to illustrate the kind of practices Liang used and how his practice diverged or converged with his articulated beliefs. Interaction analysis in the above studies made it possible to compare teachers' stated beliefs and their actual practice. Li and Walsh (2011) have argued the case for interactional analysis in researching teacher cognition. They claim:

> Teachers' stated beliefs (from the interview data) and their interactions with students (from the classroom observation data) were compared as a means of gaining insights into the complex relationship between what teachers report as belief and their interactions while teaching. Put differently, this procedure allowed us to compare what teachers say they do while teaching with what they actually do as evidenced in their interactions. The procedures used in this study also provided us with an opportunity to reflect on the extent to which classroom interaction data can enhance understandings of teachers' beliefs. (2011: 44–5)

Interactional data not only help to establish a relationship between the teachers' stated beliefs and practice, but also provide evidence of the growth of teachers' beliefs. In her 2012 study, Li showed how her participant, Fang, changed understanding and behaviour through the lens of classroom interaction:

Extract 2.2

```
1   T    so there are two types of verbs regular and irregular
2        (1.5) now we are dealing with regular verbs today (2)
```

```
3         look at these verbs on PowerPoint(2) to change to past
4         tense you need to add ed after the verb so the rule is v
5         plus ed (2.0) you must remember to plus ED after the verb
6         to change it to past tense (.) now let's look at some
7         other verbs and I want you to give me their past tense.
```

Extract 2.3

```
1   T    so ((pointing to the PowerPoint Once upon a time...)) from
2        this short sentence or from these words (1.0) what can you
3        think about it (1.3)
4   S1   [eh (.) °story°?
5   S2   [fairytale?
6   T    I heard STORY and FAIRYtale? GOOD (2.0) so and what is er
7        your err favorite fairytale?
8   S1   [°sleepy beauty°
9   T    [sleepy beauty? sleeping beauty! =
10  S3   =Cinderella [°Cinderella°
11  S4               [three bears (1.0) three bears
12  T    three what?
13  S4   three bears
14  T    [oh (.)
15  SS   [oh
16  T    mine is the beauty and the (.) beast yeah and do you
17       remember the ending of those fairytales? =
18  SS   =yeah
```

The development of Fang's beliefs was clearly evidenced in her interaction with her students. In Li's analysis:

> Several changes were observed in this session about Fang's teaching. First, instead of giving out explanations and structures using linguistic terms as she did at the beginning of the term, Fang presented a context (once upon a time) to elicit ideas from students. Establishing a context seems rather important here to the writing session. Secondly, Fang tried to develop a dialogue with students (line 5-6) after she heard students' responses rather than giving out her ideas of what they should write. The information exchange evidenced in the above excerpt suggests that Fang valued different voices in her teaching and she developed awareness of learner involvement. (Li 2012: 14)

In another study, Morton and Gray investigated how teacher educators and student teachers negotiate meanings related to various aspects of personal practical knowledge through the discourse of shared lesson planning sessions in the practice teaching component of a pre-service TESOL certificate course: Certificate in Teaching English Language to Adults (CELTA). They argue that although 'the teacher educator produced more meanings related to personal practical knowledge, the student teachers had a substantial share in the discursive resources with which meanings were exchanged', in particular in the knowledge of instruction (2010: 297).

Extract 2.4[3] (TE: Teacher Educator; ST: Student Teacher)

```
1   TE:   It's a little bit vague at the minute because you haven't
2         worked it out exactly but if you could contextualize it
3         little bit
4   ST:   If you look at this form - a lot of it's (.) they are
5         going to fill in fairly easily they're going to have a
6         good idea (.) the weather conditions they can discuss
7         what weather conditions amongst themselves and they can
8         decide where it happened and how long they saw it for (.)
9         the text that I give them leads to maybe the final three
10        or four boxes
```

In this exchange, we can see that the teacher educator prompted the student teacher to produce meaning in a clearer, more detailed fashion by requesting further clarification (lines 1 and 2). In the response, the student teacher produces the meanings relating to the knowledge of learners (lines 5–6) and knowledge of instruction (lines 5–8), claiming `they are going to fill in fairly easily they're going to have a good idea . . . they can discuss what weather conditions amongst themselves and they can decide`. The availability of the interaction between the trainer and the student teacher made the construction of personal, practical knowledge observable.

Interactional analysis advances our understanding by taking action/practice into consideration of teacher cognition, but the problem with interactional data alone is that classroom practice is only part of the social acts of teachers and it is normally used to compare with what teachers claim. The deliberate separation of 'thinking' and 'behaviours' causes problems in researching cognition, as teachers are active thinkers who 'think' and 'act' simultaneously in their work. It is inappropriate to treat teachers' thinking and understanding as one act and their actions as another. Another problem with an interactionist view is that teachers' beliefs, cognition, knowledge are all explored from an external's perspective, which does not advance our understanding of 'participants' insights'. That is, it is all interpreted by the researcher, and the teachers' own insights are not included.

METHODOLOGICAL ISSUES

As discussed, various data collection methods have been used in researching teacher cognition and in this section I describe four main issues that arise from an analysis of the different approaches to data collection and analysis:

- the fact that cognitions revealed from studies are defined by the data elicitation methods and therefore might not truly represent the cognition of those teachers;
- the lack of a shared understanding between the participants and the researcher (Speer 2005) or insights from the teachers;
- the often inappropriate distinction between beliefs and practice; and
- the relationship between beliefs (conceptions, understanding, perception) and practice might be the result of the data elicitation and might not be an accurate reflection of the phenomena researchers seek to understand (Speer 2005).

In the rest of this section, I will discuss these four points in turn. First, research on teacher cognition uses a range of data elicitation methods, each of which implies underlying assumptions about the nature of the cognitions being investigated. For example, when questionnaires are used, teacher cognition is viewed as a fixed set of the assumptions and knowledge teachers hold, which can be revealed by standardised statements. On the other hand, researchers adopting an interactionist position assume that cognition can be retrieved in the moment-to-moment interaction. Because different methods are used and different theoretical perspectives are adopted, different conceptions of 'cognition' may emerge. Second, there is a lack of 'shared understanding' between the participants and the research study, especially about the concepts involved. Take one of the key concepts – CLT – as an example. Howatt (1984) has distinguished between a 'strong' and a 'weak' version, and Richards (2006) distinguishes CLT as 'classic' and 'current'. Larsen-Freeman (2000) also proposes seven key features of CLT. It would be impossible for both participants and the researcher to talk about the concept with the same meaning, without explicitly defining it. Therefore, the shared understanding is vitally important to ensure that the researcher is interpreting and representing the concept in the same way as the participants. To resolve this issue, Speer (2005) suggests having stimulated recall as a way to achieving shared understanding.

The third issue is about the concept itself. In the literature, cognition is often defined as either professed or attributed beliefs (Calderhead 1996; Putnam and Borko 2000). These two terms are treated as different aspects of cognition, articulated beliefs versus practice, and investigating the relationship between the two has been an important research agenda. However, according to Speer, the distinction might be inappropriate as '(A)ll claims about teachers' beliefs are, to greater or lesser extents, attributed to teachers by researchers' (2005: 362).

The fourth problematic issue is closely related to the third. In the literature, inconsistency, discrepancy and mismatch between beliefs and practice were reported (see also Chapter 1). For some researchers, to some extent, negative images of teachers were produced as the latter can articulate their understandings as one thing yet their practice reveals something else. For others, they emphasise the contextual factors which account for these inconsistencies, discrepancies and mismatches (e.g. Borg 2006). However, this result might be due to issues discussed above. On the one hand, this might be due to teachers responding to data collection methods differently. Much research has been concerned with comparing teachers' practices using classroom data regarding what they think and believe, drawing on either questionnaire or interview data. The problem lies in the fact that teachers might be responding to different things that researchers have intended to investigate. On the other hand, these mismatches are related to the concept being separated into two domains, with one dealing with 'mind' and the other 'action'. Going back to Speer's argument, I would like to emphasise here that it might not be appropriate to separate 'thinking' from 'action' for two good reasons. First, teacher cognition is highly influenced by the macro- and micro-contexts within which they work. Curriculum, testing, language policy and materials all affect what teachers think, believe and understand about language teaching and learning. Other factors, for example, colleagues, school environments, students and their teaching experience also play a role. Micro-contexts, the moment-to-moment interaction in the classroom, materials and activities, also contribute to teachers moving away from their original plan to make interactive decisions. Therefore, teacher cognition is understanding, thinking and action in situ rather than a fixed object inside the head. Second, teachers are active thinkers, who constantly make decisions and justifications based on their understanding in situ. Deliberate separation of their account of beliefs from action will not take teachers' interactive decision-making into consideration in terms of their pedagogical thinking.

SUMMARY

In this chapter, I have reviewed mainstream methodologies associated with teacher cognition research and presented methodological problems associated with these approaches. In summary, most teacher cognition studies use questionnaire, interview and classroom data as a means of gaining access to the teachers' mental lives, and data are screened, sorted and interpreted according to literature or the researchers' understanding. Cognitions in such research are products of these data elicitation tools and researchers' interpretations.

Some research involves actions (e.g. classroom practice) and focuses on the relationship between what teachers say and what they do. It is based on the assumption that mental lives are separate categories from teaching behaviours. The problem with this assumption is that it ignores the fact that teachers' verbal comments and accounts are also action (behaviour) if attention is placed on how it is said. Thus, it will not be appropriate to describe teachers' cognition (including knowledge and belief) as inner, mental processes that determine, influence or impact their practices. Moreover, it cannot be assumed that teachers' comments are channels to gain access to their mental lives or cognition. Rather, teachers' comments are their cognition-in-interaction. In the next chapter, I will present a discursive psychological perspective which uses CA principles in the study of teacher cognition.

NOTES

1. Repertory Grid Technique, originally developed by Kelly (1955) for his Personal Construct Theory, is an interviewing technique using factor analysis to determine an idiographic measure of personality. It has four parts: a topic, a set of Elements, a

set of Constructs and a set of ratings of Elements on Constructs, usually on five- or seven-point rating scales. This technique has been modified to research teachers' beliefs (e.g. Munby 1982).
2. Extracts 2.1, 2.2 and 2.3 are all taken from Li (2012) with modification in transcription.
3. Extract 2.4 is taken from Morton and Gray (2010: 309) with modification in transcription.

3
TEACHER COGNITION AND INTERACTION

INTRODUCTION

As discussed in the previous two chapters, although the cognitive perspective has been dominant in research on teacher cognition (e.g. Pajares 1992; Ng and Farrell 2003), there are issues at both the theoretical and methodological level. Consequently, a cognitive view of cognition has been challenged by other perspectives. This chapter therefore offers an alternative approach to the study of teacher cognition through interaction and shows how an approach informed by DP and CA may go some way in offering a solution. This is based on the assumption that it is inappropriate to try to create two domains of teacher cognition by separating beliefs from action. Furthermore, understanding language teachers' beliefs cannot be achieved by simple recourse to what they say or do at face value. Rather, a deep understanding is needed of the complex interplay between personal beliefs and context-specific actions as depicted through interaction.

Instead of viewing cognition as the static traits of a person that remain constant in different situations and contexts, from a DP perspective cognition is viewed as an object *in* and *for* interaction (te Molder and Potter 2005: 2). Specifically, 'it focuses on how psychological categories and constructions are used by people in everyday and institutional settings' (ibid.). This chapter demonstrates the relationship between interaction and what teachers think, know, believe and do in professional contexts, and illustrates how cognition manifests itself in social interaction. The starting point is to understand the relationship between language and thought, and conversation and cognition. Following this, I will present a discursive psychological perspective on cognition and discuss principles of CA, which are adopted by researchers who take a discursive psychological perspective. Then I will illustrate how teacher cognition can be researched from a discursive psychological perspective. In so doing, this chapter makes a strong case for looking at cognition through interaction (see above) and illustrates how teachers' knowledge, understandings and beliefs are embedded in interaction.

COGNITION AND CONVERSATION

The relation of thought to word is not a thing but a process, a continual movement back and forth from thought to word and from word to thought.

In that process, the relation of thought to word undergoes changes that themselves may be regarded as development in the functional sense. (Vygotsky 1986: 218)

Here, we can see clearly articulated the relationship between word and thought – for Vygotsky, the relation of thought to word is a process, a continual movement back and forth from thought to word and from word to thought. Thought, thinking, ideas and perceptions are not fixed, static and pre-existing in people's minds, but are part of a developmental process. Interaction, therefore, is the display of such development. This is in line with the position of DP in promoting understanding of psychological matters.

DISCURSIVE PSYCHOLOGY

DP is an 'emergent discipline' with an approach to cognition that differs from other discursive approaches, e.g. sociolinguistics (Potter 2005). It is an approach to cognition 'in which the theoretical and analytical focus is moved away from the individual mind to processes of social interaction' (Hepburn and Wiggins 2005, in Roth 2008: 34). Some scholars treat DP as a methodology as it re-specifies traditional psychological topics, such as cognition, thought and conceptions in terms of the methodical, situated discursive production of mental entities (Potter and Edwards 2003). However, according to Edwards and Potter (1992), it is more than a method as it offers a framework with which to theorise traditional psychological interests in different ways. DP is, thus, not only a method of analysing everyday talk but a theoretical perspective towards it. For Potter, DP is more than a framework, it is 'an approach embedded in a web of theoretical and metatheoretical assumptions' (2003: 784–5). It is important to realise that at a theoretical level, the psychology domain 'is an object, in DP, it is practical, accountable, situated, embodied and displayed' (Potter 2005: 740). Thus, the fundamental theoretical position of DP is that 'talk is both the terrain/context and tool of human activity', and talk 'not only establishes and maintains the topic, but also establishes and maintains the activity in which participants talk about a particular topic' (Roth 2008: 35). Edwards (2005: 259) summarises three major strands in DP. These are: (1) re-specification and critique of psychological topics and explanations; (2) investigations of how everyday psychological categories are used in discourse; (3) studies of how psychological business (motives and intentions, prejudices, reliability of memory and perception, etc.) is handled and managed in talk and text, without having to be overtly labelled as such.

Roth (2008) makes the point that DP is interested in theorising the interactional work being done 'in and through talk'. He further clarifies that 'the preposition "in" means that talk is the context in which the work is being done and the preposition "through" indicates that talk is the main tool by means of which this work is accomplished' (ibid.: 35). Talk therefore not only establishes and maintains the topic, but also establishes and maintains the activity in which participants discuss a particular topic. This theoretical position leads DP to consider the relationship between everyday talk (e.g. in interviews) and cognition differently from the traditional view. In the traditional forms of conception and cognition, research employs two processes of abstraction – gross categorisation and restriction – which DP rejects as legitimate (see Edwards and Potter 1992: 5). *Gross categorisation* considers a stretch of talk as independent from the conversation as a whole, and abstracts what's being said in the talk, whereas from a DP perspective, no stretch of talk should be viewed on its own, as it is the contingent continuation of the earlier talk and a resource being referred to in subsequent talk. Gross categorisation also considers theorising what's being said as public expression whereas from a DP perspective, talk is not the reproduction of what is in the speaker's head but how the speaker displays thoughts and concepts in talk. *Restriction* mainly applies to closed questionnaires and structured interviews when participants are restricted with choices of their concepts and beliefs. Hence, rather than focusing on what people know or perceive, DP attempts to discover how issues like knowing, perceiving and believing are dealt with by participants *themselves*.

As presented in Chapter 1, DP views cognition as publicly displayed and available for analysis and comprehension, and presents itself as an approach that considers cognition as an object in and for interaction. The focus is on how psychological categories or constructions, such as memory, belief, perception and knowledge, are used by people in everyday or institutional talk. For teacher cognition, it focuses on how logical categorisations and constructions of understanding, perception, beliefs and knowledge are used by teachers in institutional settings. DP sees language as social practice[1] (Edwards and Potter 1992: 15). Thus, 'interaction can be seen as patterns of activity which take place in and constitute social situation' (Barwell 2003: 202).

> What we find in everyday talk is . . . a rich seam of concern about truth and error, mind and reality, memory and perception, knowledge and inference . . . people casually and routinely construct formulations of such things (perception, knowledge, inference and so on) as part of everyday discursive practice . . . (Edwards and Potter 1992: 17)

In DP, discourse is taken to be mainly naturally occurring interactional talk (see Potter 1997) through which people live their lives and conduct their everyday business (although sometimes using texts as well). DP applies the principles and methods of discourse but, to be specific, mainly uses principles of CA, to investigate psychological themes.

The merit of the DP perspective on teacher cognition is the emphasis on *action, context and natural talk*, which is distinct from the cognitive view of teacher cognition that stresses the cognitive psychological labels using experimental manipulations or decontextualised examples. In te Molder's and Potter's (2005) view, DP is the perspective that has addressed cognition most systematically in a psychological context (e.g. Edwards and Potter 1992, 1993; Edwards 1997; Potter and Edwards 2001).

REDEFINING TEACHER COGNITION – A DISCURSIVE PSYCHOLOGICAL PERSPECTIVE

The term cognition needs to be redefined here from a discursive psychological perspective, since it will be theoretically and methodologically inappropriate to adopt the same perspective of the construct as the cognitive view because they take different stances. A search of *The Oxford Dictionary* (2012) defines cognition as:

- the mental action or process of acquiring knowledge and understanding through thought, experience, and the senses.
- a perception, sensation, idea, or intuition resulting from the process of cognition.

A few things are worth noting about the definitions above. First, cognition *is* about mental action or the process of acquiring and understanding of knowledge and therefore it is difficult to observe or pin down. Second, cognition is related to knowledge, and, indeed, it is the cognition of *something*. The closeness of knowledge to cognition makes it difficult to separate these two issues. They are interrelated. Third, cognition develops through thought, experience and the senses. Here, we can see both internal and external forces to the development of cognition. Experience often represents external influences while thought and senses are internal. Fourth, we can see the linking of cognition to 'perception' 'ideas', 'sensation' and 'intuition'. These are considered as consequences or forms of cognition. In other words, one's *perception* about something is a way of *demonstrating* one's cognition about something. It is worth noting the relationship between cognition and feeling (sensation, intuition). Therefore, cognition is not just about knowledge, perception, ideas but also feelings towards an object/phenomenon. Finally, we can see the difficulty of investigating cognition; it is difficult to observe and even to articulate.

Based on the above definition, then, teacher cognition might mean several things. First, it is about acquiring and understanding knowledge, and in recognition of the varieties of knowledge a teacher acquires and needs to understand, this might include pedagogical knowledge, subject content knowledge and personal knowledge. Second, teacher cognition is about the thinking process. Clark and Peterson (1986) claimed that there were three stages of teacher thinking: pre-teaching, while-teaching and post-teaching thinking. How teachers think and make decisions therefore is an important feature of teacher cognition. Third, it is apparent that teacher cognition relates to teachers' own experience, both their personal learning experience and their professional experience. As Clandinin and Connelly (2000) have pointed out, teachers' beliefs and practice are a complex combination of past experience, present situation and future plans. I would like to highlight here that this is the kind of experience teachers have on a daily basis, through interaction; interaction with colleagues, with students, with mentors, even with themselves, constitutes a large portion of teacher experience. Therefore, experience must be considered as an important factor that shapes and develops teacher cognition. If we recognise the importance of experience, then there is a good argument to look at it through interaction. It is through interactions with others that experiences are encountered, developed and learned. Indeed, experiential learning is perhaps one of the most powerful influences on professional development. Fourth, 'perception', 'ideas', 'sensation' and 'intuition' are all considered as cognition. For teachers, their attitudes, perceptions and conceptions of certain aspects of teaching are *all part of their cognition*. These are also closely related to their values, emotions and feelings. Rather, cognition perhaps is more individual and developmental as teachers' experiences are ongoing and their knowledge is constantly developing and being reshaped. That is, teachers' perceptions, decisions or feelings are all context-shaped and context-evolving. It seems at this point that we need to acknowledge the complexity of teacher cognition. It is not and should not be treated as a fixed object existing in teachers' heads. Rather, it should be considered as the orientation a teacher takes towards the moment they experience, the issue they discuss or the concept they try to understand. From a discursive psychological perspective, teacher cognition is socially and publically displayed understanding, knowing, positioning, conceptualising and stance-taking that is publicly displayed in action. This is what I would like to call 'cognition-in-interaction', which is different from individually held mental states. Cognition-in-interaction is a special kind of psychological reality – not the one defined by the mental state or process, but by the participants orienting practically in an ongoing interaction. Thus, cognition is fluid and changing, it exists in situ and is shaped by the understanding of the distributed cognition in prior turns-at-talk, and shapes the development of the next turn.

A useful clarification at this stage is to distinguish an interactionist's perspective from a discursive psychological perspective towards teacher cognition. Although both perspectives place interaction at the heart of understanding and both approaches consider the importance of interaction, they do have a different take on the nature of teacher cognition. From the interactionist's perspective, it is considered to be a complex interactive system, which can be studied through the teacher's interaction within the context at both macro- and micro-levels. Cognition is viewed as entities that may be transformed or even emerge in and as a result of interactions (Skott 2001). More importantly, the perspective places a high value on examining beliefs as they relate to evidence of participating teachers' classroom practices, and very often it makes sense of teacher cognition through both what they say and what they do in classrooms (through the lens of classroom interaction). Like DP, an interactionist's perspective focuses on how issues like 'knowing' are dealt with by the participants in public through their actions and interactions, and interpretation of cognition is at the level of public interaction, rather than the private realm of the mind, which is achieved through discourse analytical approaches. However, such a perspective does not address the issue of achieving shared understanding, as methodologically it takes little or no account of the teacher participant's interpretation of their own classroom practice (Speer 2008), and still separates what teachers say from what they do in classrooms as if they are two distinctive aspects. On the contrary, DP considers the construct of cognition in and through interaction and adopts the principles of CA to explore the organisation of interactions between participants, and it addresses the issue of gaining participants' own insights and co-constructing cognition between interactants.

CONVERSATION ANALYSIS

As stated earlier, CA principles are adopted by researchers who take a discursive psychological perspective of cognition. CA does not treat language as a system independent of its use, but treats 'grammar and lexical choices as sets of resources which participants deploy, monitor, interpret and manipulate' in order to perform their social acts (Schegloff et al. 2002: 15). In principle, CA considers talk as action rather than a channel to action. Participants' understandings and views are the basis of understanding talk-in-interaction and the central focus is how sequences of action are generated (Hutchby and Wooffitt 2008: 14). In conversation, interactants display their interpretation of each other's utterance and the social actions they represent. Conversation also performs a social display of the interactants' cognitive, emotional and attitudinal states. The participants' understandings and points of view are discovered by how participants understand and interpret each other's actions and develop a shared understanding of the progress and direction of the interaction. It is important to note that CA is not able to establish the cognitive state of individuals but 'the progress of intersubjectivity or distributed cognition' (Seedhouse and Walsh 2010: 128). Intersubjectivity is the ways in which mutual understanding is achieved by interactants through their organisation of sequence, turning-taking and repair. In achieving shared understanding, interactants are constantly displaying to each other their social actions and cognitive state, and their understanding of each other's social actions and cognitive state. CA takes an emic viewpoint from inside the system and it considers this as crucial to 'the participants' perspective within the interactional environment in which the talk occurs' (Seedhouse 2005: 166). CA also has a dynamic, complex, highly empirical perspective on context and considers talk to be socially and locally constructed by participants in micro-contexts. Contrasting the traditional view of context-shaped and context-reviewing, Seedhouse (2005) pointed out the importance of the sequential environment in which contributions to interaction occur and in which the participants design them to occur. Contributions to interaction are context-reviewing because they form part of the sequential environment in which the next turn occurs:

> contributions to interaction are CONTEXT-SHAPED and CONTEXT-REVIEWING . . . they cannot be adequately understood except by reference [to the] other sequential environment in which they occur and in which the participants design them to occur. Contributions are context-reviewing in that they inevitably form part of the sequential environment in which a next contribution will occur. (Ibid.: 166, emphasis in the original)

The idea that conversations are context-shaped and context-reviewing is taken up by DP to understand the 'psychological reality' of cognitive entities, because DP takes the position that performance and action need to be understood in specific and local details of setting and procedure. In both CA's and DP's term, the 'psychological reality' is not defined as a process in the head but as an orientation to the interaction in the course of ongoing interaction – the socially distributed and negotiated cognition. te Molder and Potter (2005) make a distinction in representation in researching cognition between a cognitive perspective and CA and DP. They claim that in CA and DP, representation is not about mental entities but actual descriptions in talk or texts, and the involvement of those descriptions *in action*. In DP, discourse bears four distinctive characteristic features. First, discourse is treated as the primary medium for action, which concerns how psychological matters are done. This position is different from the mainstream psychology of language which considers discourse a pathway to mental objects. Second, discourse is situated. This position is built on the prior one that discourse is action-oriented. Third, discourse is situated *sequentially* (Potter 2012b). Discourse cannot be treated as stand-alone utterances which can be examined separately. On the contrary, discourse (action) is developmental in the unfolding of conversation. Each piece of discourse (or every action) is related to what happened and triggers what happens next. Fourth, discourse is situated *institutionally*, as action is shaped by the institutional practice and norms. Discourse in classrooms is thus different from discourse in a hospital simply because they have different institutional goals and actions. These goals and actions influence and decide the kind of discourse that can occur in these institutions. In educational settings, discourse is by and large shaped by pedagogical goals, which decide what materials and tasks the teacher chooses. Therefore, it is difficult to study cognition without considering pedagogical goals.

As discussed above, the study of socially distributed cognition cannot be separated from the study of interaction because of the embeddedness and the intertwined-ness of cognition and interaction (Schegloff 1991). As argued by Seedhouse and Walsh (2010: 182), 'CA analysis not only demonstrates *what* understandings the interactants display to each other, but *how* they do so by normative reference to the interactional organisations'. Specifically, the researcher gains access to displays of understanding in the same way that participants gain access; the researcher is, in essence, a participant observer who views the interaction in the same way as those participating.

A DISCURSIVE PSYCHOLOGICAL APPROACH TO TEACHER COGNITION

Using a conversation analytic approach, DP's goal is to understand how, why and where everyday talk mobilises psychological concepts (memory, cognition, attitudes, affect, beliefs, identity, conception and motivation). DP has taken these psychological aspects in a radically different direction because it understands the role of language in human activities very differently (Edwards and Potter 1992). Language is not considered as a channel to these mental entities, but as a resource that people use in interaction to manage public affairs. Empirically, there is very little research on teacher cognition adopting this approach, as pointed out in Chapter 1. Among the limited studies, Barwell (2006), Roth (2008, 2009) and Morton (2012) have adopted a conversation analytic lens to the investigation of the construct of teacher cognition in different settings, almost all of which concern conceptual changes in science or maths classrooms.

Roth (2009) tracked knowing (ideas, conceptions, beliefs) in real time using a fine-grained analysis of a university physics professor teaching a third-year undergraduate course. Focusing on thinking-in-action during lectures concerning an expository genre, he argues for a full implementation of the dialectical theory and method (Vygotsky 1986) concerning the dynamic dimensions of thought in action and the subordination of language to communication and thinking-in-action. One key conclusion Roth draws is that thought is a living process – by demonstrating how the professor spent considerable effort in evolving a thought, both in phenomenal and in representational space. The production of thought (the process of articulating/forming knowledge) is evidenced with hesitation, false starts and restarts, fillers, indicating that 'the lecturing in this case does not consist in reading out an already existing mental model to make it available to the audience' (Roth 2009: 309). This is further evidenced by the professor's action of discarding the idea and wishing to return to it at a later moment in time. What Roth here demonstrates is challenging the cognitive notion of thought, knowledge and beliefs, in such a way that knowledge should not be considered to be a 'fixed form' but instead one developed in the process of articulation. Roth also suggests that knowing and learning are distributed – and therefore are contingent processes – across different temporal, spatial and social scales. He particularly points out how the professor established a web of significance relations that constitute meaning using various sources (including words, gestures, body positions, body movements and prosody) in the context of inscriptions. He shows the professor formulating some facts, knowledge, ideas or concepts as certain, whereas others were uncertain. He speculates that:

> The fundamental result of such an approach is that ideas no longer can be understood as residing in the individual mind but that they come to be embodied in the setting ... ideas are forms of thought that integrate inner and outer moments ... and in integrating the inner and outer dimensions of speech in particular. (Ibid.: 310)

Morton (2012) examined a science teacher's (Isabel) use of, and reflections on, classroom talk in teaching a unit on genetics in a bilingual classroom. Based around the three stages of teaching in the literature of teacher cognition and decision-making, Morton examined the teacher's pre-active (planning), interactive (teaching) and post-active (reflection) decision-making by adopting the discursive psychological perspective of cognition. Three types of data were used to depict teacher cognition: an interview about Isabel's approach to planning and teaching the unit, fine-grained transcriptions of two video-recorded lessons which included non-verbal behaviours such as movement and gesture, and an interview based on videoclip playback. The study showed that Isabel did not have the pre-existing belief that her students had 'misconceptions' but she produced and established this belief as the result of interaction with the researcher who was doing quite a lot of work in 'pressing' her. The analysis showed that this kind of belief or conception of students' conceptual status can be specified or partially re-specified as socio-interactive and discursive. This kind of belief construction and development is also evidenced at the interactive stage (teaching). Equally, in the video-based reflection, Isabel demonstrated how she constructed her own practice as uncovering students' misconceptions and then directing them towards the 'right' ones.

Morton argues for the importance of raising teachers' awareness of the impact of their uses of classroom talk, 'from the broader level of a communicative approach to the more micro "action" level of specific interventions in teaching' (2012: 109). At a theoretical and methodological level, he suggests that it may be time to pose some questions about the use of discourse in research on teachers' beliefs about practice and 'discursive psychology tells us that we should be careful about assuming that talk can straightforwardly provide a window onto what learners or teachers "think"' (ibid.). Belief dissatisfaction, change, development, reinforcement therefore can all be approached as interactional and discursive matters.

CA provides a fine-grained analytical perspective of what's going on in talk-in-interaction. By adopting CA principles in researching teacher cognition, it is possible to focus on the nature of the cognition being socially shared, socially mediated and publically displayed. The key issues here are to use CA principles to establish a fine-grained, moment-by-moment analysis of teacher thinking, knowledge development and feeling, to gain insights into the participants' understanding of their cognition, and to uncover the 'organisation of talk' as organised by the participants themselves, rather than to approach the data from an extraneous viewpoint. That is, the focus is placed on how the participants display for one another their understanding of the situation they are in. In such talk-in-interaction, speakers display in their sequentially 'next' turns an understanding of what the 'prior' turn was about and how they are positioned and oriented to it (Hutchby and Wooffitt 2008). Data, therefore, are not approached with a predetermined set of features but are treated in a rather open manner. CA is particularly relevant in understanding interactive decision-making, in the case of dealing with unexpected answers or making a move which might depart from what teachers had planned before the lesson. The emphasis is placed on moment-by-moment decision-making.

I have argued the case for investigating teacher cognition through the lens of interaction. In the next section, I will take three data collection tools – interview, video-based reflection and classroom recordings – to illustrate how teacher cognition can be studied in the framework of DP informed by conversation analytical principles. The discursive social approach emphasises the social nature of teacher cognition in and through interaction.

DATA SOURCES AND ANALYSIS

DP works with interactional data, which happen naturally and are not staged by the researcher (Potter 2012b). In terms of researching teacher cognition, the 'naturally' occurring interaction data include semi-structured interviews, classroom data, video-based reflection, team lesson planning, one-to-one tutorials and so on. It is important to note that they are all focused talk with research and pedagogical considerations and agendas, but they develop naturally. That means that the conversation between participants can develop in any direction by any of the participants. Interactional data are recorded on digital video and transcribed in a way that captures delay, overlap, intonation and volume. It is a recording of how cognition is unfolding for the participants in the interaction – it is *not* the recording of the participants' brain (movements), but a display of how the interaction unfolds and how every bit of interaction is connected to its prior and later sequences in dealing with psychological matters (e.g. perception, memory, knowing and believing).

Within this approach, three considerations are important. First, data must be natural talk, which means that the flow of the talk is natural, without being staged by the researcher. However, we must bear in mind that institutional talk is usually not equally distributed, and it has a focused agenda and goals. Second, video-recordings are made subject to detailed transcription for micro-analysis. Pauses, gestures and intonation are made available in transcripts. Third, participants are involved in any data collection procedure; for example, classroom recordings and reflective group discussion are usually made by participants themselves to minimise the reactivity generated by extended researcher involvement (ibid.).

The transcription procedure throughout this book follows two forms of transcript. A basic transcript was generated to get an overview of what the predominant themes are in relation to teacher cognition. Then, selected stretches of conversation which deal with certain psychological matters are transcribed following broad Jeffersonian conventions (see Appendix) and are then subjected to micro-analysis.

Interviews
Interviews have been used as a useful tool to elicit teachers' understanding, perceptions and beliefs about aspects of language teaching and learning. The use of the semi-structured and unstructured interview has contributed to understanding teacher cognition in relation to personal theories and the role of context in the research adopting the cognitive perspective. The interviews normally are used to elicit data from teachers about one aspect of their teaching or beliefs, such as understanding of teaching, learning, learners, subject knowledge, self- and professional development, to allow teachers to talk about both their overarching beliefs and how they practice their beliefs for particular lessons. For interview analysis, most research conducts thematic content analysis, using either the belief literature to guide their analysis or by adopting a grounded approach. The thematic analysis can 'reduce' and 'extract' data in a systematic way. However, the danger of doing thematic analysis for teacher cognition research is that the researcher may selectively interpret and represent the teachers' points of view, and the process of how the 'belief' or 'perception' is co-constructed by the participant and the researcher is lacking. The point being made here is that it is not clear how the teacher's understanding is co-constructed with the researcher and how the belief is elicited by the researcher if a thematic analysis is adopted. Potter and Hepburn (2005) pointed out some contingent problems in the reporting of interviews, including: (1) the deletion of the interviewer; (2) the conventions of representation of interaction; (3) the specificity of analytic observations;

(4) the unavailability of the interview set-up; and (5) the failure to consider interviews as interaction. They argue that interviews should be studied as an interactional object. When studying teacher cognition, it is worth considering analysing data from a discursive psychological perspective if we are to understand teachers' beliefs from the participants' own points of view.

Let us start by considering some data. Extract 3.1 is taken from an interview with an English language teacher from a Chinese secondary school about the importance of learning English for Chinese learners.

Extract 3.1 (Ma: The teacher; I: Interviewer)

```
1   I    so what do you think is important in learning English (.) I mean
2        for your students? (0.2)
3   Ma   er(.)((clears her throat))(3.0) for my students (.) vocabulary
4        and grammar (.) definitely (.) er (.) in fact I feel
5        communication is also important (0.3) but you know the test is all
6        about vocabulary and grammar (1.2) you know that=
7   I    =yeah((laughing))I took many tests when I was a student=
8   Ma   =we all did (.) and now you have to take a test if you want
9        to gain a position in a school (1.2) even in a secondary
10       school or a good primary school(.)
11  I    so you were saying vocabulary and grammar are important
12       because they are the things tested?=
13  Ma   =yeah (.) tests are mainly about vocabulary and grammar (.) so
14       they are important for students if they want to get good
15       grades (0.2) that's the reality (3.2) I need to make sure that I
16       teach my student the important and useful content (0.8) but
17       you might disagree with me.
```

A thematic analysis of the data identifies a number of themes:

- The teacher (Ma) believes vocabulary and grammar are important for her learners.
- Her beliefs about learning English are influenced by tests.

These are important points to be made about this particular teacher's beliefs about language learning. However, more can be revealed from a discursive psychological perspective. First, we can see how the interviewer's question (line 1) orients Ma to the direction of what is important for a language learner. It is this orientation that directs the flow of the conversation and construction of the teacher's beliefs about language learning: vocabulary and grammar are important. Furthermore, note lines 11 and 12, where the interviewer summarises the teacher's point of view and seeks confirmation. Second, from a discursive psychological perspective, it is also interesting to see how the teacher displays two sets of beliefs about language learning. In lines 3–4, the teacher displays her beliefs about the importance of vocabulary and grammar, positing herself as a teacher who talks about language learning for students; in lines 4–5, she positions herself differently in responding to the interviewer's question from her own perspective – I feel communication is also important. Although these two sets of beliefs are not necessarily contradictory, it is clear that she puts more emphasis on grammar and vocabulary for which she provides a justification that a 'test is all about vocabulary and grammar' (lines 5–6). Third, it is clear that Ma's beliefs about important aspects of language learning are co-constructed by the researcher and the teacher. Note the discourse marker 'you know' 'you know that' in line 5 and 6 respectively have established a shared understanding of what is being talked about in the context. It is further suggested that the meaning of the influence of the test is co-constructed between the teacher and the interviewer, as evidenced by the latched turns (lines 6 and 7), the researcher's acknowledgement token and laughter (line 7). Then the similar experience from the interviewer (line 7) positions both the teacher and the interviewer differently this time, as a person who experienced many tests, which generates a long turn by the teacher, exemplifying the importance of tests as a gateway to entering the profession (lines 8 and 9). Fourth, this conversation suggests that the teacher holds beliefs about other matters, for example tests and being a teacher. It is worth noting that the longish pause (line 9) here has an emphatic effect on what she said earlier, suggesting that she possibly holds a strong belief about tests. After this pause, she completes her turn by commenting that teachers need to take a test even they want to work in a secondary or a good primary school. An assumption can be made that the teacher's discursive construction of her beliefs about important aspects of language learning and teaching has been extended to a wider scope in the sense that learning vocabulary and grammar is important because of the test. And the test decides a career. The importance of testing is further illustrated by her clarification (lines 13–15). After a long pause (3.2 seconds), her understanding about being a teacher is also revealed through the interview, this time projecting her identity/role as someone who teaches her students useful and important content (grammar and vocabulary). This suggests some complexity:

- She considers the importance of vocabulary and grammar in language learning, which is contextualised by the reality that students need to get good grades in tests and they are all about grammar and vocabulary.
- She also considers communication important but her talk implies that she might put more emphasis on vocabulary and grammar in practice as they are useful and important for achieving good grades.
- It seems that Ma believes that tests are very important, as in reality not only do students need to get good grades but also anyone who wants to become a teacher. It looks like the social context shapes her beliefs. However, the teacher also recognises that her beliefs about the importance of tests are open to challenge (lines 16–17).
- She assigns a strong responsibility to herself as a teacher to help students to achieve their academic goals, implying that she might not do what she believes but does what is useful and important for her learners.

This level of analysis also gives us insights into not only what has been said, but how it is said.

- Meaning is co-constructed between the interviewer and the teacher. Thus, the belief might not be purely the belief that the teacher holds, but a belief that she constructed through dialogue with the interviewer. One example is when the teacher invites the interviewer into the construction by saying 'you know that' after a longish pause (line 6).
- The flow of the conversation is oriented by the interviewer and the beliefs Ma holds unfold with the progress of the conversation.
- Shared understanding is established through language (for example, you know) and personal experience (lines 7 and 8).

```
7   I    =yeah((laughing))I took many tests when I was a student=
8   Ma   =we all did (.)and now you have to take a test if you want
9        to gain a position in a school (1.2) even in a secondary
10       school or a good primary school(.)
```

- Pauses function differently in the unfolding of the beliefs. After a long pause (3.0) in line 3, Ma starts to answer the interview question. Arguably, this three-second pause provides her a space for organising her thoughts. Clearly, Ma does not have fixed knowledge or belief about which component of English is important for her students. Her articulated knowledge and beliefs are constructed in the interaction with the researcher. Then in line 6, after a 1.2 second pause, Ma initiates a turn (you know that) for the interviewer to contribute. This pause suggests the teacher takes an active role in co-constructing meaning with the interviewer. In line 9, after Ma articulates the importance of tests, she pauses (1.2 seconds) and then exemplifies and stresses the implications of testing (even in a secondary school or a good primary school). It is this pause that stresses the importance of the implication that she brings up later. While a 3.2 second pause in line 15 marks the conclusion of her turn and she offers the floor, the interviewer, however, does not take the cue, so Ma carries on but moves in a new direction, this time talking about herself as a teacher. This shift clearly suggests that all aspects of teacher cognition (e.g. teaching, learning, students, tests and self-) are intertwined with each other. Then the brief pause after the articulating of her responsibility (0.8) indicates an invitation to the interviewer to join in the conversation as she realises that her beliefs about the test might be challenged: you might disagree with me. Again, from a discursive psychological perspective, we can see how beliefs can be articulated, shared and co-constructed through a conversation (interview) with the interviewer.

Sometimes interviews are carried out after the class, so there is something more concrete for both the researcher and the teacher to refer to in discussing aspects of teaching and learning. In the following extract, the researcher interviewed the teacher after her class, specifically talking about one of the contextual factors influencing classroom practice: the student.

Extract 3.2 (L: Lin (the teacher); I: Interviewer) (Lin 4.04_5.01)

```
1   I   er (.) what's the student level? (.)
2   L   students vary a lot in their English levels (.)
3   I   of course (2.0) er (.) your lesson today was (.)ah that (1.0)
4       er about reading? was it reading?=
5   L   =yes=
6   I   =it's a reading lesson (.) then you asked them to practice
7       speaking (.) talking about it (.)
8   L   yes (.) it was listening (.)reading and speaking (.)
9   I   so it's about [listening and reading
10  L                 [°listening reading and speaking°=
11  I   =that's right (.) listening reading and speaking (.) I
12      noticed that after you gave them homework (.) you have left
13      early during the break (.) some students went to the computer
14      at the front ((of the classroom)) to search for the topic
15      during the break they started to search
16  L   £ hmm £=
17  I   =I think they are (.) good (3.0)
18  L   ((tidying up her collar)) I think they are overall enthusiastic
19      because I am teaching students of art humanities and social
20      sciences ((flipping her hair))(1.0) these students pay a lot
21      attention to English=
22  I   =ah (.) yes (.) of course (.)but I think science students
23      should also (.) pay attention to English?=
24  L   =Science students are relatively less keen in English=
25  I   =hmmm (.) [you
26  L             [science students pay more attention to maths physics
27      and chemistry (.)art humanities and social sciences
28      students also pay a lot of attention to maths (.)((turning
29      to one of her colleagues)) isn't that right? (.)
30  I   yeah yeah yeah ((nodding her head))
```

In this extract, the researcher asks a question about student level in line 1. As a participant in the setting, the researcher opens up the space for Lin to articulate her knowledge about students, to which Lin responds immediately with a general idea (line 2). Note, following a 2.0 second pause after the researcher's acknowledgement and agreement (line 3), the researcher changes the topic to the class itself. After talking about the focus of the lesson, the researcher starts to reformulate her question about students by bringing up her observation of students' reaction after class (lines 12–15), which wins the teacher's acknowledgement. In line 17, the researcher provides her own beliefs about these students based on her experience with them during the break, which generates a more detailed response from the teacher after a long pause (3.0). In responding to the researcher's comment, the teacher elaborates her belief that they are 'overall enthusiastic' about English (line 18) and provides *evidence* for her elaboration that describes her temporal conception about students who study Art Humanities and Social Science – they pay more attention to English (lines 19–21). Then the researcher shows understanding by agreeing and confirming: ah (.) yes (.) of course, followed up with her own opinion that science students should also pay attention to English. Note the function here of emphasizing should implies that she thinks Lin suggests that students who are studying science subjects are not enthusiastic about English. Upon hearing her comment, Lin provides an immediate response to *confirm* and *reformulate* her conclusion that science students are less keen in English (line 24). This is followed up by a further *clarification* and *elaboration* that science students pay more attention to Maths, Physics and Chemistry (lines 26–7). Note in this clarification, she also refers to students studying the Art Humanities and Social Sciences to support her claim that Maths is more important for students, this time *reformulating* her statement to relate it to all students, rather than just a single group (lines 27–8). The teacher also seeks support from her colleagues to verify her statement (line 29), to which the interviewer responds with confirmation of repeated yeah yeah yeah with a nodding gesture (line 30).

In this interview, we see that Lin made public her knowledge and feeling about her students through interaction with the researcher. In her view, students vary in their proficiency level and she is pleased with her students being engaged in the task she set. We can also see clearly that she associates her beliefs about students to their disciplines: Science students are less keen on English while students in Art Humanities and Social Sciences are enthusiastic. Clearly these students are assigned as two distinctive groups with different attitudes towards English. We can also infer Lin's beliefs about her subject: Maths is important since all students pay attention to Maths. From a DP perspective, we do not only see these, we also see how Lin displays her ideas in the interaction with the researcher. She reformulates (line 18, 24, 27–8), confirms (lines 24, 29), clarifies and elaborates (lines 26–8) her ideas and uses other strategies, such as providing evidence (line 18), holding the floor (line 26), seeking verification from colleagues (line 29). So in sum, we do not only see what is said about Lin's understanding of the importance of learning English, but *how* it is said and displayed in Lin's articulation.

Classroom interaction
According to Ellis (1998: 145), teaching is a 'series of interactional events'. Any understanding of these 'events' therefore should focus on the turn-taking and exchange structures in operation and pay attention to the collaborative nature of the discourse between teacher and students. Understanding the ways in which classroom talk is 'accomplished' (Mehan 1979) is crucial to an understanding of decision-making. Put simply, an understanding of classroom interaction lies at the very heart of an understanding of teachers' cognition.

There are at least three reasons for studying teacher cognition through analysing classroom interaction. First, classroom interaction provides evidence of teachers' pedagogical stance. According to van Lier (1996: 5), 'interaction is the most important element in the curriculum'; a position that is echoed by Ellis who claims 'learning arises not through interaction, but *in* interaction' (2000: 209; emphasis in the original). So what teachers want to achieve in and for learning is reflected in their interaction with students in class. Put simply, if a teacher understands learning as memorisation, then in his/her interaction with students, drilling and strategies for memorising will likely be evident. Conversely, if a teacher perceives participation and engagement as learning, he/she will try to create space for participation and engagement (cf. Walsh and Li 2013). Thus, teachers' understanding of learning is embedded in the interaction and can be studied through and in their classroom interaction. Second, it casts light on teachers' cognition-in-interaction with students, which arguably influences what they know, believe and think. Research following different perspectives shares the same view of the importance of including classroom practice in researching teacher cognition (e.g. Li 2013). That is, the moment-to-moment interaction in the classroom is in essence a socially-mediated display of teachers' knowledge, understanding and beliefs. Traditionally, classroom interaction in teacher cognition research is analysed as a way of accessing what teachers know, believe and do. However, a discursive psychological perspective places the emphasis on *how* teachers interact with students in teaching at a micro-level. I would endorse Speer's argument here to say that not only do classroom practices need to be considered in researching teacher cognition, but they need to be studied at a micro-level. Third, a focus on interaction gives teachers insights into their own local contexts, which is a very important aspect of teacher cognition research. The obvious starting point for discussing beliefs is the local context in which teachers work; an understanding of that context would surely facilitate better understandings of how teacher cognition is shaped by the context. Related to this are the opportunities to empower teachers to become reflective active thinkers who are able to draw on sources to understand their own pedagogy and, hence, improve teaching and learning. In short, understandings about teachers' beliefs must acknowledge the importance of interaction given that interaction lies at the very heart of teaching, learning and professional development.

Extract 3.3 is taken from an English class of Year 10 students in a Chinese secondary school, where the teacher is discussing fact versus fantasy with students. This is a young male teacher, who was just into his third year of teaching English.

Extract 3.3 (C 24:35_25:28)

```
1   T    ok just now er we have talked about something about er facts
2        and fantasy (.) next I will give you something different
3        ((showing a PowerPoint slide of the Loch Ness Monster)) (1.0)
4   SS   ((1.0 unintelligible))
5   T    what's that? (0.8)Name!=
6   S1   =the monster of=
7   T    =the monster of::(1.0) what!=
8   S1   ='lake'(.)
```

```
 9   T    lake (1.1) yes is lake but we always use this word ((writing
10        loch on the blackboard)) lo::ch it's a Scottish word (.)
11        Loch's monster. Is it er (.) fact or fantasy? (1.0) is it a
12        fact or °fantasy°? We don't know (.) Maybe it's a fact (.)
13        some er some people believe it's true(.) some people
14        don't(1.0) some people think just invented such a things so
15        we cannot say it's a fact or fantasy (.) We just say it's a
16        mystery a legend (.) er, this is the first one(.) next one?
17   T    ((showing the next slide))does anyone know this?
```

This extract illustrates how this teacher understands teaching and learning and his role in this process. It is clear that he views acquiring vocabulary as an important feature of learning English and he puts emphasis on accuracy of language use. He has a clear strategy to embed vocabulary in his interaction with students. In this extract, he is eliciting the Loch Ness Monster as an example of distinguishing fantasy from mystery. Note that when he asks the question, quite a few students take the cue but he nominates a student after he is not completely sure what they are all trying to say (line 5). The student then takes the turn (line 6), which he follows immediately without letting the student finish (line 7). It is important to note the 1.0 second pause and the sound stretching of 'of', suggesting that his interruption was a confirmation of the student input and this space is kept for the student to continue to complete his turn. The same student then completes his turn with 'lake' in a soft voice, suggesting the uncertainty of his answer. The teacher first repeats the student input 'lake' and then after a longish pause (1.1), he provides feedback with confirmation. Note the emphasis on 'yes', which suggests a great degree of confirmation. He then follows up to explain the accurate word for this occasion would be 'loch', a Scottish word. This follow-up suggests this teacher does not only focus on meaning but also on form, and he has a strong desire to create opportunities for students to acquire vocabulary in context – loch, a Scottish word, meaning lake, in this particular case.

He then carries on, distinguishing mystery from fantasy, using the Loch Ness Monster as an example. First, he presents a question (lines 11–12), which is followed by a one-second pause that allows time for a response. When there is no indication of responses from students, he repeats the question and provides his view that 'We don't know' (line 12), followed by his own answer to the question. Then he goes on to give several speculations and tells students that 'We just say it's a mystery a legend' (lines 15–16). This long turn suggests that he is very comfortable to act as knowledge provider and that accuracy (of the choice of the vocabulary and the concept) is very important. Taken in combination with his earlier interruption, it looks much more as though he wishes to move things forward quickly, allowing little time for student contributions. The focus does appear to be on providing information, but not entirely at the expense of cutting out opportunities for students to respond.

Again, the point here is that without this micro-level analysis we might draw simple conclusions that this teacher is student-centred, communication-oriented as evidenced by student contributions. However, this interaction suggests that this teacher 'shows' several things about teaching and learning and how they have emerged in the interaction:

- He makes efforts to engage students by involving them in authentic materials, by introducing 'loch'.
- He sees the importance of accuracy in language learning, including choice of vocabulary and concept understanding by emphasising the differences between fantasy and fact, and mystery.
- He allows space for student contributions but perhaps is more comfortable with being a knowledge provider through extended turns and close control of the flow of the conversation.
- Vocabulary learning is embedded in feedback and contextualised.

Video-based reflection

Breen (1991) recommends that teachers should be encouraged to make connections between classroom action and personal theory to facilitate curriculum change (both in teaching and teacher training). He stresses the need to understand teacher beliefs by asking teachers to evaluate their beliefs based on 'actual classroom events'. Speer (2005) takes a different position, arguing that this procedure would provide opportunities to assess and generate shared understanding between the researcher and teachers. Her argument is based on the assumption that inconsistencies between teachers' beliefs and practice might be simply the consequence of a lack of 'shared understanding' between the researcher and the teacher participant. She argues a case for using a video-based reflection to achieve, as far as possible, a shared understanding between the teacher and the researcher of the construct being discussed. Video-based reflection is used based on video-recordings and playback of the teacher's classes to allow the researcher and the teacher to talk about what was happening in the classroom. The focus is placed on 'reflections upon descriptions, explanations and justifications given in the course of a talk' (Gellert 2001: 35) and the teacher's interpretation and understanding of what was happening. Speer argues that the benefit of using videoclip playback as a methodological technique in researching teacher cognition to collect data on beliefs is that it is tied to specific examples of teachers' practices. In her words, '(c)oarse grain sized characterizations of beliefs and general descriptions of teaching practices appear unlikely to do justice to the complex, contextually dependent acts of teaching' (2005: 224). Studies in teacher cognition also exemplify the advantages of such a technique for understanding teachers' beliefs in relation to their behaviours. This research strategy has been adopted by different researchers. Morton (2012) used the videoclip-based comment procedure to ask the teacher (Isabel) to reflect on her classroom talk, as shown in Extract 3.4.

Extract 3.4[2] (R: Researcher; I: Isabel)

```
1  R   so what was your purpose with this
2      with these questions
```

```
 3   I    my purpose
 4   R    at the beginning of this
 5   I    yeah what I wanted was to find out
 6        what they what mm
 7        what conception they had about a mutant
 8        the word mutant sounds so weird [you know=
 9   R                                   [mm hm hm
10   I    =I wanted to find out
11        .hh what their eh knowledge about mutants was.
12        just that
```

When Isabel was asked about the purpose of talking about mutants, she clearly identified it as 'finding out their conceptions'. Morton's analysis shows that it is clear that what Isabel was targeting in her classroom talk was to identify what 'conception' (line 7) and 'knowledge' (line 11) students had so that she could possibly change them. From a DP perspective, the focus is placed on how language is used to achieve particular soci(et)al practice in that context (e.g. reflection in this instance). After the researcher asks the question, 'so what was your purpose with this with these questions' and makes a further clarification (line 4), Isabel explains that her thinking regarding asking this question was to find out what conception the students had about a mutant. She further provides her own *understanding/perception*: 'the word mutant sounds so weird' (line 8). Note that the discourse marker 'you know' in line 8 and the researcher's acknowledgement using back channel 'mm hm hm' in line 9 show a degree of shared understanding. Morton also commented that Isabel's stated purposes neatly fit the interactive/dialogic communicative approach (ibid.: 108). Then Isabel reformulates her answer that she wanted to find out the students' knowledge about a mutant. The issue for the discursive psychologist now is not whether and how cognition and conception are correlated within Isabel's mind but rather how Isabel and the researcher managed to make meaning together. In other words, how participants achieve social meaning in context is more the concern of DP than what are the mental states of the participants.

SUMMARY

This chapter has presented a discursive psychological perspective towards the study of teacher cognition, which challenges the cognitive view of teacher cognition as a static and fixed assumption held by teachers. A discursive psychological approach, using principles of CA, considers different types of data to illustrate the discursive nature of teacher cognition, which can be and needs to be studied through an interactional lens. The next chapter focuses on pre-service teacher cognition by looking at the process of knowledge and belief development in a teacher education programme.

NOTES

1. *Conversation and cognition* (te Molder and Potter 2005) was the first time perhaps that experts in interactional analysis were brought together to address the issues of cognition through the lens of interaction, including ethnomethodology, conversational analysis and discursive psychology. The relationship between cognition and conversation can be explored from different perspectives.
2. This extract is taken from Morton (2012).

PART B: ANALYSIS

4
LEARNING TO TEACH AND PRE-SERVICE TEACHER COGNITION

In Chapter 3, a discursive psychological perspective of teacher cognition was presented. To recap, the main arguments for adopting a discursive psychological perspective to investigating teacher cognition through the lens of social interaction are:

1. Teaching is a social practice and interaction is central to effective teaching and learning.
2. Teacher cognition is about teachers' knowing, understanding, conceptualising and doing their work in their professional context; it is not a static mental object held by teachers. Rather, it is one outcome of the interaction with the context, which is highly shaped and defined in situ.
3. Interaction is not a channel for cognition but the action of cognition.
4. Meanings are co-constructed by participants through various interactional strategies. Meaning is produced not only through what is said, but also how it is said.

This chapter focuses on pre-service teacher cognition – the kind of beliefs, conception and knowledge teachers in preparation display as they undertake a programme of teacher education. Using detailed transcripts of group discussions, interviews, teaching practice and video-based teacher reflections, this chapter provides insights into pre-service teachers' thinking, decision-making, knowing and understanding about language teaching and learning, and about being a language teacher.

PRE-SERVICE TEACHER COGNITION

It is widely acknowledged that pre-service teachers begin their professional learning with relatively established pedagogical beliefs, which originate largely from their prior experiences of learning a second language, particularly in secondary schools or formal classrooms (Kern 1995; Peacock 1999). This is known as an 'apprenticeship of observation' (Lortie 1975). Much research in pre-service cognition has already suggested that these prospective language teachers have many preconceived ideas about how languages are learned and how they should be taught, and these beliefs and conceptions: (1) play a pivotal role (as filter) in their acquisition and interpretation of knowledge in their professional learning; (2) strongly influence their teaching behaviour (Bailey et al. 1996); and (3) tend to be reinforced during TESOL (Teaching English to Speakers of Other Languages) courses.

The majority of research on pre-service teacher cognition rests on the stability of the concept and the impact of teacher education on its development. For example, Peacock (2001), in a longitudinal study, showed that teachers' beliefs changed little in training and that teacher education had little effect on the development of teachers' beliefs. Likewise, Borg (2005) concluded that little change in teachers' beliefs was noted in the context of the CELTA (Certificate in Teaching English Language to Adults). These studies seem to confirm the pessimistic view that 'preservice programmes are not very powerful interventions' (Zeichner et al. 1987: 28).

However, some research has questioned the stability of teachers' beliefs over time (e.g. Kern 1995; Mattheoudakis 2007). These contradictory views might be due to the different contexts in which these studies were situated, or the validity of the instrument they employed. Much of this research relies on the questionnaire created by Horwitz (1985), Beliefs about Language Learning Inventory (BALLI), an instrument which might be seen as being rather subjective since data are presented at face value without supporting evidence from classroom or interview data. This said, M. Borg (2005) did use a case study approach but her study was restricted by the length of the programme (four weeks) and it is unlikely that any changes would be observed over such a short period of time. Although research on pre-service teacher cognition has been expanding, Borg (2009) argues that the process of language teachers' cognitive change has as yet remained relatively unexplored. Furthermore, Wright (2010) correctly points out that there is a lack of research on pre-service teachers' learning in formal teacher education. Perhaps one of the very few longitudinal studies to date was that conducted by Li (2012). She investigated two student teachers' belief development on a one-year Master's TESOL course adopting a case study approach. Various types of data, such as interviews, classroom data and written reflections on the teaching practicum, were used to describe and depict the development of these two pre-service teachers' beliefs and practice, and Li concluded that 'teacher education (including course structure, tutors and teaching practicum) can have a powerful influence on pre-service teacher development' (2012: 50). She further claims that pre-service teacher cognition development is a reflection of teacher identity, which includes confirmation/consolidation of pre-existing beliefs, realisation beyond pre-existing beliefs, expansion of pre-existing belief systems, integration/addition of new ideas to pre-existing beliefs, and localisation/reconstruction of pre-existing and newly established beliefs (ibid.: 51).

TEACHER KNOWLEDGE AND KNOWING

Traditionally, L2 teacher education has centred on the learning theories of second languages to develop competent language teachers, rather than on teachers as learners of teaching (Freeman and Johnson 1998). Such an approach also focuses on developing teachers' content knowledge and how this is learnt. Therefore, emphasis is placed on the knowledge in teacher education and much of the research in teacher cognition focuses on exploring deficit teacher knowledge and making suggestions on correcting teachers' knowledge and beliefs. These areas are investigated in such a way that that knowledge is treated as a concrete product that we are able to observe and examine. However, we also know that knowledge is developed in a social cultural context through interaction with people around the person, and cognition can develop as the result of interaction with the environment. Knowledge therefore is not something that teachers should acquire but an understanding that they develop in their local contexts.

At a very broad level, the term *teacher knowledge* is used as an umbrella term to cover teachers' theoretical and practical knowledge. This might overlap with beliefs, dispositions, values and propositions. In education, Shulman (1986) categorised content knowledge into several areas, including disciplinary content knowledge, pedagogical content knowledge and curricular knowledge. Shulman (1987) then subsequently developed the categories to include general pedagogical knowledge, curriculum knowledge, pedagogical content knowledge, knowledge of learners, knowledge of educational context and knowledge of educational ends. This set of categories is defined as the core issues underlying teachers' understanding of effective pedagogy, although Shulman cautions us that this categories of knowledge base 'remains to be discovered, invented, and refined' (1987: 12). Elbaz proposed a concept *practical knowledge*, which she defines as 'teachers' knowledge of subject matter, curriculum, instruction, classroom management, school and community, learning styles, as well as knowledge of their own attitudes, values, beliefs and goals – all shaped by their practical classroom experience' (1983: 5). *Practical knowledge* was further developed and expanded by Clandinin and Connelly (1987) as *personal practical knowledge*, as they believe that the knowledge teachers hold and refer to in their professional life is constructed and reconstructed through their stories and process of reflection. As explained in Chapter 2, this line of inquiry is largely focused on the personal side of teacher knowledge and this has been done through narrative inquiry. Kumaravadivelu (2012) reviewed these different concepts of teacher knowledge and proposed that for teacher preparation we should aim for a set of manageable and meaningful types of knowledge, and proposed three types of knowledge: professional knowledge (about language, language learning and language teaching), procedural knowledge (classroom management), and personal knowledge (personal endeavour). This framework attempts to synthesise various insights from the literature, despite the concept of professional knowledge being vague and blurry. On the other hand, Johnson (2009a) points out the need to turn our attention to the process of teacher knowing – how teachers come to know what they know, how certain concepts in teachers' consciousness develop over time, and how their learning processes transform them and the activities of L2 teaching. This suggests that teacher education perhaps needs to move from developing language teachers' knowledge to raising their awareness of the process of knowing.

Teacher learning plays an important role in developing pre-service teachers' knowledge. Teacher learning is an interactive, reflective and experiential process in which interaction with peers and experts (e.g. tutors), and negotiation in the community to become a teacher, are important features. Given the importance of teacher learning and the role of teacher education in developing and shaping teacher cognition, this chapter is dedicated to this concept in order to explore the kind of teacher cognition pre-service teachers have and how such cognition is embedded in social interaction. Since the position of DP is that cognition is situated sequentially and institutionally, it is inappropriate to even address the question of whether pre-service teachers' cognition changes over time. Thus, this chapter focuses mainly on pre-service teachers' cognition-in-interaction, paying particular attention to how they display their knowledge, understanding and positions in social interaction in lesson planning sessions with tutors, reflections on teaching, individual teaching and team teaching.

The dataset for this chapter rests on 741 minutes of data from pre-service teacher education programmes in different contexts. The data consists of 404 minutes of group teaching (where teachers work as a small group and share responsibility for a lesson) and 336 minutes of individual teaching, 127 minutes of self-reflection and peer evaluation of lessons, and 212 minutes of lesson planning discussion with the teachers' tutors and work group. In my view, this is a reasonable dataset for investigating teachers' knowledge, conception, beliefs, thinking and practices. In reviewing the dataset, it is clear that student teachers' concerns are generally with understanding subject knowledge, instructional methods, teacher explanations and establishing relationships with students. These areas are important for teachers as they represent the immediate need of a teacher in the profession. A number of themes of interest emerged, including 'developing content knowledge', 'developing pedagogical knowledge' and 'developing self as a teacher'.

DEVELOPING CONTENT KNOWLEDGE

For language teachers, a number of concerns in relation to language and literacy teaching are noticed, among which increasing learners' performance as measured by examinations and developing communicative abilities have indicated a need to increase teachers' 'knowledge about language' (henceforth KAL). In this dataset, KAL is a concept that relates to knowledge about language as system, as discourse, as ideology and as social practice. In a way, these conceptions are similar to some of the categories that Cook proposed (2007, 2010). Language as system is very much similar to the view that language is a set of sentences which are governed by rules and the ultimate goal of learning a language is to work out how words produce meaningful sentences. Language as discourse is concerned more with its meaning in a particular community, whereas language as ideology concerns the function of the language in the society. Finally, language as social practice sees language as action. Words are no longer just words, they have meanings and consequences.

LANGUAGE AS SYSTEM

Johnson (2009a) summarises that the knowledge base of L2 teacher education has drawn heavily from the disciplinary knowledge of linguistics and SLA to define what L2 teachers need to know about language and L2 learning (Freeman and Johnson 1998). Yet, how language is defined and how SLA is understood in a teacher education programme decide what is to be presented to student teachers. As shown in the dataset, language as system is somewhat overemphasised in such contexts. Language as system refers to the rules that govern language systematically in all aspects of linguistic form, such as phonology, lexis and grammar. The phonology system considers the sounds of a language, including phonological and phonemic systems and how these systems relate to words, stress, intonation and pronunciation. Knowledge about lexis is knowledge about words, including semantics (meaning) and etymologies (the origins of words). The syntactic system deals with the rules and structure of grammar.

In Extract 4.1, a tutor (T) is conversing with two students (ST1 and ST2) who have just finished their lesson planning session.

Extract 4.1 English is too complicated (interview)

```
1    T      how's the class?=
2    ST1    =um (0.5) um (.) hmmm ((looking at her friend)) not really good=
3    T      =>why? What's wrong?<=
4    ST1    =>no no no< (.) we learnt a lot (.) °it's just English is too
5           [complicated°
6    ST2    [we didn't know that be going to not necessarily mean
7           [future tense
8    ST1    [future tense er
9    T      °hhhuh huh°=
10   ST1    =the tutor told us today that if you [plan with someone(.) ]for
11   ST2                                         [°have an arrangement°]
12   ST1    example say I invite Sherry for dinner next Monday((looking at
13          her friend)) you can also use be going to but it doesn't mean
14          future=
15   ST2    =no it means arrangement plan (.)although next Monday is future
16          (0.8)but anyway you know what I mean=
17   ST1    =the focus is on the plan bit not the future tense (.) so we
18          didn't know this (.) so er the lesson planning session was a
19          disaster (0.5) now we need to £learn grammar again£
20          ((laughing with embarrassment))
21   T      °hhhuh huh°(.) a grammar book (.) it might help.
```

The tutor initiates the conversation by asking the students' opinions of the session. A preferred response in this situation would be a positive response. In this extract, student 1 displays hesitation (line 2), notably a 0.5 second pause, a hesitation marker um followed by a micro-pause (.) and another hesitation marker hmmm, indicating a potentially negative response. The carefully constructed dispreferred response was received by the teacher as a surprise, as indicated by an immediate reply Why? What's wrong? and at an unusually fast speed. In response, the same student suggests nothing is wrong and they have learnt a lot. But after a micro-pause, she provides a further explanation to her earlier comment in a noticeably softer tone that English is too complicated. What is interesting here is that the student uses a subtle way to display her position shift from possibly criticising the session to their own understanding of the content. Note that student 2 overlaps student 1 and claims insufficient content knowledge (line 6) (Koshik 2002) and this claim is once again evident later on in the interaction (line 18). This insufficient knowledge claim displays a knowledge base before the session, and in this interaction we can see these two students are doing work to show their sufficient knowledge status (from lines 10–17). For these two students, this interaction clearly demonstrates their knowledge and belief about the subject – English is a complicated system. Here they particularly refer to the syntactic system (lines 4 and 5). That knowing English is complicated is evident in the process of the knowledge or understanding co-construction by providing explanations and clarifications, and illustrating the acquired knowledge of 'be going to'. Not being able to fully understand the meaning of 'be going to' in the lesson plan is considered a 'disaster' (lines 18 and 19), which suggests the importance of grammatical accuracy in their teaching. This belief is further illustrated by their solution to the disaster, we need to £learn grammar again£. The smiley voice and embarrassed laughter displays their beliefs about their subject knowledge and themselves as knowledge source (line 20). This is understood by the teacher who provides confirmation °hhhuh huh° (.), and a suggestion to use a grammar book. From both the tutor's and students' perspectives, grammar is important – knowing and being able to explain the grammar point is critical in teaching.

LANGUAGE AS IDEOLOGY

Another prevailing view is English as a tool, a resource, a channel to gain access to another culture and community and a means that can help people to gain opportunities in work or life in general. The extract below is from an interview with a TESOL student, demonstrating how this understanding is co-constructed and shared in a conversation.

Extract 4.2 English is a very important subject (interview)

```
9    I    so why do you want to teach English?
10   ST   um (2.3) I um (.) I am interested in English an- it is
11        very important subject (1.5)
12   I    important subject at school?=
13   ST   =yeah (.) it's important subject in school cos everyone
14        has to learn it (.) you get students' respect an- (0.7)it's
15        important when you leave school (.)you go to study abroad
16        or go to work (.) English is important=
17   I    =so it's important because it gives people opportunities=
18   ST   =yeah. opportunities for example um (.) the chance you
19        get a better job is bigger (1.3)
20        hmmm (.) in a way it is a resource (.)so it's useful
```

In the interview, the first pair part which the interviewer produces sets the agenda for this conversation, signalling an expected answer to be something about English, not why she wants to be a teacher. The student teacher follows the cue and provides a relevant but brief second pair part that she is interested in the subject and it is important (lines 10 and 11). This is followed by a longish pause (1.5), indicating turn completion and giving. The interviewer then takes the turn and follows up the claim of (English as an) important subject and steers the conversation in this direction. Here, particular attention is paid to why language is important as a school subject and the rising tone can be interpreted as seeking agreement, clarification and elaboration (line 12). The student teacher provides further elaboration to highlight the functional aspects of the language (line 14). In this extract, the power that English has is obvious because her understanding of the importance and usefulness of the language as a tool or resource is displayed in three different situations (lines 14–15, 18–19): (1) you get students' respect; (2) you go to study abroad; and (3) the chance to get a better job is bigger.

We can see in this extract that English is initially viewed as an important and useful subject at school, but it is also assigned significant value at a societal level where English could be a gateway to studying abroad and securing a job, or as a power that gives the teacher respect. Here, the interviewer and the student teacher co-construct the idea that English gives people opportunities (lines 17–18). The shared understanding between the interviewer and the teacher is established through the talk of the importance of English as a subject, which has a strong impact beyond the context of school.

English as power is widely shared by pre-service teachers as it does not only lead to a better job and better life potentially, but also to a higher status. Consider the following dialogue between two trainee teachers about teaching practice where their understanding of the power of English is illustrated.

Extract 4.3 Her English is so beautiful (peer reflection)

```
1    STA    all students like Rebecca (1.2) you know (0.2) she just
2           attracts attention=
3    STB    =yeah I like her (.) her English is so [beautiful
4    STA                                           [yeah (.) but it
5           doesn't mean she's a good TEAcher (.) what I DON'T
6           understand is her mentor likes her. hhhh even she makes
7           mistakes (.) students love her and they all respect her (.)
8           as if she's a good teacher
9    STB    but. she is not (.) they like her because her English is
10          good. I think it's better than her mentor
11   STA    I am stress-out to teach the same class (0.8) they just keep
12          saying Rebecca pronounces the word this way (.) ((sighs))
```

During peer reflection on a teaching practice, these two student teachers focus on their work relationships with colleagues. Student teacher A starts with a statement that all students like Rebecca with a longish pause (1.2). This pause could be interpreted in various ways. It might indicate a turn completion and giving, or it might indicate that the student A is taking the time to structure what she is going to say.

Here, judging from what follows, it might be the latter as the student teacher A is trying to express unhappy feelings in relation to Rebecca. The discourse marker 'you know' and the brief pause suggest that she is establishing a shared understanding that Rebecca attracts attention with her colleague. This indicates that she is complaining about Rebecca rather than complimenting her. Student teacher B immediately follows up with an affirmative answer to co-establish the fact and points out the reason – Rebecca's popularity is due to her beautiful English (line 3). Rebecca's beautiful English is established through the interactional work between the two student teachers by talking about her relationship with the mentor, the pupils and her colleagues (e.g. student teacher A). As we can see here 'beautiful English' gives Rebecca a special status, although she is not recognised as a good teacher by her fellow colleagues (lines 5 and 9). Student A also puts herself in a position of suffering from Rebecca's special status because children keep challenging her authority by comparing her with Rebecca. Apart from displaying the power that English has in shaping student teachers' role and identity, what student teacher A articulates here is a display of negative experience in practice, which might result in negative emotions about teaching (Farrell 2001).

LANGUAGE AS SOCIAL PRACTICE

For some student teachers, language is regarded not only as a system, a discourse, an ideology, but also as a social practice. Johnson argues that '(F)rom a language as a social practice perspective, meaning is central; not in the service of form or function, but as the expression of deeply embedded concepts that denote ways of feeling, seeing, and being in the world' (2009a: 46). Thus, student teachers who take such a stance display their understanding that language only has meanings through and in the way it is used, and helping students to realise how language is used to express meanings lies at the heart of language teaching. It is also interesting to note that the student teachers' understanding of language as social practice is to some extent related to their own study experience when they use the English language for social purposes. Language and its meaning do not exist as a form of grammar, a set of vocabulary or ways to pronounce, but as a practice in everyday life. Such understanding is more evident at the later stage of the course when student teachers have been exposed to various ideas about teaching and have experience in using English as social practice.

In Extract 4.4, student teacher Fiona is talking about her lesson plan with her tutor and fellow colleague, Georgie.

Extract 4.4 Use of English in everyday talk (lesson planning conference with the tutor)

```
1    STF    er (.) my idea (.)I think it's important to get students
2           understand hmmm (.)use English in everyday talk (.) English
3           is real (.) so I am thinking of er:: asking them to talk
4           about the Chinese festival↑(1.2) to start the class
5           (1.8)
```

LEARNING TO TEACH AND PRE-SERVICE TEACHER COGNITION 83

```
6     T      hmmm so you ask them to talk↑ (1.2) um it's a bit vague
7            so(.)anything specific? (0.4)
8     STF    yeah (.) I will elicit the topic from them (.) and ask them
9            to share something about their experience =
10    STG    =might be a good idea if you also share YOUR experience (.)
9            it's like fake otherwise (.) I mean they need to experience
10           using English for COMMUNIcation (.)
11    T      [good idea
12    STF    [yeah(.) maybe that's the way that help them understand (.)
13           learning English (.) isn't (.) shouldn't be like learning
14           grammar
```

The idea of language as social practice is implemented in the lesson plan as Fiona articulates her thinking (line 1). Here, she specifically refers to lexical choice of I think, my idea in expressing her understanding about the role of language. In her articulation, language as social practice is considered as her teaching purpose and teaching method (lines 3 and 4). Instead of confirming Fiona's ideas, the tutor carefully scrutinises the idea by seeking confirmation (line 6). The rising tone here implies that it is not a confirmation or approval of the student's idea, rather it is a subtle way to challenge the viability, and possibly ask for more details. The longish pause in line 6 (1.2), indicates the completion of the turn and turn-giving, which Fiona does not take. The tutor then takes the turn again to provide a clear assessment of the plan (slightly vague) and rephrases the request as a question to ask for more specific information on how this is going to be done (line 7). Fiona takes the cue to provide a second pair part containing both how she is going to implement the plan and what kind of information is desired (lines 8–9). At this point, we can see that the idea of language as social practice is also taken up by another student teacher, Georgie, who follows up with a suggestion for giving students experience of using English for social purposes. This idea is immediately approved by the tutor and taken up by Fiona, who confirms that this is the way to get students to understand language (lines 12–14). In this extract, we see how Fiona's idea of English for social practice is developed with the help of the tutor and her colleague from an abstract and vague idea to a concrete plan for a lesson. This idea is then practised in peer teaching.

Extract 4.5 FioTe5 (05.24_08.33) a special day

```
9     F      do you know there is some special day on Thursdays.
10           it's a very special day ((hand going from right to left
11           showing excitement))(.) do you know what day is on
12           [Thursday?
13    S2     [Valentine's day? =
14    F      =what? ((looking at this student))=
15    S3     =<Chinese new year:::>=
16    F      =yes Chinese new year ((nodding her head)). So do you
17           remember how you celebrate your last Chinese new year?=
18    S4     =YES
```

```
19   F    ((moving her body towards the student with a surprised face))
20        how?=
21   S4   =er..I had er a big dinner with my family=
22   F    =[oh
23   S4    [and we watched [spring (.) festival gala as they call it
24   S5                    [°tv°
25   S4   (.)and we played mahjong
26   F    [ah..((laughing))
27   SS   [(((laughing loudly))
28   F    that's quite interesting. you remember that you celebrated
29        with your family last year yeah?=
30   S4   =yeah
```

In Extract 4.5 Fiona is using a question and body language to elicit spring festival from students, with the emphasis on special day (line 9). Fiona rephrases her question immediately (lines 11–12) when a student takes the cue and overlaps Fiona's question. The immediate response suggests the topic is of interest to students. Clearly, the student's response is unexpected as Fiona shows surprise (line 14). A second student then takes up the cue with an expected answer. Note the stretches at the end of his answer and the stress further indicate that this is the obvious answer and his surprise at the first student's reply. This time, Fiona follows up with confirmation: a positive assessment with a repetition of the student's response yes Chinese new year and paralinguistic signs (e.g. body language) to suggest approval (line 16). Fiona then initiates another question (lines 16–17), which a third student immediately answers. Again, this is an unexpected answer from the teacher's perspective, as suggested by her surprised face and a question how? (line 20). The student provides a response (lines 21 to 25) with 'assistance' from his peer (line 24). Note that in line 22 Fiona shows acknowledgement to the information provided. Here, oh is also produced as a 'change of state' token (Heritage 1998); it registers a change in Fiona's state of knowledge or information. This student's contribution has definitely aroused the students' interest as well as the teacher's, evidenced by their laughs (lines 26 and 27). Here, an interesting thing to note is that the cultural norms, playing mah-jong during spring festival and watching Festival Gala, are appreciated by both the teacher and the students. The language for communication and social practice is evident in this extract where the students and the teacher share their experience of celebrating a festival. Further, meaning is focused and there is no attendance to the form.

One might argue that student teachers display a strong understanding of language as social practice because they are teaching their peers and they practise the methods and ideas they learnt in the course, as with those teachers who were described in Breen et al.'s study (2001). This could be true. However, what this extract suggests is: first, student teachers do possess and display different understandings about the subject knowledge, (e.g. their conception of language), and such knowledge is displayed in interaction; and, second, the belief about the content knowledge is constituted in a micro-context (e.g. lesson planning episodes, lead-in stage of a lesson) as evidenced in the above extracts.

DEVELOPING PEDAGOGICAL KNOWLEDGE

Pre-service teacher cognition about pedagogy or pedagogical knowledge often refers to their understanding and knowing about teaching methods and activities. In this dataset, student teacher cognition is distributed in two main areas: developing understanding of teaching methods, and teaching procedures. It is clear that student teachers orient towards the teaching methods they learnt from their course and attempt to use them in their own teaching. They also develop a strong awareness of teaching procedure, including staging a lesson, using personal information in teaching, giving feedback, giving instructions and dealing with unexpected events. These themes are displayed in their designing activities, theoretical understanding and classroom teaching.

DEVELOPING KNOWLEDGE OF TEACHING METHODS

The understanding of teaching methods is represented by students as dichotomies: communicative approaches versus linguistic form-based approaches. Student teachers display confusion of these concepts and difficulties in understanding the link between theory and practice, which is illustrated in the following extracts.

Extract 4.6 is taken from a lesson planning session where a student teacher is articulating her teaching method.

Extract 4.6 I don't know

```
1    ST1    so my teaching is £CLT£ °I think°=
2    T      =what do you mean by CLT? It's a bit vague (.) isn't it?=
3    ST1    =yes (.) it's vague (.) I don't know really (0.5) I
4           guess (.) it's teaching speaking and listening more↑
5    T      hmmm (.) teaching speaking and listening more is
6           communicative? (.)
7    ST1    no (.) that's not what I mean (.) I can't give you example
8           or something (.) I don't really know
```

Despite the fact that she labels her pedagogy as CLT (communicative language teaching), she displays confusion and a lack of confidence in understanding the concept, as indicated by the smiley and very low voice (line 1). Rather than telling the student what her design is, the tutor follows up with a clarification request to help the student teacher to articulate what CLT is. Not only that, the tutor also challenges the student teacher by providing feedback on her claim of using CLT (line 2). The student teacher's uncertainty now is further displayed by confirming the teacher's feedback on her understanding of CLT being vague (line 3), and then a withdrawal of the idea as she claims insufficient knowledge (line 3). This exchange demonstrates how this student teacher's understanding about pedagogical approach changes. At the beginning, she claims to be using CLT and then she withdraws the idea and claims insufficient knowledge (Koshik 2002). This is followed by her attempt to exemplify what she means by CLT. I guess and the slightly rising tone suggest that she is still not sure about her explanation or understanding (line 4), which is picked up by her tutor who challenges with a confirmation check (lines 5-6). The student quickly clarifies that teaching speaking and listening being communicative is not what she meant and further makes a claim of insufficient knowledge (line 8). This display of pedagogical knowledge from knowing to not knowing is typical in this dataset. Student teachers very often feel they know what a certain teaching method means and claim that they are using such a method in their teaching, yet in dialogue with their tutors or colleagues they face the difficulty of pinning down the practice matching the theory. The development of awareness of pedagogical knowledge through scrutinising and negotiation suggests that a teacher's awareness could be a result or consequence of interaction with others. It is very typical for novice teachers to think they are following a certain method as they lack confidence and flexibility in teaching (Gatbonton, 2008).

Lack of confidence and flexibility emerge while teaching when teachers produce long teacher turns and control the floor so that students have minimum space to intervene. This said, when student teachers do have awareness and knowledge to relate their practice to classroom situations they become more flexible and confident in making pedagogical decisions. Extract 4.7 is taken from Xie's teaching which reflects typical teacher talk by student teachers at the beginning of their journey in learning to teach.

Extract 4.7 XieTe4 (00:00_03:23)

```
1    STX    um: look at your email I really need you to um download
2           this pdf (1.0)an(d) um because I am going to teach
3           reading so um I really need you to read this (2.4)an-
4           because we are short of time so er: can you just start
5           reading from the summary↑ un:til the end of the first
6           page (.) I will give you ((looking at the screen)) it's
7           not a difficult article so: I will give you hmmm three
8           minutes to finish it (.)and then we will start with
9           some questions ok↑
```

This extract starts with an instruction to get students to download the article they need to read (line 1), a pedagogical aim (lines 2-3) and an activity for students (line 3). Here a long pause (2.4) indicates the end of the instruction and the start of the activity. At this point, we can see that Xie changes her plan by asking students to read from halfway through the article after realising the time constraint in class (line 4). Judging from the article length and level of difficulty by looking at the screen, Xie concludes, it's not a difficult article so: I will give you hmmm three minutes to finish it (.) (lines 6-8). Here we can see the teacher's ability to judge a situation and make a new plan in situ, especially in giving an indication of the time in which she expects her students to complete the reading (lines 7-9). Here, Xie gives instructions, positioning her students as being able to complete the task within a given time and produce answers. This extract, from a discursive psychological perspective, raises two useful points. First, not all teacher learners follow their plans rigidly and it is possible that student teachers can develop competence in making interactive decisions based on the situation. The ability to be able to make a good and effective decision is closely related to the concept of expertise, which perhaps should be taken into consideration for every teacher education programme. Second, this teacher's knowledge about pedagogy is developed in teaching, notably in the way that she changes her plan. The knowledge of students needing to start from halfway through the article and complete it in three minutes does not exist in her head, but has emerged from her judgement of students, materials and perhaps interaction in the class. Therefore, it is important to examine the moment-to-moment decision-making in learning to teach or teacher learning.

DEVELOPING KNOWLEDGE ABOUT TEACHING PROCEDURE

Student teachers' pedagogical knowledge about teaching procedure specifically concerns staging a lesson. The difficulty in general relates to a lack of interactional competence to achieve the pedagogical goals. For example, staging in class is very difficult, in particular in two aspects: opening class in a natural way and making a smooth transition from one activity to another. The former concerns the natural lead-in while the latter concerns moving the class forward smoothly.

Staging class: opening class is difficult

Extract 4.8 EJTe5 (00:00_00:10)

```
1   STF   £ok£ good (.) afternoon (.) class?
2   SS    good afternoon °teacher°
3   STF   um (.) so. how's your weekend?
4   S1    busy=
5   STF   =busy↑ (.)
6   S1    yeah=
7   STF   =yeah? (.)
8   S1    yeah!
9   STF   ((nodding her head))(0.3)ok↓
```

Extract 4.8 is an example of a student teacher displaying difficulty in opening the class in a natural way. The teacher asks students about their weekend (line 3), to which one student responds (line 4). Here, the teacher displays difficulty in moving the dialogue forward or linking it to her pedagogical objective. As shown in line 5, the teacher echoes the student's contribution with a slight rising tone, requesting confirmation, which the student provides (line 6). It would be natural for the teacher to move forward either to ask further questions or make a comment. However, the teacher carries on to make another confirmation check (line 7) and the student responds in an affirmative (line 8). Then the teacher confirms with body language and moves on, as indicated by a pause and discourse marker with a falling tone ok↓ (line 9). The difficulty for this student teacher in opening the class lies in the ability to either provide appropriate feedback or follow up the student's turn to move the topic forward. The skill or knowledge of being able to interact naturally in the classroom is defined as classroom interactional competence (CIC) (Walsh, 2006) (see more in Chapter 5). The lack of such a competence results in making a link between the opening of a lesson and her pedagogical objectives.

Staging lessons: problems of transition
Effective classroom management is key to the creation of an environment for successful learning (LePage et al. 2005), including being able to create a cohesive lesson, transiting the lesson smoothly, and maintaining students' engagement and attention. Not surprisingly, student and novice teachers often cite classroom management issues as their greatest challenge (Burnard 1998; Silvestri 2001). Gaining and maintaining engagement has been identified as one of the concerns for effective teaching (Acheson and Gall 2003; Nolan and Hoover 2008), and consequently managing transitions can be particularly difficult as it is possible to create problems, including disengaging students from the current task and re-engaging them in a new task. Successful transition is essential to a successful lesson, therefore it is obvious that many teachers spend quite a big chunk of their management time in transition. In this dataset, student teachers clearly have developed ideas about the importance of transition and display difficulties in transiting from one stage to another in teaching. In Extract 4.9, Emma is teaching vocabulary – *forget* and *remember* – and the consolidating activity is to ask students to make up sentences.

Extract 4.9 EmTe4 (24.25_25.56)

```
11    E     so can you give me some sentences by using remember and
12          forget (.) you? ((pointing to one student)) first (.)
13    S1    I remember er I remember going out with a friend last week
14          but I forget the name of the place=
15    E     =uh (.) so you remember you went out but you forgot the
16          name↑ of the place?=
17    S1    =yeah=
18    E     =yeah↓ ((turning to another student)) how about you? (0.2)
19    S2    I forgot to bring money today but I will remember to do it
20          tomorrow (0.3)
21    E     so you have made sentences er (.) it's important you can
22          use the tense correctly (.) so um: (1.2) next ((looking at
23          her notebook)) we will read a story and I will ask you a
24          few questions
```

In line 11 Emma asks a question to request students' contributions, and makes an individual selection (line 12). The nominated student provides a relevant answer (lines 13–14), to which the teacher provides a back channel as an acknowledgement receipt (line 15). This is followed by a confirmation check (lines 15–16) as indicated by a repeat from Emma with a rising tone (line 16). The student confirms and the teacher moves on to nominate the next speaker (line 18). After the second student's contribution, Emma consciously starts to move to the next activity as she does not provide any feedback on this student's contribution and the discourse marker 'so' here suggests the teacher is ready to move to the next activity (line 22). The transitional work is also done through the teacher summarising the current activity (line 21) you have made sentences er (.) and emphasising the importance of using the correct tenses. The natural flow of this lesson would have been some activities on tenses. However, Emma follows her lesson plan (note she is checking her notebook) to move to the next activity: we will read a story and I will ask you a few questions. From this, we can say that Emma displays difficulty in making natural and smooth transitions in her interactional work with students in the following regards:

- She does not provide any feedback on the contribution by student 2, indicating the completion of the first activity and moving on to the next one.
- After her summary of the previous activity, Emma demonstrates difficulty in moving on, notably by the long pause, hesitation and sudden change of the activity.
- Emma also has to refer to her lesson plan and uses transitional words to move from one stage to another. In line 22, after the long pause, Emma chooses to use the transition word – next – to indicate the transition.

Although Emma starts a new activity, it is hard to say this is a successful transition as she failed to help the student understand the connections between the two activities and there is no clear learning objective. In this case, having two disconnected activities might disengage students.

PERSONAL EXPERIENCE

In this dataset, student teachers in particular make use of their own personal experience of teaching to contextualise the learning materials, to expand learning opportunities and to increase topic and task authenticity. Extract 4.10 is an example of a teacher using personal experience to engage the students and to build a relationship with students.

Extract 4.10 MayTe1 (00:00_01:31)

```
1    May    um good morning everyone (.) welcome to my class↓ (.)
2           um::: to begin with (.)one of my friends has recommended
3           a very interesting TV programme to me and today I wan:t
4           to show it with you <ALL OF YOU> ((her hands moving in
5           rhythms)) and first let's to hear what my friends says
6           ((operating the computer))
```

In Extract 4.10, May shares her experience of watching a very interesting television programme that her friend recommended to her and that she is going to show to her students (lines 2–4). In this short extract, we see the various things May does to engage students. First, she uses emphatic tones in different places and gestures to show her excitement. Second, the personal experience certainly provides authenticity and she indicates that she wants to share her experience with the whole class. The slow but loud speech of <ALL OF YOU> brings everyone into this activity (line 4). For her and her students, they are not teaching and learning English but sharing experiences. Using personal experience certainly engages the students, and from this teacher's perspective the purpose of learning a language is to use language to access information. The use of personal experience is closely related to teacher emotion in a professional context. It is evident that there is a strong link between teachers' emotions and their curriculum, pedagogy (Zembylas 2002, 2003, 2005, 2007; Hargreaves 2005) and relationship with students. Making jokes, using humour and sometimes tolerating misbehaviour are all part of reconstructing pedagogy based on students' reaction (Demetriou et al. 2009). The fine-tuning of the lesson reflects the teacher's ability to building rapport and engage students.

GIVING FEEDBACK

In a classroom, teachers routinely find themselves in the position of responding to learners' displays of knowledge or giving feedback to their contributions. In any classroom, the ubiquitous, three-part IRF (Initiation-Response-Feedback) exchange (Sinclair and Coulthard 1975) is said to account for around 70% of classroom discourse (Wells 1993), and research suggests that feedback is an important component of learning when the teacher is in the position to accept, reject, evaluate or comment on the student's contribution. Much research has been done in this area (e.g. see Lerner 1995; Seedhouse 1997; Waring 2008), and one particular relevant point is that teachers' knowledge and competence in providing appropriate feedback is critical in creating or suppressing learning opportunities (e.g. Waring 2011; Walsh and Li 2013). Clearly, knowledge about giving feedback is one important element for pre-service teacher cognition. However, surprisingly, student teachers demonstrate little understanding of the importance and strategies of giving feedback. In particular, lack of feedback, teacher repetition, preferred and dis-preferred feedback are the major themes, which merit a further discussion.

Lack of feedback

The dataset suggests that a predominant theme is a lack of appropriate feedback, with the F position being occupied by a form of *sequence-closing third* (SCT) in CA terms (Schegloff 2007) or teacher repetition. SCTs, for example the use of *oh, okay*, or assessments (i.e. *great*), are designed not to project further turns within the sequence and therefore minimally expand on the foregoing adjacency pairs (Schegloff 2007). The use of SCT and teacher repetition is shown in the following extracts.

Extract 4.11 CJTe4 (11.27_11.39)

```
1    J    who can tell me among these four words ((looking at
2         the screen))uh how many how many of these words have
```

```
3          two (0.7) meanings↓
4          (1.2)
5    S1    li[ft↑
6    S2      [lift↓
7    J     um ok (.)
```

In Extract 4.11, Joan produces a first pair part demanding a response with a word having two meanings on the screen. After a longish pause, student 1 makes an attempt to respond, with the second student overlapping part of the same answer (lines 5 and 6). Clearly, both students have produced the preferred response, and instead of giving clear feedback which might lead to the use of this word or its meaning, or its part of speech, Joan simply displays SCT to complete the sequence with a discourse marker ok (line 7). In the videoclip-based reflection, Joan realises the issue of a lack of feedback in her teaching.

Extract 4.12 Post-teaching reflection

```
49   J    the third problem is I think I should give some um praise
50        for students when some of them answer my question=
51   Tu   =give praise↑ no matter what what they say?=
52   J    =I should I mean give them feedback um so maybe not just
53        praise(1.1) it can be corrections as well
54        I should give them feedback
55        er so I think this is my problem.
```

Lack of feedback as a problem is highlighted at the beginning and end of this exchange (lines 49–50, 55). In this extract, the knowledge of a problem with feedback is developed through the course of the video and discussion with her tutor. Note that at the beginning Joan constitutes the problem as one of not giving positive assessment (e.g. praise), which is challenged immediately by her tutor, evidenced by repeating Joan's reflection with a rising pitch, indicating a clarification request or a subtle challenge and the need to discuss it further (line 51). This is closely followed by a further question, to which Joan responds (lines 52–55). Joan clarifies her idea by rephrasing 'giving praise' as feedback (line 53). After a rather longish pause, Joan develops this idea further to include the possibility of corrective feedback, which is usually considered as negative feedback (Gass and Mackey 2006). There are two things worth noting in this extract: (1) Joan's understanding about feedback is refined through and in interaction with the tutor; and (2) it is through the video-based reflection that the student teacher is able to conceptualise a lack of feedback as a problem and orient towards a solution to it. Being able to reflect on their teaching based on real data offers teachers an opportunity to develop. This indeed could be an area for growth in professional learning.

Teacher repetition as feedback

In this dataset, quite a lot of what occupies the F position is teacher repetition. Researchers working on classroom discourse recognise that teacher repetition is an important element in shaping the classroom discourse cohesion from a social interactional perspective, although they might have different understandings of the role of teacher repetition. For example, Norrick claims that repetition is a 'neutral and objective way for the teacher to ensure comprehension by the whole group' (1987: 253), whereas Hellermann (2003) strongly holds the opposite view, suggesting that teacher repetition cannot be neutral due to the sequential placement of the teacher repetition following a student's contribution. For Hellermann, the functions of teacher repetition could be acknowledgement and evaluation of student participation with the reshaping and revoicing work to meet the teacher's pedagogical goal and 'to shape the trajectory of the immediately following discourse' (ibid.: 83). He further argues that the function of teacher repetition as a feedback move is closely linked to its prosody. In this dataset, it is interesting to note that student teachers use repetition as positive assessment and acknowledgement of student contribution. Extract 4.13 is taken from Yu's class where she is organising students to play a word-guess game.

Extract 4.13 YuTe3 (0:53_1.31)

```
27   T    we will have a game (.) er based on my descriptions (.)
28        can you guess the words (1.0)related to the winds↑ (1.0)
29        according to the degrees (1.2)ok? (0.5) first ↑=
30   S    =°gust°=
31   T    =just (.) after my descriptions
32        ((students laughing loudly))
33        the first is er gentle wind er (.) can you think of the
34        words? (.)
35   S1   drizzle↑
36   S2   breeze↓
37   T    bree:ze↓ next
```

In this extract, Yu gives instructions about playing a game of guessing words based on her description (lines 27–8). After Yu's first description (lines 33–4), two students provide two answers; note that the first student's word is produced with a rising tone, indicating uncertainty (line 35) while the second student uses a falling tone to indicate the confidence in his reply (line 36). In the teacher's feedback move, Yu selects an appropriate answer, which is a repetition of the second student's word and pitch (line 37). The teacher repetition of the student's contribution with a slightly stretched sound indicates the acknowledgment of the student's response as relevant, whereas the relative matching of student pitch level and intonation indexes alignment with the student's contribution, a positive assessment (Hellermann 2003).

Preferred and dis-preferred feedback
In language classrooms, what is sequentially and affectively preferred may be pedagogically and developmentally dis-preferred (Waring 2008). The balance between providing positive feedback and achieving the pedagogical goal is an important issue

for teachers, and is challenging for many student teachers. Extract 4.14 is taken from Emma's class, where she is teaching verb tenses.

Extract 4.14 EmTe4 (11.05_12.14) Forget

```
22    E     now↓ forget (.)Carol can you give me the past tense first?
23    S3    =forgeted=
24    E     =ok forgeted (.) can you spell it for me? (.)
25    S3    g-e-t-e-d=
26    E     =e-d right? (.)
27    S3    yes=
28    E     =past perfect?=
29    S3    =forgeted=
30    E     =so it's the same (.) right?=
31    S3    =yeah (.)
32    E     but (.)it's a good try you know the pattern very well and
33          (3.0) this is the ((writing on the board)) this is not the same
34          as previous verb (.) this is a special one (.)for forget the
35          past tense is forgot ((3.0 writing on the board)) and the past
36          perfect is forgotten ((4.0 writing on the board))clear? (.)
37          yeah? (.) ok↓
```

Extract 4.14 began after a few exercises on the past tense of regular verbs. Emma asks a student to provide the past tense for *forget*, to which the student responds (line 23). This is a dis-preferred response, since it is incorrect, yet Emma's feedback move is to confirm the student's response and request its spelling (line 24). The student provides the ending of the word (line 25), to which the teacher seeks clarification of adding the suffix of -*ed* (line 26). The student confirms (line 27). In this interactive work, Emma seems to be confirming the student's contribution by repeating the student's responses and does not take any opportunity at this stage to offer corrective feedback. Engaging students in interactive work and encouraging students' contribution is affectively and sequentially preferred; however, in examining the pedagogical goal focusing on the accuracy of the form, this feedback move is dis-preferred.

In line 28, Emma follows up with a request for the past perfect and the student responds immediately, as evidenced by the latched turn (line 29). In what follows, the teacher seeks confirmation from the student (line 30), to which the student confirms (line 31). The feedback move Emma now takes is to first provide a positive assessment and then follow up with a long pause (line 33), indicating an indirect rejection of the student's answer. Then Emma produces a long explanation to point out that this verb is not the same as other verbs they have just learnt and 'forget' is a special verb. Emma's explanation is accompanied with writing on the board and confirmation check (lines 36 and 37). After a very brief pause, Emma produces a sequence closing the turn. Here, the discourse marker ok with falling pitch indicates she is ready to move on to the next topic. The low pitch level is one prosodic resource for closing the sequence (Brazil 1997, cited in Hellermann 2003). This time, although Emma does not provide direct corrective feedback, she makes an effort to provide indirect feedback through an extended explanation. In this case, the feedback move is pedagogically preferred. The ability to assess the feedback together with the pedagogical goal is important and should be encouraged in teacher learning. It is also clear to us that even for one teacher, the feedback strategy can vary in different situations in classrooms and therefore awareness of the feedback move will contribute to developing effective teaching in general.

GIVING INSTRUCTIONS

The importance of giving clear and proper instructions and the ability to use language to engage students and achieve pedagogical goals is another recurring theme in the dataset. In other words, student teachers demonstrate insufficient CIC and display difficulty in giving instructions, as shown in the following two extracts.

Extract 4.15 HeTe3 (16.18_17.05)

```
7   H    so er (.)so how much words I have to teach you to use
8        is also most of them I think most of words could be
9        very complicated and boring words for you but (.) I
10       think (.) if you want to learn the words↑ that words is
11       necessary so at my part (.) I I just want to help you
12       to ˚know˚ how to just remember those words↓ my you can
13       understand in this way so I just took four words from
14       them
```

In Extract 4.15, the student teacher Henry gives an incomprehensible explanation to students. In this incomprehensible explanation he also displays his beliefs about teaching and learning English, as well as his understanding of being a teacher. First, for Henry, English vocabulary for students is somewhat complicated (line 9) yet necessary (line 11). Second, learning involves knowing and remembering (line 12). Third, his role in teaching is that of someone who gives students such knowledge as he displays himself, the one who has to teach (line 7), decides what to learn (line 13), and an instructor who can assist learning (line 11).

Classroom interaction also suggests that teachers often follow the IRF sequence in which they occupy long turns with minimum student input. In many cases, students are restricted to the role of repeating after the teacher as the following extract suggests. Clearly, in such interactive work, the teacher shapes and directs the flow of the interaction. For example, in the following extract, the teacher is opening the class by introducing a television programme and learning objective: celebrities talking about themselves when they were twelve years old.

Extract 4.16 MayTe1 (05.23_07.44) (continues from Extract 4.10)

```
7   May   so my friend has recommended her tv programme (.) this
8         tv programme is called 12 again: and today↑ we will (.)
```

```
9          have (.) invited three celebrities ((mispronunciation))
10         to talk about themselves about (.)themselves when they
11         were twelve years old (.) and FIRST let's us to learn
12         some new words
13         ((operating the computer))
14         the first one goofy read after me GOOFY=
15   SS    =goofy=
16   May   =goofy=
17   SS    =goofy=
18   May   =goofy mean:s silly and especially in a very special
19         especially in a funny and pleasant way (.) so we always
20         called this man is very goofy and next one↑
```

In this extract, May introduces the topic and activity (lines 7–11). After a brief pause, she starts some vocabulary work, which might assist understanding of the television programme (lines 11–12). The sequencing work is done not only by using the sequential word, but by using a louder voice. For May, reading after the teacher is an effective way to learn new words (lines 14–17). Teacher explanation is another useful way to help the students learn new vocabulary as the teacher first explains the meaning of the word and then provides an example. Clearly, here the teacher dominates the sequence and this view of learning is closely associated with her view of being the teacher. The role of the teacher and his/her identity is also an important theme in the dataset and this will be discussed further in the next section.

DEALING WITH UNEXPECTED ISSUES

Because of the interactive nature of teaching, unexpected events happen all the time and the ability to improvise is a strong characteristic of effective teaching. Effective teaching requires teachers to be able to make judgements and good decisions in the moment in relation to their pedagogical goals. Typically, 'good' interactive decisions are those which have a positive effect on learning, or which create learning opportunities (Walsh 2011). Unexpected events happen for various reasons but student teachers can display difficulty in making good interactive decisions perhaps due to lack of professional knowledge or first-hand experience.

One type of unexpected event happens when students display sufficient target knowledge in the subject. A typical reaction from student teachers to this kind of unexpected event is to carry on with the lesson plan without making any changes. There are perhaps two reasons for this: first, student teachers feel it is important to follow their plan as ditching or changing a plan halfway through the lesson could cause additional unexpected events and introduce chaos into the teaching; second, because student teachers are still learning to teach they feel less confident and competent in improvising.

Extract 4.17 is taken from Nina's classroom, who is teaching vocabulary before reading.

Extract 4.17 NiTe 1 (3.21_3.34) Department store

```
24   Ni   anybody know what does department store mean?
25        (2.3)
26   SS   yeah: ((laughing with certainty))
27   Ni   let me tell you((reading from the note)) department
28        store is a lar:ge st:ore with some varieties of goods
29        and it's usually organized in different sections (1.0)
30        yeah↑ just like this one ((pointing to the picture))
31        read after me department store=
32   SS   =department store
```

Nina checks the meaning of a phrase with students (line 24). After a rather long pause, all students produce a confirmation in unison, with a long stretching sound possibly displaying confidence (line 26). The teacher, however, proceeds with the lesson according to the plan to provide a definition of the word and a visual explanation (lines 27–30), and then follows up with an activity of reading after the teacher.

A second type of unexpected event observed in student teachers' teaching is extended pauses, long silences when teachers expect students to participate or contribute. Long silences can be interpreted by teachers as disengagement and non-attention (Shen et al. 2009). In dealing with long silences, student teachers very often try to fill the gap with their own speech. In so doing, the teacher intends to facilitate thinking and contributing, but sometimes the strategy may have the opposite effect, for example obstructing opportunities for participation and contribution. Li (2012) suggests that a long pause is necessary after a teacher's question as it might provide students with space for thinking, organising their thoughts and rehearsing their reply before they speak out. Equally, Walsh (2011) identifies the extended wait time as one of the characteristics of CIC on the teacher's part, as it shows the teacher's ability to provide space for learners to think and formulate a response. When the wait time is less than a second, or when the teacher rushes to fill the gap, the result can be insufficient time for learners to respond (e.g. see Budd Rowe 1986). In Extract 4.18, although the teacher employs an extended wait time and utilises different strategies, she has to close the sequence due to a lack of response.

Extract 4.18 MariTe1 (24.07_24.45)

```
1   STM   which is most like you? Sharon?
2   Sh    um most of things [like her
3   STM                     [yeah (.) for sure (.) especially for women
4         what about you Linda?
5         (3.0)
6   STM   I mean would you take all the things with you? Or just basic
7         things (.) like?
8   Li    um (1.2)
9   STM   ok (.) ok
```

In this extract the teacher, Marion, asks a question which requires students to choose between two types of travelling styles. There is no space for self-selection in this sequence as she immediately nominates an individual (line 1). Sharon, the student, provides a brief answer, with the teacher's feedback overlapping with her last two words (lines 2-3). The orienting of the teacher's overlap and the positive assessment yeah suggest that the teacher is satisfied with Sharon's input and is ready to move on to the next student (line 3). In line 4, Marion nominates a second student, Linda. Linda does not take the turn, hence there is a long pause (line 5). The long pause could be interpreted as dis-preferred response, which causes Marion to reformulate her original question as a polar question (lines 6-7). It is clear that Marion utilises different strategies with different students. In the case of Sharon, Marion's feedback overlaps the end of the student response (but at a point where the essential information has already been conveyed), whereas with Linda she allows adequate time (3.0) for a response and, when this is not forthcoming, she reformulates her question to make it easier for Linda to respond. However, despite her efforts, in the end Marion has to close the sequence due to the lack of student responses. As we can see, in line 8, Linda takes the turn indicated by a hesitation marker um with another longish pause. However, Marion takes over the turn to close the sequence (line 9), as indicated by the sequence closing marker, ok (.) ok. When students experience difficulties in delivering expected responses, the teacher will assist the students by reformulating the question and providing space to develop their thinking, or by closing the sequence in order to move the lesson forward. In this context, learning is not necessarily facilitated.

DEVELOPING SELF AS A TEACHER

'(L)earning to teach – like teaching itself – is always the process of becoming: a time of formation and transformation, of scrutiny into what one is doing, and who one can become' (Britzman 2003: 31). In other words, the process of learning to teach is a process of constructing meaning of teaching and professional growth in planning a lesson, designing an activity, choosing appropriate materials, implementing the plan in the classroom, giving feedback and assessing students. Teachers are constantly defining and redefining themselves, and evaluating the role they play in this process consciously or unconsciously. Learning to teach is thus consequently a process of understanding 'who I am' and identity development (Clarke 2008), rather than just learning subject knowledge and pedagogical skills.

BEING A KNOWLEDGE PROVIDER

For language teachers, one particular area that deserves attention is that of what makes a good language teacher. Research suggests that a perceived good foreign language teacher is one who can create a good language environment, encourage students to practise and use the language, and use appropriate materials and classroom activities (Riddell 2001). In particular, they should take different roles in teaching, such as organiser, participant, resource controller and assessor. However, for pre-service teachers, being a good teacher is to a large extent more about being a knowledge provider or being knowledgeable in the subject matter. The knowledge domains that consistently are displayed in the interaction in teaching, interview and stimulated recall are again subject knowledge, for example knowing the rules and having a vast knowledge of vocabulary, along with pedagogical knowledge, in particular the skill of being able to explain the subject knowledge well. Being knowledgeable about English and being able to teach students something new – such as vocabulary, grammar rules, strategies to learn words, cultural norms and something students can take away with them – are characteristic of a good teacher. This is often displayed in classroom teaching with long teacher turns, explaining grammar rules or the usage of lexis. This collective identity of being a knowledge provider, however, is 'socially constructed but individually enacted' (Miller Marsh 2003: 10). In the following extracts, student teachers' knowledge and beliefs about themselves are displayed and shaped in the interaction with the important others, such as peers, their tutors and students.

In Extract 4.19, Paula is teaching about Poland and positions herself as an incompetent teacher due to a lack of target knowledge.

Extract 4.19 PauTe3 (08.35_08.57) Chopin

```
1    STP    how about the um Chopin Chopin ((incorrect pronunciation))
2           he is from Poland too=
3    S1     =what↑ °what°=
4    STP    =do you know piano music? [Chopin ((gesture of playing piano))
5    S2                               [Chopin ((correct pronunciation))=
6    STP    =[yes Chopin (with right pronunciation)
7    S1      [oh
8    SS     ((laughing))
```

Paula starts with a statement to suggest a connection between the famous pianist Chopin and Poland (line 1–2), but with wrong pronunciation of the musician's name. A student clearly is not following her and shows confusion and seeks clarification (line 3). In responding to the student's clarification request, Paula poses a question to indirectly help the student to establish the link as well as repeating the musician's name and a gesture of playing piano (line 4). The second student produces a response overlapping the teacher's explanation with a correct pronunciation. This overlapping indicates that the second student is happy to provide the clarification and move on. Paula then confirms the student's contribution with a positive assessment and corrects her pronunciation, whereas the confused student displays understanding (line 7). This exchange ends with the students laughing. It seems that the pronunciation of Chopin is the key to the understanding of the message despite the teacher's efforts to explain by using gesture and providing a context. The teacher as a knowledge provider here is dispositioned by the takeover from the second student. This moment was highlighted in the stimulated video-based reflection with the tutor, and Paula self-evaluated herself as having performed poorly. Extract 4.20 highlights how Paula conceptualises her role in teaching.

Extract 4.20 They corrected me

```
1   STP   this is bad (.) isn't it? (.)
2   Tu    don't worry about that (.) that happens=
3   P     =I should have checked it but I thought I knew it (.)
4   Tu    it's ok and you corrected it quickly=
5   STP   =yeah but really it's <they CORRECTED ME > (.)
6   Tu    [hmmm
7   STP   [and I am the teacher and er I was teaching them some
8         cultural knowledge but (.) °it didn't go this way°
```

As a first pair part, Paula evaluates this moment as bad, as she mispronounced the word (line 1), and the tutor produces a relevant second pair part to comfort Paula (line 2). However, for Paula, being corrected by a student seems to be a big deal. In line 3, she blames herself for not having checked the pronunciation before the class and for having taken it for granted. It is the following tutor turn (line 4) that triggers her negative feelings about being corrected by her student; note that she emphasises this point with a slower speed and louder voice (line 5). This is a very interesting turn, which suggests that the teacher does not like the fact that students corrected her mistake and is not comfortable with the situation because she positions herself as the knowledge source (line 7). This exchange is completed by Paula explaining that the pedagogical objective was to teach students some cultural knowledge but it did not work due to the issue of the mispronounced word (lines 7–8). In this extract, although Paula does not explicitly express her authoritative role in the class, her interaction displays such a belief since she is not happy nor comfortable with challenges from students. Insufficient subject knowledge might have a strong impact on Paula's confidence, as Murdoch claims that for non-native teachers, 'language proficiency will always represent the bedrock of their professional confidence' (1994: 254). This will also influence the way they manage teaching, materials and access to language resources (Farrell and Richards 2007). Indeed, as Tsui (2003) suggests, subject knowledge influences how teachers use textbooks: the less proficient the teachers are, the more prescriptive they are. So the target language proficiency is an important factor in becoming a teacher. Richards et al. (2013) make this point explicitly:

> teachers need to have an advanced level of TL proficiency so they can also provide meaningful explanations, rich language input for learners and respond spontaneously and knowledgeably to their learners' questions on language and culture. Teachers also need an advanced level of proficiency in order to take learners beyond the beginner level of study. (Ibid.: 244)

For non-native speaking (NNS) student teachers, developing pedagogical knowledge and awareness is especially difficult because they are still in the language learning stage and will pay more attention to their subject knowledge rather than their pedagogical knowledge. Nevertheless, a common assumption is that if students are proficient in the target language and have rich linguistic knowledge they are able to transfer this knowledge to classroom teaching. Research suggests the opposite is true (Johnson 2009b), and the link between linguistic knowledge and instructional decisions in teaching is not promising (Bartels 2005). Therefore, although linguistic or subject knowledge is important for language teachers perhaps pedagogy is more important, and perhaps student teachers need to be aware of this, and perhaps teacher education should focus less on knowledge and more on pedagogy. These two issues will be discussed in Chapters 7 and 8 respectively.

ESTABLISHING AUTHORITY

As suggested earlier, teachers learn to develop close relationships with students when learning to teach, and building close relationships with students is important for teaching. Hargreaves (2000, 2005) warns that a failure to establish such relationships may make teachers prone to experiencing emotional misunderstandings. However, because newly qualified teachers very often feel challenged and subject to comparison with other teachers, they also demonstrate the importance of establishing authority during learning to teach. Li (2012) demonstrates two non-native English-speaking pre-service teachers' authority moves in attempting to manage the classroom. Authority can be established through demonstrating subject knowledge, class control and reinforcement of the gap between the teacher and learners. In the following extract, Tina establishes her authority by controlling the floor, the activity and for how much time each participant speaks.

Extract 4.21 TiTe 2 (00.00_01.32)

```
1    ST    er have you understood all (.) all these expressions↑
2          (1.0)
3    SS    [yes
4    S     [yeah but=
5    ST    =and now we are going to practice this and er:: by talking
6          about our past is experiences (.) and er a:: each I (.) I
7          want you to working in pairs (1.0) °in pairs°
8          (4.0)
9          >°you working in pairs°< (.)
10   S     what↓ about what ↓
11   STQ   and er each of the group I will give you one topic (.) and
12         you talk to each other (.) on this topic (.) and er you will
13         go(t) got one minutes to prepare (.) and then you talk about
14         to each other for four minutes (.) so each of you will have
15         two minutes to talk (.)
16   S1    o↑k↓ (.)
17   STQ   [ok?
18   SS    [((students laughing))
19   STQ   and er you should remember that you need to (0.5) use er
```

```
20              these expressions (.) as many as possible ((underlining
21              those on the board)) (.) here ˚these two↑˚ (.) ˚these three↑˚
22              and er ˚where is it˚ ((2.0 looking at the board)) ˚here here˚
23              (1.0)    ˚ok?˚
24              and er now er after you finish it er I will need some of you
25              um to present to (0.8) told the class (.) what you have done
26              for other one so (.) when other is talking↑ you must listen
27              very carefully (.) ok?
28    S1        ok=
29    SS        ((other students check with each other))
30    STQ       =and er now please draw ((giving out the topic))
```

Tina spends 1.32 minutes in setting up pair work. First she checks that all students understand the expressions (line 1). After a 1.0 second pause some students confirm this, while there is one who clearly has some issues (line 4). However, Tina does not provide space for that student to elaborate but carries on with her plan to move to the next activity (line 5). Then she gives an instruction (line 7) and after a 1.0 second pause, she repeats the instruction, although in a rather low voice as if she is trying to avoid saying it (line 7). This is followed by a 4.0 second pause, and then Tina repeats her instruction again, this time at a faster speed and soft voice (line 9). This is followed by a brief clarification request from a student (line 10), indicating that the instruction is vague. It is interesting to note that Tina neither acknowledges the student's question nor gives feedback on the student's remark, but simply carries on to give her instruction, in a very long turn (lines 11–15). Note here how she controls the topic (line 11), how much time there is for preparation and for how much time each participant will speak (lines 12–15). This kind of instruction is quite unusual in real-life classrooms simply because it is impossible to control the development of the dialogue between two interlocutors, as is suggested by one student's response (line 16). The falling and rising tone in line 16 suggests the unusualness of the prior turn. Despite the student's reaction, Tina again carries on to mark the end of her instruction, using a discourse marker ok (line 17). Note here that the students produce laughter (line 18) overlapping her further instructions (line 19). The cohort's laughter here suggests that the students treat the self-selected student's reaction in line 16 as funny.

In the next long teacher turn (lines 19–27), Tina gives further instructions, this time requesting that the students use the taught phrases as many times as possible as a method to practise these expressions. It is worth noting that Tina also underlines those expressions to help the students to remember which ones they need to use. This is done by her pointing out where these expressions are located on the board, rather than what they are (lines 19–22). This long turn again finishes with her intention to let the students start the task, indicated by the discourse marker as a comprehension check (line 23). However, she follows up to provide further instruction – this time detailing what the students need to do after they talk to each other and a request for students to listen to each other carefully (lines 24–7). Note the instruction she gives here is partially incomprehensible (lines 25–6): what you have done for other one. Although she again finishes her rather long instruction with another comprehension check, clearly there is only one student who follows her as he acknowledges (line 28), while others are checking with each other (line 29). This instruction displays Tina's knowledge of being a teacher through organising an activity. Clearly, for Tina, being able to closely control the class is a priority. This is done through detailed instructions, long teacher turns and the use of resources (e.g. gestures, voice pitches and speed, and board work).

Establishing authority is also reflected in the way that the teacher sets up rules in the classroom, such as 'who' has the right to speak. Consider the following extract in which the student teacher, Elaine, sets the rules on how to answer questions or raise a question.

Extract 4.22 ElaTe3 (1.23_1.35) Listen to the teacher

```
1    E1    now listen to the teacher (.) if you have problems (.)or
2          questions (.) please raise your hand and the teacher will
3          answer your question
4          (2.0)
5          yeah? do you understand me?=
6    SS    =Ok
```

In this exchange, Elaine makes sure that the students understand how to ask a question. The rule-setting is one key element of classroom management. Here Elaine manages the class to show that she has the absolute authority of 'knowledge' and the right to speak. The teacher's instruction is followed by a 2.0 second pause. Then she follows up with a comprehension check to require confirmation from the students (line 5), to which the students respond. It is clear that Elaine would like to control the class to a degree that students only ask the teacher questions, and it is her role as a teacher to answer them. From a discursive psychological perspective, it is how Elaine does this that is of interest. In this extract, first Elaine refers to herself as 'the teacher', indicating her status in the classroom; second, she explains how to ask questions or to bid for a turn to speak, setting the rule for the classroom structure; and, finally, she takes the responsibility of answering the questions or providing knowledge, again indicating the different roles that the students and teacher play in the learning process.

Shifts from learner to teacher

Teacher education in general entails the formation of a professional identity (Danielewicz 2001; Clarke 2008) and for student teachers it is a process of shift from learners to teachers. Shifting from learners to teachers and back to learners is a trajectory of learning to teach, and it involves several areas, such as accumulating their subject knowledge by talking and using metalanguage. Every profession has its own professional language (jargon, for example), and Woods (1996) notes that language teachers share common language, including terms such as 'proficiency', 'grammar', 'cloze' and 'input', and such phrases as 'learner-centredness', 'communicative approach' – although the precise understanding of what is referred to by such terms may vary. Being able to talk about their teaching using common language reflects their own identity of being language teachers.

Extract 4.23 Talking about terms (post-lesson reflection)

```
1   St1    er (0.8)first of all my stage of practical teaching mmh is
2          pre teaching (.)an'd' my aim is to achieve learners' schemata
3          re:lated to the topic ermm: first I think er (1.0) my pre
4          teaching related to er our er text hmmm and I tried to elicit
5          some uh: important v vocabulary from student (1.0) but er:
6          (2.5)I↑ didn't er pay attention to check if they KNEW the
7          vocabulary means er I just er do some er drills and er: some
8          uh knowledge check (.) so from my feedback and before I ask
9          student to repeat the words (.) I need to KNOW whether they
10         understand the meaning er (.) that's mine (0.3) how about
11         your zoey↑
```

In Extract 4.23 we notice that the student teacher defines her stage of teaching as pre-teaching and talks about her teaching aim. The list of vocabulary – schemata, topic, pre-teaching, text, elicit, vocabulary, check, means, drills and knowledge and so on – belonging to these language teachers is evident throughout the dataset, highlighting the subject knowledge that teachers expect themselves to master and the language they associate with this profession. It is worth noting that this teacher identity is also associated with how this teacher views learning; here, the teacher refers to knowing in two specific places, indicating her beliefs about knowing as learning (lines 6 and 9).

SUMMARY

This chapter has looked at pre-service teachers' beliefs and knowledge and how they are displayed and developed in interactions. Drawing on various interactional data, this chapter sheds lights on pre-service teacher cognition from a discursive psychological perspective. That is, pre-service teacher education or teacher learning is a process of teacher knowing. Knowing, as shown by the data, is a process of developing disciplinary knowledge of and beliefs in how to learn and what is important, of negotiating pedagogical knowledge between theoretical and practical aspects, and of developing a sense of being a teacher and roles. These areas of knowing or developing are displayed in how student teachers interact with 'the others' in different settings, and are shaped by the situations. This knowing process is important for developing effective pedagogy and has strong implications in teacher education. I will discuss this in Chapters 7 and 8.

5

DEVELOPING EXPERTISE AND IN-SERVICE TEACHER COGNITION

INTRODUCTION

Expertise is a key element of effective teaching and an important factor influencing teachers' decision-making, which is referred to as an important agenda in researching teacher cognition (e.g. Borg 2011). Understanding expertise has potential for teacher learning and development. Berliner (1995, 2001) asserts the importance of uncovering the characteristics of expert teachers as they can be used to help novice teachers to attain a greater competence. Gatbonton (2008) further argues that comparing these two groups of teachers might help us see how expertise is developed and identify key moments for teacher to grow. However, previous research has not yet depicted the nature of expert teachers' work and to what degree the novice and expert teachers' work differs at a micro-level. As Fagan noted, 'most have not taken into account the intricate constructions of classroom communication, which may mean they fail to detail the systematic nature of novice and expert teacher talk-in-interaction' (2012: 111). To address this issue, it is therefore important to show the expert's action in teaching (Tsui 2003). The aim of this chapter is to identify the expertise of in-service teachers and how it is displayed in their practice and professional context. Specifically, this chapter addresses the following questions: What are the critical differences between expert and novice teachers' cognitions? And how do these differences exist or display in interaction in their professional contexts? This chapter uses detailed transcribed data of teachers' professional activities – for example teaching, lesson preparation and reflections (video-based interviews) – as a means of discussing how novice and expert teachers differ and how expertise is distributed in interaction.

EXPERT VERSUS NOVICE

Expertise, according to Dreyfus and Dreyfus, is the ability of *'knowing how'* to use knowledge one has to deal with cognitively demanding problems rather than *'knowing that'* knowledge in decontextualised situations (1986: 4; emphasis in the original). In the literature on expertise, the most commonly associated topic is the study of experts. Tsui suggests that experts in their profession should possess certain qualities, such as 'being very knowledgeable in their field; being able to engage in skilful practices and being able to make accurate diagnoses, insightful analyses, and the right decisions, often within a very short period of time' (2003: 1). As far as teacher expertise is concerned, research has differentiated experts from novices in task performance: novice teachers tend to follow context-free rules (Berliner 1994), have difficulty in addressing issues emerging from interaction (Westerman, 1991), and have difficulties in bringing together theories and contemporary methodology in teaching (Tochon and Munby 1993). In practice, novice teachers tend to deal with problems from a more superficial, short-term perspective, focusing on the 'here and now', while expert teachers are able to connect the problem at hand to a long-term goal and deal with it at a deeper level, bring learning theories to bear on their teaching, and are able to handle curricula demands (e.g. tests) (Li 2013). Because of the differences between novice and expert teachers in handling problems, research concludes that novice teachers are using a bottom-up approach in dealing with a situation, as opposed to experts, who use a more top-down approach (Glaser 1987; Foley and Hart 1992). Further, Bereiter and Scardamalia (1993) point out that expert teachers are willing to take on a problem that will increase their expertise, such as continuous experimentation and reflection 'in action' as well as 'on-action' (Schön 1983), as opposed to novice teachers who 'tackle problems for which they do not need to extend themselves' (Bereiter and Scardamalia 1993: 78).

Studies on novice and expert teachers are still rare in the L2 teacher education field, as only a handful currently exist (e.g. Akyel 1997; Richards et al. 1998; Tsui 2003; Gatbonton 2008). It is not surprising that there is 'yet no established common criteria for identifying experts' (Tsui 2009: 190). Identifying novice and expert teachers is problematic as there is no reliable way of distinguishing them, and previous research has adopted different criteria to identify expert teachers. Work experience has been used to distinguish expert from novice. For example Gatbonton (2008) suggests that experienced teachers are those who have at least four to five years' work experience and novice teachers 'are those who are still undergoing training, who have just completed their training, or who have just commenced teaching and still have very little (e.g. less than two years) experience behind them' (ibid.: 162). Tsui (2003) used a combination of criteria which included experience, reputation, recommendation and classroom observation. In some cases, expert teachers were identified by educational authorities as well as by using additional criteria, such as student achievement, supervisor and peer nomination and recognition (e.g. Li 2013), and similar criteria are adopted to identify novice and expert teachers in this book.

Clearly, relevant experience has a strong relationship with developing expertise as expertise is unique to a specific domain of activity and requires thousands of hours of practice within that domain (Berliner 1994; Palmer et al. 2005; Gatbonton 2008). Of course, experience does not necessarily lead to expertise (Ericsson et al. 1993) and that is why some experienced teachers remain non-expert (Tsui 2003). In fact, deliberate practice is critical in the development of expertise (Ericsson et al. 1993). Deliberate practice, is an activity that is 'specially designed to improve the current level of performance', 'requires effort and is not inherently enjoyable' and 'the individual can engage in' (ibid.: 368). Based on this claim, Palmer et al. suggest that 'the primary determinant in achieving expertise is purposeful engagement of the individual in the practice of their expertise. This engagement is characterized by both direct instruction and extensive reflective practice by the individual who is motivated to acquire the expertise' (2005: 15).

DISTRIBUTED AND MULTIPLE EXPERTISE

The various differentiated criteria adopted by researchers suggest that there are no commonly accepted criteria or methods for identifying expert teachers because expertise is developed in and shaped by the context in which teachers work. So, expertise is 'domain bound and context bound' (Palmer et al. 2005: 21). It is, then, perhaps more meaningful and important to study how expertise is displayed in a situation rather than considering what expertise is in an abstract manner. That is, expertise thus is not a state but an ability displayed in a particular situation. Because of the close relationship between expertise and the situation, it is more appropriate to talk about distributed expertise as teachers engage in the interactions with the context (including colleagues, students and materials) to appropriate their knowledge and to apply their knowledge in different situations (Tsui 2003).

Equally, an expert teacher does not have expertise in every aspect of teaching and learning. For example, a novice teacher could have expertise in certain areas while remaining novice in most aspects of teaching (e.g. Tsui 2003), and equally expert teachers could be a novice in an unfamiliar situation and become 'temporary novices' (Rich 1993: 139). Thus, expertise could be multiple and it is perhaps more meaningful to talk about expertise in areas of specialisation (e.g. activity design, material development) rather than to use general terms like expert teachers.

In what follows in this chapter I will illustrate how (non)expertise is distributed in interaction and how multiple expertise exists. The data consists of 415 minutes of teaching and 122 minutes of interviews from expert teachers, and 584 minutes of teaching and 208 minutes of interview from novice teachers. It is not this book's intention to make strict comparisons between novice and expert teachers, but rather to offer some insights into their practices and demonstrate how expertise is displayed in teaching.

DISTRIBUTED EXPERTISE

This section presents and exemplifies differences between novice and expert teachers. An attempt has been made to include a representative, though by no means comprehensive, comparison through a sample of discourse. In examining the dataset, it is clear that what distinguishes expert from novice is found in three distinctive, yet interrelated, areas:

- Conceptions of knowledge
- Classroom interactional competence
- Classroom management

Conceptions of knowledge

The knowledge domains articulated by Shulman (1986) have been widely used in assessing expertise (e.g. Hogan et al. 2003; Tsui 2003). As presented in Chapters

1 and 4, the knowledge needed for teaching is of three types: content knowledge (knowledge of the subject matter); pedagogical knowledge (knowledge of how to teach in general); and pedagogical content knowledge (how to teach the subject area) (Shulman 1987). It is clear that an expert teacher is one who possesses numerous domains of knowledge needed in language instruction and is able to implement them in classroom practices, in particular in subject and pedagogical knowledge domains (Richards and Farrell 2005). It is also clear that expert teachers display differences in their contextual knowledge from novice teachers. In a nutshell, novice teachers usually have minimal or 'textbook' knowledge and thus rigidly adhere to taught rules or plans with little situational perception. Experts, on the other hand, do not rely on rules, guidelines or maxims but display flexibility and confidence (Tsui 2003). In the discussion below, expert and novice teacher cognitions in interaction are presented according to three domains of knowledge: content (subject) knowledge, pedagogical knowledge and contextual knowledge.

Conceptions of content knowledge
It is common to see a pedagogical focus on linguistic form and accuracy in a language classroom, especially in an L2 context, across both expert and novice teachers' classrooms. Typically, linguistic-focused teaching requires teachers' explanation and student repetition of the teacher's utterance. However, what differs between expert and novice teachers is how such a focus is interpreted and dealt with by the teacher. Specifically, novice teachers tend to display less interrelated knowledge and language is approached as isolated and individual items. Conversely, expert teachers possess a rich and integrated knowledge base which they draw on in approaching the language. Language knowledge and skills are connected and situated in a wider curriculum and syllabus, and contextual information and materials available are considered. The following extracts illustrate how a novice teacher differs from an expert one in conceptualising the subject knowledge and their approaches to it in preparing the same lesson.

Ban is a novice teacher who is in her second year of teaching. In this extract, Ban is sharing her ideas about a new lesson for Year 7. The unit 'She often goes to concert' is in Module 8: 'Choosing presents'. According to the textbook, one of the key learning points is to correctly use adverbs of frequency like *often, sometimes, usually* and *always*.

Extract 5.1 Translation activity is good

```
1  I    tell me about this lesson=
2  B    =um (.)it's about adverbs .hh like often (.) sometimes
3       (.)always and usually
4       (1.0)
5  I    ok (.) so um can you talk about your lesson plan?=
6  B    =yeah (1.2) my plan is (.) um I think most of children
7       already know these words (.) so I am going to ask them
8       to provide Chinese meanings first and then I will give
```

```
9          them some [exercises
10   I               [£what if they don't know these words?£=
11   B     =um yes (.) they do (.) but I need to make sure they
12         know accurate Chinese translation (0.8) so I think a
13         translation activity is good (.) I can check whether
14         they know exact meanings of these words
```

Extract 5.1 clearly shows that Ban's understanding of the content is about form and accuracy, in that the accurate and precise understanding of the Chinese meaning of these adverbs is what she requires from the students. In articulating what the learning objectives are and how to achieve these, Ban clearly displays her understanding of subject knowledge – vocabulary and its precise meanings. This extract shows that Ban emphasises the importance of knowing the accurate meaning of the vocabulary and translation is a good way to achieve this goal (lines 12–13). Her pedagogical considerations also indicate her conception of subject knowledge in the interaction. For Ban, knowing the exact Chinese translation of English words means learning and the vocabulary are treated as individual words. The context in which the vocabulary can be used is not taken into consideration. This extract also suggests her conception of teachers' and learners' roles. She positions herself in relation to the learners as the one who gives instructions (lines 7–9), takes responsibility for learning to happen (lines 11–12), and holds the knowledge (lines 13–14).

Expert teachers display integrated and contextualised knowledge. In particular, expert teachers are able to make use of this integrated knowledge, which includes disciplinary knowledge, pedagogical knowledge, contextual knowledge and their years of experience in the process of planning a lesson and teaching. They demonstrate flexibility in approaching teaching content and rich knowledge about how the teaching content is positioned in the curriculum and presented in the textbook. They are able to draw upon their knowledge about students, the curriculum, pedagogy and assessment to make a decision to distinguish the long-term and short-tern goal of learning (Li 2013). An expert teacher with integrated knowledge demonstrates an ability to judge the difficulty level of the content, learners' needs and their prior knowledge. In summary, the kind of knowledge that expert teachers exhibit and are able to use in making decisions is integrated and related. Consider the interview in Extract 5.2 with an expert teacher, Han, who is reflecting on a lesson taught using the same material as that presented in Extract 5.1.

Extract 5.2 Developing social skills and emotional knowledge

```
1   I    tell me about this lesson=
2   H    =well this lesson is part of a big module of choosing
3        presents (.) and this unit is reading and writing about
4        (.) how often one does something=
5   I    =so it's about adverbs of frequency=
6   H    =yeah (.) but all my students know these (0.5)
7        words (.) so um I think I have to change the lesson=
```

```
8   I   =what do you mean by changing a lesson? =
9   H   =well instead of reading the passage and learn the
10      vocabulary (0.3) I think we will talk about hobbies
11      and um use hobbies as a way to identify right presents
12      and um (1.2) so it's (.) um about developing social
13      skills and emotional knowledge
```

As an expert teacher, Han is able to approach the content in a holistic way. In Extract 5.2, Han positions the lesson as part of a large module in terms of content with emphasis on the skills rather than individual vocabulary. Language is referred to as its function, for example line 4. The learning content is situated within a wider curriculum plan, a large module of choosing presents in this instance, and this idea is further developed when Han describes her teaching plan (lines 9–12), and subsequent teaching objective (lines 12–13) Again, this pedagogical consideration of focusing on developing social skills and emotional knowledge comes from her knowledge about the students (line 6). Han displays her expertise in understanding the content in relation to the students' existing knowledge when she considers modifying the lesson (line 7). Changing the lesson here shows her flexibility and integrated knowledge of the curriculum and syllabus. Being flexible refers to the ability not to follow the curriculum closely but to 'stretch' the curriculum based on the students' existing subject knowledge.

Conceptions of pedagogical knowledge

Pedagogical knowledge is about how teachers teach and what they focus on in instructional activities. In most cases, it is very personal and contextualised and closely related to the teacher's own learning and teaching experience, hence the personal, practical knowledge.

Overall, novice teachers display a lack of flexibility and confidence in their pedagogical considerations and they tend to follow the rules and their lesson plans rigidly; they also display difficulty in practising learner-centred pedagogy in spite of having such awareness; novice teachers also display and prioritise a desire to establish authority in classrooms and show a lack of reflection.

A lack of flexibility seems to be relevant in many areas in novice teachers' considerations, such as lesson plans, the use of materials (textbooks), the teaching content and assessment methods. Newly qualified teachers or novice teachers feel less confident and flexible in their job because they are still at the 'launching phase' and lack experience (Gatbonton 2008). In this sense, there is clearly a strong relationship between experience and expertise, and establishing authority does seem to be relevant and important for novice teachers. On the other hand, this might be due to the fact that novice teachers have not gained the skills in deliberate practice to actively and purposefully engage in their application. Certainly, there is not sufficient 'reflection-on-action' and 'reflection-in-action' (Schön 1983). Reflection-on-action is illustrated in Extract 5.3, a post-lesson reflection from a teacher.

Extract 5.3

```
1   Tea   I don't like the reading passage in this lesson (.)
2         it's boring=
3   I     =why didn't you use something else instead?=
4   Tea   =no (.) it's not realistic (0.2)um I uh I don't change
5         the reading passage because (.) there are key words
6         they ((students)) need to learn (.) I am worried if I
7         change they will not learn (.) cos they
8         are important um (.) then it's um it's my fault=
9   I     =but can you teach these important phrases through
10        some interesting readings? (0.3)
11  Tea   I don't know (.) I am not experienced (.) I don't have
12        enough experience I am a new teacher
```

In Extract 5.3 a teacher is expressing her dissatisfaction with the teaching content (line 2). This subtle, negative assessment on the learning materials implies her knowledge of what constitutes interesting material for her students and of material evaluation for a specific purpose. However, she also demonstrates that there is a tension in using different materials because of the important vocabulary and phrases to be learnt (lines 5–6). Essentially, she is concerned that any change in materials will mean that the new words are not learned. The lack of flexibility in material choice is further revealed through a possible suggestion from the interviewer. Here the interviewer raises a possibility of using different materials (lines 9–10), which is rejected by the teacher immediately. The rejection here suggests a lack of flexibility and confidence in making changes to the teaching content. Interestingly, the teacher attributes this rejection to a lack of experience.

Closely related to the lack of flexibility is the lack of confidence in using a student-centred approach, although novice teachers very often demonstrate awareness and knowledge about student-centred pedagogy. There seems to be a tension between their understanding of the principles of student-centredness and implementing the approach in actual teaching. One important factor affecting their ability to do so is confidence in teaching. In Extract 5.4, a novice teacher was interviewed about his pedagogical considerations.

Extract 5.4

```
1   I     what's your teaching approach?
2   Tea   (5.0)I am (.) my teaching approach is communicative
3         approach (3.0)
4   I     aha (.) so could you say more?
5   Tea   (2.0) it's £student centred£ (.) yeah (.) my approach
6         is STUDENT CENTRED and I consider students' needs (.)
7         um (.) style (.) and er (3.0) >and I use< real life
8         materials if I can=
9   I     =that sounds [very good=
```

```
10   Tea              [but I am not sure=
11   I       =why?
12   Tea     (.) I don't know whether it is work (.) so I am not
13           confident (.) I am more comfortable when I follow the
14           traditional teaching method (2.5) I feel I am teaching
15           and er students think they learn
```

Extract 5.4 displays this novice teacher's thinking about pedagogy. After a long pause (line 2), he makes the claim that his teaching approach is communicative. When further elaboration is required (line 4), there is quite a long pause before the teacher reformulates his claim of using a communicative approach to a new claim about using a student-centred one. Then he repeats with an emphasis on STUDENT CENTRED with a further elaboration of what he means by a student-centred approach. Here this elaboration implies that the teacher does have awareness and knowledge of a student-centred approach (lines 5–8). This, however, is followed by the teacher's uncertainty about the approach (line 10) when the interviewer provides a positive comment (line 9). The lack of confidence is displayed in the interaction as the teacher sees traditional teaching as a proper way for teaching and learning (lines 12–14). This uncertainty and lack of confidence is very common among novice teacher across the dataset and the confidence issue is also closely related to a desire of teachers to gain their students' trust and respect, and of establishing their authority in the classroom.

Turning now to expert teachers, they display expertise in their pedagogical knowledge in four distinctive but related areas. Specifically, they display flexibility and confidence in pedagogical decisions; they have clear and measured teaching objectives; they are competent in embedding accuracy in meaning-focused activities; and there is awareness of taking contextual cues in their pedagogical decision-making.

Expert teachers display their expertise flexibly in many aspects of their teaching, for example making pedagogical decisions based on the context, designing activities and using materials to address student needs and learning styles. Han, in Extract 5.2 above, shows confidence and flexibility in changing her textbook based on her knowledge of her students. Her contextual knowledge about students' prior linguistic knowledge allows her to choose a topic which will interest the learners but will also practise the vocabulary in that unit.

Expertise is also displayed in having specific, clear and measurable teaching objectives with a focus on meaning and understanding. When expert teachers talk about their teaching plan, they normally have specific teaching aims and know exactly what activities will help them achieve such aims, and how long it will take to do so. This kind of expertise reflects personal and practical pedagogic knowledge that teachers accumulate over years. For example, in Extract 5. 5 Xiao talks about her lesson plan regarding activities.

Extract 5.5

```
1   I       ((pointing to the textbook))so this is today's lesson?=
2   Xiao    =yes (.) this can be an interesting lesson cos it's
```

```
3            about future life (.)
4   I        hmmm (.) =
5   Xiao     =and my focus is on developing their speaking skills (.)
6            so they are able to talk about future life as a plan or
7            (.) a ˚dream˚ (.)=
8   I        =ni↑ce (.) so what's the plan?=
9   Xiao     =I use a song to introduce this topic and I will ask them
10           to talk about their immediate future (.) um (.)then
11           we learn some new words (.) um (.)words they need to use
12           and the follow-up activity is to um take one aspect of
13           life and brainstorm some ideas in groups (.) then they
14           develop it as a presentation (.)
15  I        so (.) you are expecting a good presentation (.)
16  Xiao     yes (.) they know what a good presentation is (.) or not
17           and they are encouraged to have self (.) peer evaluation
18           (.) but (.) yeah I will give them feedback too um (0.3)
19           it's not just the language (.) we also consider
20           presentation skills (.) content (.) speech style and
21           design (.) all that=
22  I        =that sounds interesting
```

This extract clearly demonstrates Xiao's expertise in developing and planning a lesson by providing a clear, measurable and engaging teaching objective (lines 11–14). As an expert teacher, Xiao knows how to engage students through a series of well-designed activities – from listening to a song about future life and talking about their immediate future to working collaboratively on a project (lines 9–14). Note that Xiao in her articulation of the lesson plan presents a workflow of the activities. Here she sequenced the actives in order of complexity and built the lesson step by step. This decision-making relies on her experience with students, knowledge about students and an understanding of how learning happens. For Xiao, learning is doing rather than having; therefore, we see her understanding of learning displayed in the plan as a social practice – learners work together towards a common goal of producing a presentation. Again, the focus is placed on the process rather than the product, although she is expecting a good presentation (line 16). The elaboration of a good presentation and what it entails suggests that Xiao has a clear and measurable teaching objective which will contribute to a positive learning experience (lines 19–21). Xiao in this lesson does not treat students as passive knowledge receivers but as active participants. Students are encouraged to reflect and evaluate their own presentation, provide feedback on their peers' presentations, engage in collaborative talk and so on. The traditional view of teacher in this lesson is minimised as Xiao displays herself as a director, an organiser, a listener and an evaluator. The multiple roles Xiao has adopted in providing students with different learning experiences in different activities reflect her knowledge of effective teaching.

One aspect worth noting from the practice of expert teachers is that they are able to embed accuracy and linguistic knowledge in meaning-focused activities. Focus on form is not separated from focus on meaning, rather expert teachers are able to address these two foci together. For example, in Extract 5.5 Xiao talks about learning vocabulary in a context (line 11). Because students are able to see the immediate relevance of learning the vocabulary or grammar structure, and because the targeted words are taught in a meaningful context, learning is treated as participation in a local context. Extract 5.6 is another example, and is taken from Yun's class.

Extract 5.6 (3.19_4.52)

```
1    Yun    let's see((showing a picture of Beckham))
2           who is he?=
3    SS     =[Beckham
4    Yun    [Beckham (.) Beckham is visiting our ci↑ty↓
5           and er (1.0) he is going to buy some tea to
6           bring back home >but< he doesn't know where
7           (1.2) how to get to the tea market (0.3) yes
8           (.) so↑ if you were Beckham
9           如果你是Beckham ((if you were Beckham)) (.)
10          what would you say?
11          what would you say↓ (.) yes↑ ˚hhhuh huh˚?=
12   S1     =um where is the tea market?=
13   Yun    =right? yes? yeah↓=
14   S2     =how do I [get
15   Yun              [how
16   S2     to the tea city?
17   Yun    how do I get to the tea market yes thank you
18          how about you? (.)
19   S3     could you tell me the way to the market?=
20   Yun    =could you tell me the way to (.) yes
```

In Extract 5.6 Yun is creating a context to elicit ways of 'asking for directions' from students. Yun's pedagogical purpose here is to help students practise asking for directions in a given situation, and she does this by using a role-play situation in which students are the famous footballer, David Beckham, who is looking for the famous tea market. In this task, students are able to use their contextual knowledge to participate and the focus is to use the target language for communication. Here we can see the relevance of the topic and the footballer, David Beckham, to the students. Yun first introduces the character by showing a picture and makes an information request (lines 1–2), which excites the students as indicated by their raised voices when they respond (line 3). In lines 4–11 Yun provides the context for students to practise 'asking for direction'. Student 1 self-selects to produce a relevant second pair part, a correct answer (line 12), for which Yun provides positive feedback (line 13). Another student takes the turn and self-selects to produce another relevant second pair part, a different correct answer (lines 14 and 16), to which Yun provides positive feedback by repeating the student's contribution (line 17). Then Yun nominates a third student (line 18) who produces another relevant second pair part (line 19), to which Yun provides positive confirmation. From this extract, it is clear that an expert teacher, through a process of elicitation, acceptance and affirmation of correct responses, is able to teach the language in context and address both the form and the meaning.

Contextual knowledge
Contextual factors were widely reported to be the most influential factors affecting what teachers think and do (e.g. Andrews 2003). Various contextual factors have been reported in the literature, including policy, the curriculum, testing, textbooks, students, parents and school culture. Li (2013) suggests two types of contextual knowledge: macro-contexts (policy, testing, school culture and so on) and micro-contexts (classroom conditions and the moment-by-moment unfolding of a lesson).

Tests and school norms and culture seem to be the most influential factors among many mentioned contextual factors on novice teachers' decision-making and understanding of teaching and learning. This knowledge is concerned mainly with the macro-context; very little evidence exists in the dataset to suggest that novice teachers are specifically concerned with the micro-context, i.e. what's happening in the classroom. Sofia, a newly qualified teacher, for example, displays her understanding about the significance of tests in the interview in Extract 5.7.

Extract 5.7

```
1   I       what level do you teach?=
2   Sofia   =I teach senior two (.) and they are going to take
3           university test next year=
4   I       =what's your teaching like?=
5   Sofia   =£boring£ but useful (.) I am not doing much
6           communicative activities (.) I just focus on what's
7           in tests and um (.) lecture I suppose (.)
8   I       why not communicative activities? (.)
9   Sofia   well you know the test is very important for
10          students to get a place in university (.) I am
11          £realistic£ (1.5) and um I want to be a good teacher=
12  I       =°yeah°
```

When talking about her students' English level, rather than giving a proficiency level, such as lower-intermediate, Sofia refers to the official year group, followed by a further explanation of what it means (lines 2–3). The stage of learning and level of proficiency is recognised by what tests are relevant to students. Then when asked about her teaching style (line 4), Sofia uses two adjectives to describe it: boring but useful. After a very brief pause, Sofia explains the boring but useful approach is to lecture (line 7). Note that she contrasts communicative activities with lecturing as potentially interesting activities but less useful to serve the purpose of tests (lines 5-7). The importance of tests is displayed in how she teaches (lines 6 and 7). The further clarification of not using communicative activities again highlights the important role of the tests, this time to both learners and herself as a teacher. The importance of the test to students is that it is a gateway to the university (line 10). Her idea of being a good teacher is defined by her ability of effectively assisting students to secure a university place by helping them achieve good results in their English test. As we can see in this conversation, Sofia's approach to teaching and the idea of being a good teacher is very much shaped by the test.

Another recurring theme is that school culture and norms influence teachers' thinking. For most teachers, it is important to adhere to what is appropriate in the school's practice, which normally means being consistent with what the more established teachers or the majority of teachers do. This could be applied in many different aspects of teaching and learning, for example teaching materials, teaching methods, class activities, feedback strategies, rapport for students and even the relationship with students. Extract 5.8 is an illustration of how school norms and culture shape teachers' practice. Specifically, Julia, as a novice teacher, talks about changing the way she teaches in order to fit in with the school culture.

Extract 5.8

```
1   J    school norm and value is very important (.) for what
2        we do and um how we do our job (.) you kind-a do what
3        other teachers do and not stand out as someone(.)very
4        different (1.5) it's not a good idea to stick your
5        neck out=
6   I    =°uh huh°=
7   J    =it's like I stopped trying different group work (.)
8        after a while (.) cos most of teachers don't do that
9        (.)and um it's like I am wasting students time(0.3)
10       I don't want to be different anyway (.)yeah (.)so um
11       you kind of adjust yourself (.) I do a lot of drills
12       now (.) it's kind of normal (.)
13  I    °yeah° (.) I guess you need to fit in=
14  J    =absolutely
```

In this extract, Julia explicitly expresses the importance of school norms and values for her job (line 1). For Julia, fitting in means doing what other teachers do and not standing out as someone different, because being different could mean being marginalised (lines 4-5). From Julia's perspective, the negative influence of being different could jeopardise her career in the school. In the next turn, she gives an example of having stopped using group work because most of her fellow teachers did not do that kind of work and possibly did not recognise it as good practice. Using group work could be interpreted by other teachers and students as wasting students' time (line 9).

Because Julia attaches great importance to following other teachers, she adjusted her teaching to performing a lot of drills now, which is kind of normal (line 12). From this short conversation, probably we can infer that school norms and values are very important to Julia in the sense that she would like to fit in with the local culture and be part of it without causing any disturbance. The normality of this culture is closely related to what teaching is and how it should be done. We can also see the potential clash between her own understanding and the constraints arising from her understanding of the context. As a newly qualified teacher, her choice is to adjust to becoming a member of the community.

Novice teachers' understanding of what teaching entails is influenced by students and the important others, including fellow teachers or, sometimes, parents (Kang and Cheng 2013). It clearly suggests that '(T)he classroom is a world unto itself' and teaching is an activity closely related to the society, institution and participants involved in the process (Van Lier 1988: 179). Thus, teaching is a social activity and the classroom is a social place in nature (Tudor 2001; Hall 2011) where participants (both teachers and learners) follow its norms and culture.

Turning now to expert teachers, there are types of contextual knowledge that expert teachers display which novice teachers lack. First of all, expert teachers display understanding of students' difficulties in learning, as displayed in Extract 5.9.

Extract 5.9

```
1    I      what are the main things you think about when you plan
2           teaching? (.)
3    Cai    um (.) main things (.) are (1.2) content (.) the topic
4           >and students< these are the things=
5    I      =what do you mean you when you say the students?=
6    Cai    =they are important (.)the the language points and
7           my teaching aims all about students↑ (.) yeah they are
8           important (0.2) affect my teaching (0.8) hmm. like what
9           they already know (0.3) what they like (.) is it
10          appropriate for them is the question I ask all the time
11          and the thing is (.) yeah (.) their level (.) their
12          needs and how difficult the new content is for them
13          (2.1) yeah all this kinds of things °I can't really
14          name everything° (.)
15   I      so students decide how you teach?=
16   Cai    =yeah (.) definitely
```

In Extract 5.9, an expert teacher is talking about the principles behind his planning cycle. Clearly, students are one of the key elements in preparing a lesson (line 4), for example language points and teaching aims (lines 6–7). He further elaborates this point through a series of questions he would ask himself when preparing a lesson, including students' prior knowledge and preferences (line 9), the appropriateness of the content (line 10), student level, needs and difficulty (lines 11–12) and so on. Cai attaches great importance to students in his teaching by claiming that students are influential in many aspects of teaching. From the questions he poses to himself when preparing for a lesson, we can infer that Cai puts himself in a learner's position. This repositioning provides Cai with insights into the difficulties students might face in learning and how he might go about addressing them. Expert teachers often attribute this knowledge to the many years of teaching experience they have. Clearly, there is a strong link between experience and expertise (Tsui 2009). However, what data also suggest is that expert teachers gain this type of knowledge through critical refection or 'reflection-in-action' (Schön 1983), and they have a positive attitude to teacher learning in the professional context.

As discussed in Chapter 1, the concept of practical knowledge is knowledge 'broadly based on (teachers') experiences in classrooms and schools and is directed toward the handling of problems that arise in their work (Elbaz 1981: 67). However, it does not mean that teachers with years of experience will necessarily have sufficient pedagogical practical knowledge for effective teaching. Only when teachers engage in reflection critically with regards to students' learning styles, interests, needs, strengths and difficulties, and instructional techniques and classroom management issues, can they develop practical pedagogical knowledge. This fundamentally decides whether a teacher can develop expertise.

Second, expert teachers are able to consider both the macro- and micro-context in making judgements in many aspects of teaching, including material choices, activities and their role in teaching. In fact, the micro-context, such as students' reactions in class and the interaction between the teacher and students influences what expert teachers do. Their sensitivity to what's going on in the classroom enables them to make a swift change sometimes in class in order to address students' needs and difficulties. This kind of decision-making is interactive and requires expertise in making a good decision online. It is an outcome of the moment-by-moment interaction with students, materials and activities.

In Extract 5.10, the teacher, Sue, is guiding students to find the right information from the text to answer her questions, and the following takes place as a result of students' contributions.

Extract 5.10 (8.52_11.30)

```
1    T     so just now we are talking about all kinds of gifts
2          bought from shops (.) if we want to buy something from
3          shops what maybe <the most important thing that we
4          need>=
5    SS    =money=
6    T     =money ok (.) so we need money (.) and as Amy just
7          mentioned that daming's mother always buy expensive
8          clothes (.)what if daming doesn't have that much money?
9          and <he still wants to buy some presents for his
10         mother> what can you do (3.1) you? ((hand gesture))
11         (2.8)
```

```
12  S1  maybe er daming can borrow some money from her um
13      from his father er maybe s and um=
14  T   =still use parents' [money]
15  S1                      [um when daming have got um (0.6)
16      lot of moneies and he can give it back to his father=
17  T   =maybe one day he can return the money °ok° zhouwan (.)
18  S2  um I have another rea another way he can make the
19      clothes for your mother (.) I think it's very cheap and
20      also you can draw clothes (.) you know (.) I know a very
21      cheap way (.) on the website you can buy a clothes you
22      can draw it you draw a picture you like=
23  T   =very creative ideas (1.0) ((hand gesture to another
24      student)) more ideas?=
25  S3  =eh we can pick up some photos and er (2.0) £and er£
26      sell it and then we can earn some money=
27  T   =you can earn some money yourself (.) that's a good
28      choice (2.0)
29  S4  um I think er (1.0) daming can do some housework for
30      his parents and then he will get the money and buy the
31      clothes=
32  T   =((nodding her head)) earn the money himself (1.0) Ann=
33  S5  =um I think maybe just give his mother something he owns
34      because for the parents er anything from the child is
35      special=
36  T   =that's your idea (.) any more different ideas?
37      (3.0)
38  S6  um I think like pretty clothes don't have to be
39      expensive he could just look around and buy something
40      he could afford but his mother would like(.)
41  T   any more different ideas? (.)
42  S7  well I think if daming decided to buy his mother
43      a dress (.) he can start saving money um before his
44      mother's birthday and that I think the money will be
45      enough to buy one=
46  T   =very good (.) you have very creative ideas
```

Because the students mentioned buying gifts from shops Sue decided to bring the topic of money to the discussion, and one of the pedagogical concerns here is to help students be aware of a genuine problem associated with buying presents (especially expensive clothes suggested by a student earlier). Clearly, the decision Sue made was the outcome of one student's contribution, which she also refers to (lines 6–7). This extract spans 2 minutes 38 seconds in 46 lines, with contributions from seven different students. As we can see, Sue successfully elicits the topic from students (line 5) by following up an earlier discussion (lines 2–4) and engages students with a real-life problem to challenge students (lines 7–8). Here the question what if daming doesn't have that much money? is genuine and authentic, and aims to enable students to develop their language skills rather than knowledge. In the students' contributions, we can see that Sue is not trying to rush to a conclusion but instead allows students to express their opinions. This is evidenced by several invitations from her to contribute (lines 10, 17, 23-4, 32, 36 and 41), and a challenge (line 14) to enable more than one idea to be put forward. We can also see that learners' contributions are longer than the brief answers that are observed in many language classrooms. Clearly, the pedagogical goal is to provide students with a space to develop their solutions to the problem. It is also clear that the teacher uses various interactional strategies to help the learners to develop their ideas, such as a challenge (line 14), reformulation of the student's contribution (line 17), positive feedback (lines 23, 27-8 and 46) and a summary of students' contributions (lines 27 and 32). The judgement and decision Sue makes to move the lesson forward and develop immediate learning opportunities makes her an expert teacher and different from novice teachers.

Third, expert teachers displays competence in differentiating long-term from short-term goals (Li 2013). That is, expert teachers are competent in considering both long-term and short-term goals in their teaching and address them accordingly. This involves shifting priorities and making the right decision for the moment. They are more flexible in deviating from their plan, especially when there are immediate learning opportunities they could exploit. The flexibility over the lesson and the looseness that the expert teachers have in teaching is one of the key features of expertise. In Extract 5.10, Sue moves away from learning language items to developing students' social and problem-solving skills in that students' understanding of managing money becomes a priority. This focus shift is done through utilising a topic raised by a student (line 6) and problematising the suggestion by the student in a real-life context (lines 8-10). At this point, although the focus of the activity is choosing the right present, Sue moves away from it to prioritising the long-term educational goal – developing students' social and problem-solving skills. In short, when considering how to facilitate learning, expert teachers are able to 'make the right choice at the right time' (van Lier 2000).

Classroom interactional competence
The classroom is the place where learning opportunities can be exploited. Teachers play an important role in providing, managing and developing such opportunities, where students might encounter the conscious choice of language by teachers or the unconscious consequence of natural interactions between members of the classroom. This is mainly done through engaging students, providing scaffolded help when necessary (i.e. feedback) and managing students' contributions through the use of classroom interaction. Therefore, teachers' ability to manage and shape student contributions is vitally important in developing space for learning (see Walsh and Li 2013). Expertise in teaching also lies in the understanding and creating such opportunities. In classroom interaction research, such an ability is also termed as classroom interactional competence (CIC): '[T]eachers and learners' ability to use interaction as a tool for mediating and assisting learning' (Walsh 2006: 132). Rather than fluency, interactional competence is concerned with the ability and act of making spoken

language fluent *together between* speakers. Essentially, interactional competence is 'a relationship between participants' employment of linguistic and interactional resources and the contexts in which they are employed' (Young 2008: 100). With regards to a classroom environment where English is taught as a foreign language as a subject and a skill, CIC on the part of the teacher is extremely important as it is the teacher who guides the teaching and learning activity and the direction of interaction.

According to Walsh (2013) and other relevant work in this area, the key features of CIC are:

- Teachers' ability in using language which is both convergent to the pedagogical goal of the moment and which is appropriate to the learner. The use of interactional strategies are appropriate to the teaching objective and are adjusted in relation to the co-construction of meaning and the unfolding agenda of a lesson.
- Teachers' ability in facilitating the interactional space which learners need to participate in the discourse to contribute to the class and to receive feedback on their contribution. In short, CIC creates space for learning (Walsh and Li 2013).
- Teachers' ability in shaping learners' contribution by accepting it and making it relevant to the class through using different interactional strategies, such as paraphrasing, reformulating, extending and scaffolding, and appropriately using code-switching and a multi-modal learning environment (Sert 2015).

In a nutshell, novice teachers typically demonstrate low levels of CIC whereas expert teachers have high levels of CIC. The differences largely exist in interactional structure with particular attention to initiation and feedback, and interactional strategies. Seedhouse's work is relevant here. He proposes 'three interactional properties which derive directly from the core goal, and these properties in turn necessarily shape the interaction' (2004: 183). He further suggests that:

> these three properties follow in a rational sequence and constitute part of the unique fingerprint of L2 classroom interaction and part of its context-free machinery:
> 1. Language is both the vehicle and object of instruction
> 2. There is a reflexive relationship between pedagogy and interaction, and interactants constantly display their analyses of the evolving relationship between pedagogy and interaction.
> 3. The linguistic forms and patterns of interaction which the learners produce in the L2 are potentially subject to evaluation by the teacher in some way. (Ibid.)

In studying classroom interaction and learning, Seedhouse (2004) refers to the overall organisation of an L2 classroom as interactional architecture, which constitutes the organisation of turn, sequence and repair. In the following, I will examine these aspects from both novice and expert teachers' classrooms.

The organisation of turn-taking and sequence
Much work has been done to explore the nature of classroom interaction (e.g. Seedhouse 2004; Walsh 2006, 2011) and it is generally agreed that the IRF (Initiation-Response-Feedback) pattern predominates (Sinclair and Coulthard 1975).

The three-part exchange starts with an initiation from the teacher, and questions are typical of an initiation move (Tsui 1995; Cook 2008). This is then followed by a response from students and a non-compulsory feedback move from the teacher. Teachers have many pedagogical purposes associated with the questions they ask in the initiation, for example checking students' understanding, eliciting information and engaging students. Hall (2011) also suggests that teachers use questions to exert control over learners. That is, by using a question the teacher can allocate speakership to students, determine the relevance of the learners' turn and how long the turn might be. The analysis of this dataset suggests a clear dominant presence of the IRF interactional pattern in novice teachers' classrooms. For example, in Extract 5.11 we can see the interaction between the teacher and students follow a clear pattern of IRF: Initiation (lines 1 and 4), Response (lines 2 and 5) and Feedback (lines 3 and 6). In this typical IRF exchange, questions are used by the teacher as a way to manage her teaching objective of checking learners' understanding of these adverbs. More importantly, the teacher uses questions to orchestrate the classroom interaction. She is using questions to control who speaks and for how long in this instance.

Extract 5.11

```
1   T    what does always mean? (.)
2   S1   always is 总是 ((Chinese translation always))=
3   T    =ok (.) sit down please.
4        what does often mean?=
5   S1   =常常((Chinese translation often))=
6   T    =good(.)
```

A question can be classified by its nature as an open or closed, or referential and display, question. An open/referential question can be broadly defined as a question that is open for interpretation and the teacher does not have a fixed answer to the question or does not know the answer to it, whereas a closed/display question has a fixed answer or the teacher knows the answer to it. Although in many cases, a yes/no question is regarded as a closed/display question whereas a wh- question is considered as an open/referential question, the distinction between these two types of question is more complicated than that. For example, in Extract 5.11 the teacher asked wh- questions but they are closed or display questions as the teacher knows the answer to the question and the questions do have fixed answers to them. In the dataset, novice teachers asked more closed/display questions than the expert teachers and one of the possible reasons is that novice teachers have rigid lesson plans and their intentions are to stick to the textbook and curriculum.

122   PART B: ANALYSIS

In the expert teachers' classrooms, interactional patterns are less structured although IRF is also observed. However, careful examination suggests that there are differences in the use of IRF in expert educators' teaching. Again, I will consider the IRF structure and the nature of the initiation. First, there is evidence of spiral IRF which the teacher utilises in opening up the discussion rather than closing it down (Li 2011). A spiral IRF operates like a chain of initiations and responses, before a feedback move is made. A spiral IRF is not necessarily a series of questions and answers between the teacher and one student. In fact, more than one student can be involved. For example, in Extract 5.12 the teacher is using a spiral IRF to engage students in the discussion.

Extract 5.12

```
1    I1      T     okay (.) do you think it's a good idea to increase
2                  the tube fare?=
3    R1      S1    =no (.) it's-makes people can't afford=
4    I2      T     =who do you mean by people here? (.) you? me? (1.2)
5    R2/I    S1    I think many [people like those who do not have high
6    R       S2                 [it depends on how much fare is up
7    R2      S1    salary and people who are visitors=
8    R       S2    =but visitors can afford and they only visit once (.)
9                  no? (.)
10   I3      T     so how much should the fare be increased then? and do
11                 we increase the fare only to £visitors£? (.)
12   R3      S2    I think local people should benefit from a reduced fare
13                 and visitors can pay a bit more=
14   F/I4    T     =Ok (.) we have some ideas (.)now discuss in group an-
15                 try to come to a conclusion (.) five minutes
```

In this extract, the teacher initiates a question (I) (line 1) and a student self-selects herself to provide a response (line 3). In a typical classroom, a teacher should follow up with the feedback move, but instead of giving an evaluative feedback the teacher follows up with another question which can be interpreted as a new initiation (line 4). In line 5 and 6 there are two responses from students, with one answering the second initiation (line 5) and the other one less clear. At face value, the response from the second student could be a response to the teacher's initial question in line 1 or a response to the contribution from student 1 (line 3). Then when we consider what follows this turn, it's clear that student 2 is responding to student 1 in this case (lines 8 and 9). So the interactional structure does not follow an IRF pattern in this case but contains several teacher initiations and student responses, one student initiation and a feedback (see Figure 5.1). The spiral IRF provides students with opportunities to engage in genuine discussion and in these exchanges, meaning is prominent.

In terms of initiation, we can see that the teacher has different pedagogical purposes, such as eliciting opinions (line 1), probing and seeking for clarification

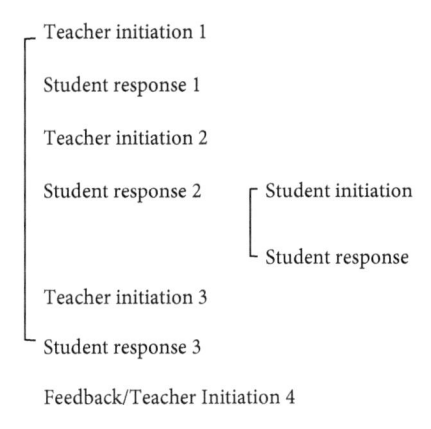

```
                    ┌─ Teacher initiation 1
                    │
                    │  Student response 1
                    │
                    │  Teacher initiation 2
                    │
                    │  Student response 2      ┌─ Student initiation
                    │                          │
                    │                          └─ Student response
                    │
                    │  Teacher initiation 3
                    │
                    └─ Student response 3

                       Feedback/Teacher Initiation 4

                    Figure 5.1    Interactional patterns
```

and elaboration (lines 4, 10 and 11), and giving instructions (lines 14 and 15). It's also worth noting that referential questions are generally preferred in expert teachers' classrooms. For example, in this extract the teacher asks four referential questions in her initiations to engage students in discussion (lines 1 and 2, 4, 10 and 11) although two of these questions are yes/no questions. It is this openness and flexibility which expert teachers demonstrate in teaching that suggests that they have expertise in facilitating learning or creating learning opportunities.

The organisation of repair
Repair is one of the key moments when learning opportunities can be offered to learners. Repair can be in various forms but direct feedback is the predominant repair in novice teachers' classrooms. Traditionally, feedback is evaluative in nature, which is also a key feature of the novice teacher's feedback strategy. There are two characteristics of feedback from novice teachers' classrooms: first, they tend to provide positive feedback such as 'good' or simply move on with an acknowledgement of receipt of the contribution; second, if there is need for a corrective feedback, novice teachers' feedback also usually entails a 'telling'. In short, direct corrective feedback is the normal feedback strategy employed by the majority of novice teachers' practice in this dataset. Extract 5.13 is a typical illustration.

Extract 5.13

```
1   T    open your workbook (.) page twelve ok↑ page twelve (0.5)
2        let's go over the exercises one by one (0.3) now have
3        you done all?=
4   SS   =yes/no/ (.)
5   T    ok it's important that you do all the exercises in the
6        workbook (0.4)
7        now we are going to cover all of it
```

```
8          ((eye gaze with one student)) now number one (.)
9     S1   Lucy went shopping on the way to home (.)
10    T    ((shaking her head)) it's wrong (.) Lucy went shopping
11         on the way what? home not to home ok?
```

In Extract 5.13, the teacher is going through exercises with students and nominates a student to complete exercise one using mutual gaze (line 8). The student provides a relevant response (line 9) to which the teacher provides feedback (line 10). The feedback contains, first of all, an evaluation, a negative feedback with a disapproval gesture (line 10), and, second, an explanatory correction (line 11).

Expert teachers, on the other hand, demonstrate an ability and competence in utilising feedback strategies to facilitate learning. In other words, expert teachers are able to use feedback to create 'space for learning' (Walsh and Li 2013). There is evidence that when the teacher's third turn is used for more than evaluation, it encourages and facilitates 'dialogic interaction' (Hall and Walsh 2002). When examining expert teachers' feedback, various strategies are employed, including:

- providing embedded repair or modification or a space for self-correction (Li 2013)
- utilising learners' contribution to develop the activity (Cullen 2002)
- seeking for clarification or asking for confirmation (Lee 2007)
- encouraging learners to elaborate (Wells 1993; Liu 2008)
- reformulating or shaping learners' contributions to make them more comprehensible (Walsh and Li 2013).

Extract 5.14 is an example in which a teacher is eliciting information from students about how English people spend their Christmas.

Extract 5.14

```
1     T    can you tell me about how er (.)
2          English people spend their Christmas (.)
3          what do you know about English Christmas?
4          (2.1)
5     S1   hmmm (.) they buy each other presents (.)
6     T    they? (.) who?=
7     S1   =family members uh an- friends (.)
8     T    family:: ((gesture for more))
9     S1   family and friends buy each other presents (.)to wish each
10         other good luck (1.3)
11    T    yes family exchange presents to give each other best
12         wishes (0.3) and?=
13    S1   =they er they get together to eat a nice food=
14    T    =yes they get together to have a nice meal (.) right?=
15    S    =yes (.)
16    T    what do they have for the big meal? do you know? (.)
```

```
17   S1    um that thing (1.2) 火鸡 ((turkey))=
18   T     =[tur::=
19   S2    [°chicken°?
20   S1    =um turkey and potatoes (0.3) and they have a nice meal (.)
21         and watch TV
```

Throughout this extract, it is apparent that the teacher is attempting to get one student to contribute to his question about 'how English people spend Christmas'. In line 3, for example, the teacher asks an open question which gives students space to contribute any relevant information. The teacher's questions here can be interpreted as a genuine request or 'pre-announcement' (Terasaki 2005). When a student self-selects himself to produce relevant information (line 5), the teacher provides immediate feedback for seeking clarification (line 6) to help the student to develop the idea precisely. Here, it is obvious that the student and the teacher are engaged in a conversation when the student clarifies that 'they' in his earlier response refers to family and friends (line 7). The teacher here uses gesture and stretched sounds (indicated by :: on the transcript) to invite the student to carry on to clarify his contribution (line 8), and it is clear that the student is able to produce a relevant second pair part with accuracy and make the clarification with assistance from the teacher (lines 9–10). After a longish pause, the teacher reformulates the student's contribution. Here, we can see the teacher has different pedagogical purposes with his reformulation. First, he makes the student's contribution relevant to the whole class and, second, he follows up the contribution to invite further ideas, notably with the invitation and? in line 12. This invitation again generates an immediate response from the same student, who contributes a different idea (line 13). Although the focus is on communicating ideas, the teacher provides an embedded feedback to foster accuracy (line 14), which is clearly received by the student as evidenced in line 20. The embedded feedback does not obstruct the students in communication; on the contrary, it helps the student to be precise about his ideas. We can also see that the teacher uses different interactional strategies to help the learner to develop his ideas and to engage in the conversation, notably the use of a follow-on question to seek elaboration (line 16). When the student displays difficulty with vocabulary, the teacher uses a strategy, hinting at the correct response by providing the first part of the word (line 18). It's worth noting that another student also provides help by giving a similar word here (line 19). With the teacher's help, the student manages to remember the word and produces the sentence. It seems that the teacher is helping the student to achieve great precision in meaning in this conversation. The follow-on questions not only provide assistance for the student to develop precise and meaningful information, they also provide the student with an opportunity to engage in a natural conversation.

Classroom management
Classroom management is a key element to move the class forward smoothly and it is 'the central element of every teacher's daily professional experience' (Wright 2005: 1). Classroom management is broadly referred to as how teachers use the available time and resources to organise and direct effective learning with learners (Thornbury,

2006). Therefore, classroom management can be as broad as including everything in the classroom. However, what this section mainly focuses on is how teachers perform the role of manager to maintain the natural and smooth flow of the lesson and it pays particular attention to teachers' management of students' classroom behaviour problems. This is also a practice in which novice teachers differ considerably from expert teachers, typically showing more concern for students' behaviour problems than expert teachers (Borg and Falzon 1998; Kokkinos et al. 2004). Non-expert teachers and novice teachers are reported as having more difficulties in finding effective solutions to the problems than expert teachers do, while expert teachers spend less time in dealing with behaviour problems (Shen et. al. 2009).

Classroom behaviour problems are of particular importance in understanding the dynamics of the classroom and the effectiveness of teaching. In this dataset, novice teachers place emphasis on managing learners' behaviours and setting up classroom norms and rules. In essence, there are far more managerial modes in novice teachers' classrooms and the majority of these are about disciplining and managing behaviours. One possible reason for novice teachers to spend excessive class time on dealing with behaviour problems is that they have negative attitudes towards student misbehaviour and they are not confident in dealing with them effectively. There is strong evidence that teachers' perceptions of classroom behaviour is a strong indicator of their confidence and their reaction to the misbehaviour (Arbuckle and Little 2004; Decker et al. 2007). Novice teachers spend considerable time dealing with misbehaviours such as daydreaming (non-attention), turn-taking problems (i.e. talking out of turn), unwillingness to follow rules and listen to teachers' instructions, being withdrawn (being quite). For example, in Extract 5.15 a novice teacher is doing some language exercises with students and she deliberately talks about what she expects students to do and how students should participate in the activity.

Extract 5.15

```
1    T    ok pay attention (.) listen carefully (.)I am going to
2         ask one of you to give me an answer if she can't get it
3         right (.) I am going to ask you (.)o↑k (1.2)
4         raise your hands if you know the answer (0.5)
5         why only seven?! put up your hands (.)
6         the first one?
```

For this teacher, it is important to make sure that students follow the rules of classroom participation – the teacher asks questions and the students answer them. Students should pay attention to what the teacher says and listen carefully so as to be ready to respond (line 1). Here, the teacher sets the rule that only one student has the right to speak at a time as she makes it explicit that: I am going to ask one of you to give me an answer. The other students will have opportunities to speak if the first selected student cannot get it right (lines 2 and 3). The teacher also makes the rule clear that students need to bid for an opportunity to speak by raising their hands. She also displays her ideology of the role of students by first complaining that only a few students know the answer and then telling them to put their hands up (lines 4 and 5). From this short extract, we can make three observations: first, it is important for the teacher to set the rules of participation in class: who can speak and when; second, it is a method for the teacher to help learners to stay mentally engaged as keeping students on track and stopping them from daydreaming is a challenging issue and one of the most frequent and troublesome behaviour problems (Shen et al. 2009); and, finally, the raised hand is a method for the teacher to check students' knowledge and for students to take a turn-at-talk. Indeed, in many cases, a raised hand indicating self-selection performs the action of the second pair part of an adjacency pair such as question-response.

Another unique feature of novice teachers' classrooms is how they manage their own behaviour – the way they speak to students and follow their teaching plan. Novice teachers pay particular attention to their performance in class, especially when they have made a mistake or moved away from their plans. 'I forgot to ...' or 'I should have ...' are frequent phrases used in novice teachers' reflections. This might be related to the learning phase novice teachers are at in their first few years as they are in the process of developing understanding about what their profession means. The fact that reflection is very often focused on their own teaching behaviour might also be related to confidence levels as newly qualified teachers are less confident about what they do and constantly check their own behaviours in accordance with what might be seen as 'standard procedure'.

In contrast, expert teachers are more flexible in the classroom and there is less evidence of them maintaining order or establishing norms. In fact, expert teachers seem to spend very little time in dealing with misbehaviour in class and are more tolerant of such problems. Nevertheless, there is strong evidence that expert teachers develop students' learning strategies and their metacognitive awareness, and develop learning opportunities. Extract 5.16 is taken from a classroom in which the teacher is guiding students to use the internet to conduct their projects.

Extract 5.16

```
1   T    ok I noticed some of you are taking notes next to the
2        new words when reading (.) that's very good (.) it's a
3        useful strategy for you to identify those words (.)
4        you don't know (.)
5        what would you do when you meet a new words? (3.0)
6   S1   look in dictionary (.)
7   T    ok check dictionary an-?
8   S2   (1.0 unintelligible)=
9   T    =yes guess (1.0) you guess from the context and
10       sentence before and after (.) yeah? (1.2)
11  S3   ˚prefix and suffix˚=
12  T    = use the lexical roots(.) prefix and suffix very good
13       (0.3) remember that you don't have to know every single
14       word when you try to get a gist of a passage ok?
```

In this extract, the teacher notices the strategies learners are using to complete a task and she takes this as a long-term learning opportunity to develop students' knowledge about learning. First of all, the teacher identifies what she sees from some students (lines 1 and 2), and she provides positive evaluative feedback (line 2). Note here that the teacher makes this strategy relevant to the whole class (lines 3 and 4). Then the teacher goes one step further to expand the learning opportunity to elicit some information from students on how to deal with unknown words (line 5). The first student makes an attempt by making a reference to using a dictionary (line 6). The teacher provides positive confirmation with an embedded correction (line 7). Then the second student makes an attempt in line 8, to which the teacher again provides a positive confirmation (line 9). This time, the teacher makes a further elaboration on the student's contribution to develop the precise meaning of guessing (lines 9–10). After another longish pause, a third student makes an attempt to answer the teacher's original question, this time referring to lexical rules of using the prefix and suffix (line 11). Again, the teacher expands the student's idea to fully develop the meaning of using lexical roots and so on. Then the teacher summarises and emphasises that knowing every single vocabulary item is unnecessary as an overall understanding of the text is more important (lines 13–14). It is clear that in this exchange the teacher's focus is on developing students' knowledge about a vocabulary learning strategy. The ability of noticing students' learning behaviour and developing this as a learning opportunity demonstrates the teachers' expertise in managing learning.

The above extract also indicates that expert teachers are able to develop learning opportunities based on their observations of students' reactions. Expert teachers are able to make moment-by-moment decisions, bearing in mind their teaching objectives and goals at a particular point in time. Extract 5.16 is such an example. In this extract, the teacher notices the learners' problems with vocabulary and makes this a learning opportunity for everyone. It is this sensitivity to the students' problem and her flexibility in adjusting the pace and organisation of the class that suggests her expertise in understanding the curriculum and her students.

MULTIPLE EXPERTISE

As presented in the first section of this chapter, expertise is not fixed or static but rather is a fluid and context-bound ability which is portrayed in teachers' understanding and practice. In this regard, expertise is multiple, meaning that expert teachers can temporarily be a novice, especially in an unfamiliar context or due to insufficient knowledge. Equally, novice teachers may demonstrate expertise in areas where they have confidence and competence.

Expert as a Temporary Novice

Gina is an experienced teacher who I would consider to be an expert teacher in many aspects, in particular her awareness of student needs and pedagogy. She recently changed her job and there is evidence that the expert has become a temporary novice. The following conversation happened in the fourth week of her new job.

Extract 5.17

```
1   I   how's everything? (.)
2   G   about the job (.) er a few days ago (.) that's the
3       I don't know which week (.) about the halfway through
4       the second week to the third week I am feeling a bit
5       (.) a bit disappointed (1.0)
6   I   why?
7       (1.0)
8   G   hmmm because (1.2) I feel this school is like (0.8)
9       because seventy five of this school actually are male
10      students (.) so the dynamic is very different from
11      those schools of half girls and half boys (1.0)
12  I   hmmm (.)
13  G   so the dynamic in classroom is really different (0.4)
14      then I feel comparing the school I used to work (0.5)
15      you know we also had science classes full of [boys
16  I                                                 [hmmm
17  G   >but probably I think students are more cooperative<
18      yeah (.) they are well behaved (.) and it's just like
19      they listen to whatever [I say
20                              [hmmm
21      >and they respect the teacher< (.)
22  I   yeah=
23  G   =but here it is quite different (1.2) hmmm I feel that
24      they are very autonomous (0.5) er:: because many of
25      them go to cram school so (0.3) when I teach the
26      content they've learnt they are uninterested (.) >but
27      actually< they are not good (.)
28  I   hmm
```

On reflecting on her new job, Gina displays disappointment at work (line 5), which is further elaborated through her understanding of classroom dynamics. For her, this is a different type of school, consisting of 75% male students, which results in a different classroom dynamic from those mixed schools (lines 8–11). In this conversation, she repeatedly emphasises the different dynamic by comparing her present workplace to her previous one (lines 10–13). She then compares the science classes in her previous school, which were also dominated by male students, to draw a conclusion that the students in her previous workplace were more cooperative (line 17). Here we can see how subtly Gina displays her dissatisfaction with her current students. She uses a strategy of comparing and contrasting to indicate that she is being challenged and displays unhappiness about the situation (lines 17–27). The previous students are described as cooperative and well-behaved, students who listen to teachers and show respect, while the current students are autonomous. However, the meaning of autonomous here is negative. Because many students go to cram school, they are not interested (when I teach the content they've learnt they are uninterested) and consider her teaching to be superfluous. This could further indicate potential cockiness – even arrogance – on their part. Gina portrays her students as unpleasant work partners (line 27) and this contributes to her disappointment at work.

Insufficient knowledge can also position an expert as a novice temporarily. In Extract 5.18, for example, Yuan, an expert teacher, displays insufficient cultural knowledge and becomes a temporary novice. Here, the teacher is eliciting information from the class about how English people celebrate Christmas. Before this extract, he had contributions from two students and now he is inviting a third student to contribute to the class.

Extract 5.18 (4.04_5.15)

```
1    T    anything else? Lina (.) what about you?=
2    S    =um (.)mistletoe=
3    T    =sorry?=
4    S    =mistletoe
5    T    (4.7)((reading the book))
6         of course something from the ↓book=
7    S    =[er. . .
8    T     [I didn't ask you to find anything from the book (.)
9         I want you to tell me [anything=
10   S                          [can I say something about
11        mistletoe ((in Chinese))
12   T    =ummm (.) well (7.2) ((looking down at the book))
13        um something like a mistletoe something like a
14        mistletoe (.) yeah mistle::toe=
15   S    =um people er on on Christmas would put mistletoe
16        on [something erm (.) if you stand under the mistletoe
17   T       [something like mistletoe
18   S    every people can kiss you and um you can't er
19        £refuse£=
20   T    =you cannot refuse?!=
21   S    =yeah=
22   T    =when people kiss you (.) you cannot re↓fuse=
23   S    =no=
24   T    =so if you happen to stand under this kind of tree (.)
25        right?=
26   S    =you can expect a lot of them((kisses))(.)
27   T    oh::I really don't know (.) thank you for your
28   I    information ok↓
```

The student brings up the topic of mistletoe (line 2), for which Yuan requires a clarification (line 3). When the student repeats her response (line 4), Yuan turns to reading the book without acknowledging the student's turn as if he is ignoring the student. After this rather long silence, Yuan takes a turn to try to identify the source of the topic (line 6). In line 7, the student is trying to take a turn while the teacher interrupts and clarifies his request for the contribution (lines 8-9). The student takes the initiative here and interrupts the teacher by asking if she can talk about mistletoe using her first language (L1) (lines 10-11). The choice of language here is interesting as it suggests that her earlier request in English was ignored by the teacher and she is using the L1 to make it clear what she wants to speak about. Rather than granting the student permission or encouraging the student to contribute, Yuan once again hesitates with a very long pause (7.2 seconds) and checks the book (line 12). The student takes a turn and makes her contribution about mistletoe (lines 15-16, 18-19). It is a rather long learner turn and in the middle, Yuan attempts to interrupt (line 17) but the student is able to hold the floor to complete her turn (line 18). Upon receiving this information, the teacher first of all displays surprise (line 20), which can be interpreted as seeking confirmation. Then follows the intended positive feedback from the student (line 21), which is interpreted as negative. Yuan reformulates the student's original contribution in line 22 as a second attempt for seeking confirmation, and this time the student provides a definite positive feedback (line 23). It seems that Yuan is unsure about this message and he seeks clarification again (lines 24-5), this time receiving an indirect positive feedback from the student who completes the teacher's turn (line 26). This student's persistence and contribution presents a challenge to Yuan, hence he tries to confirm the message and seek clarification. This long exchange between Yuan and this student is completed with a claim of insufficient knowledge from the teacher (lines 27-8). It is the teacher's attempt to understand the message by seeking confirmation and clarification, and the claim of insufficient knowledge, which suggests that the teacher is a temporary novice regarding the cultural aspect of the topic. It is obvious that due to insufficient cultural knowledge the teacher is unable to continue this discussion or expand the information to make it relevant to the whole class as an immediate learning opportunity. In this context, the teacher has no choice but to complete the turn and move on, as indicated by the discourse marker ok↓ pronounced emphatically and loudly.

Novice as a Temporary Expert
Novice teachers can become expert when they are able to address students' needs, consider both macro- and micro-contexts, utilise their subject knowledge and display confidence in teaching. The confidence in what students know, what they are (not) interested in, what experience the teacher can bring to teaching and how much the teacher knows will enable the teacher to be flexible – one criterion of expertise. For example, in Extract 5.19, the novice teacher demonstrates her flexibility in teaching and displays her expertise in bringing together the macro-context, the students, technology and her personal experience. In this extract, the teacher is reflecting on a lesson she created based on the outcome of the last lesson.

Extract 5.19

```
1   I    how did you come up with this topic? (.)
2   T    um (.) this topic (.) is when I was teaching last week
3        I realize that students don't know much about Beijing
4        Olympic games (.) you know (.) it was a big event (.)
5        and students know little about it (0.3) so:: when I told
6        them I was a volunteer for the game (.)
7        £I could tell£ they want to know more=
8   I    =I bet they would (.) so this is why this lesson?=
9   T    =yes (.) I think the children should know something
10       about it an-(.) I created this topic (.) this lesson
11       Beijing Olympic games today (.)
12  I    so you created this lesson? (0.3)
13  I    yeah (.) I used a personal video and pictures (.)
14       official website um and I also wrote some stories=
15  I    =that's a good idea=
    T    =yes (.) students really enjoyed the lesson
```

This extract shows the teacher's awareness of student knowledge. Specifically, she realises that the students do not know much about the Beijing Olympic Games despite the fact that it was the biggest sporting event China ever held. We can see her expertise displayed in two ways: first, she noticed the lack of knowledge about the Beijing Olympic Games and the desire to know about it from the students (lines 3–6); second, her own insider knowledge and experience makes her confident in creating this lesson (lines 6, 13–14). The flexibility she demonstrates here in terms of lesson content (topic) and materials relies on her own experience, confidence and knowledge about the topic.

There is also evidence that novice teachers demonstrate high levels of CIC and ability in encouraging student participation and contribution, using different interactional strategies. In Extract 5.20, the teacher is eliciting information from the students about the text they have read.

Extract 5.20 (7.47_8.51)

```
1   T    now can you tell me what the general idea of this text?
2        ((gesture to invite a student))(.)
3   S1   en um some problem that the computers can cause=
4   T    =some problems that computers can cause (.) ok (.) any
5        example? (1.3)like what problems?
6   S1   (0.5) uh maybe if you can't use it well er it will hurt
7        us (0.3)is not very good for us=
8   T    =hmmmm (.) sounds reasonable (.) you mean if computers
9        are not used well (.) they will cause problems to us?=
10  S1   =yes=
```

```
11  T   =so what do you mean by not used well then?=
12  S1  =if computers are used by bad people (.) they can steal
13      people's money and cause problems (0.3)
14  T   right (.) computers could be used for crimes
15      ((turning to another student)) you want to say something?
16  S2  I think this passage um tell us um some problems computer
17      makes an- um so also computers give us good things about
18      (0.3) it also make er also make us um um problems
19      like physical problems (.)eye (.) eyesight as well=
20  T   =ok it might cause bad eyesight
```

This extract starts with a teacher's invitation to a student for a contribution. The student makes his first attempt (line 3), followed by the teacher' repetition as a confirmation of his contribution and a request for an exemplification or elaboration (line 5). The student tries to elaborate (lines 6–7), which the teacher follows up with a confirmation request (lines 8–9). This time the teacher reformulates the student's contribution to make the meaning clearer. The student confirms the teacher's request, and the teacher follows up with a further clarification request on the meaning of not used well, and this time the student gives an example (lines 12–13). This exchange with the student finishes with the teacher's summary of the student's point. At this point, the teacher also notices that a second student is bidding to speak and the teacher then makes the invite (line 15). The second student makes a rather long turn and provides an example of the harm that computers might bring to users (lines 16–19). The teacher then confirms this contribution and moves on. Clearly, the teacher takes this comprehension question as an immediate participation opportunity to allow students to express their opinions. She uses various interactional strategies to maximise opportunities for students to participate and to enable the clarity of their contributions. This teacher demonstrates high interactional competence by using limited embedded correction (line 4), an elaboration request (lines 4–5), repetition of a student's contribution as positive feedback (line 4), a clarification request (line 11), reformulation (lines 8–9, 20) and confirmation (line 8), summarising a student's contributions (line 14), and positive feedback (lines 4 and14).

SUMMARY

This chapter discusses teacher expertise by comparing novice and expert teachers, with a particular focus on conceptions of knowledge, interactional competence and classroom management. Expert teachers' conceptions of subject knowledge are more integrated, whereas novice teachers' knowledge remains more isolated and separate. In terms of pedagogical knowledge, expert teachers are more flexible and skilful in integrating a focus on form with a focus on meaning, whereas novice teachers typically display a lack of confidence and flexibility, and concerns in establishing authority. Conceptions of contextual knowledge is another area in which expert teachers differ from novice ones. Expert teachers are able to differentiate long-term goals from short-term goals, and to address students' difficulties, whereas novice teachers focus more on following school norms and culture, and on 'fitting in'. With regard to CIC, expert teachers maintain high levels of competence in interactional work to allow and develop learning opportunities in class, while novice teachers follow rigid IRF patterns and tend to bypass or close down learning opportunities. In particular, we can see from the data that expert teachers are able to use various interactional strategies, such as confirmation checks, clarification requests, paraphrasing, elaboration, and so on, to push and shape learners' contributions. Novice teachers tend either to accept the learners' contributions without further development or provide direct repair. In terms of classroom management, there is strong evidence that expert teachers focus on learners' reactions in teaching and on teaching learners how to learn, similar to developing learning strategy and metacognition, whereas novice teachers focus on classroom behaviour issues and tend to focus on their own teaching behaviours.

From the data and discussion presented in this chapter, it is apparent that expertise is distributed and multiple. In fact, expert teachers temporarily can become novice teachers, especially in a changing context or due to insufficient knowledge. By the same token, novice teachers may attain a level of expertise in various areas to become a 'novice expert'. One key message from this chapter is that expertise is displayed in interaction – a useful means of accessing expertise and characterising its multiple manifestations and qualities.

6

INTERACTIVE DECISION-MAKING AND TEACHER COGNITION

INTRODUCTION

The metaphor of teacher-as-decision-maker (Nunan 1992) reflects how teachers conceptualise their work and the kind of decision-making underpinning teaching (Tsang 2004). Lessons are dynamic, unpredictable and interactive in nature, and are, therefore, characterised by constant change. Teachers, as active decision-makers, are constantly making choices to maintain students' interest and engagement (Richards 1998a). Perhaps it is true to say that a teacher who follows the planned lesson rigidly or ignores the interactional dynamic of the development of a lesson is less likely to address learners' needs. Research has specifically discussed teachers' decision-making and thinking at different phases, such as pre-active, interactive and post-active phases (see Chapter 1). Much research has been done to elaborate what teachers think and do in both pre-active and post-active phases, in particular in relation to how teachers interpret materials and the curriculum, plan a lesson and design a specific task. The kind of decisions are broadly affected by many factors, such as what peer teachers do, learners' characteristics and needs, socio-cultural educational beliefs about teaching and learning, and available resources and time. However, teachers also make interactive or 'online' decisions 'in the moment-by-moment progression of a lesson and in the context of competing pressures such as time, the attention span of the learners, curricular demands, exam pressures and so on.' (Walsh 2006: 48; see also Tsui 2005). Such interactive decision-making constitutes a major part of teachers' classroom behaviour (Li 2013). Walsh (2006) suggests that teachers vary in their ability to create learning opportunities and make good interactive decisions. Making good interactive decisions requires teachers to have the ability to observe the class to find alternatives and select the best one to fit the specific immediate teaching context and address the pedagogical goal of that moment; therefore, it is an important consideration of teachers' classroom practice (Li 2013: 176).

This chapter focuses on critical moments in teaching and explores why and how teachers make their interactive decisions (Tsui 2003), and how the decision-making of a moment displays deeply rooted beliefs and conceptions, by looking at classroom data and self-reflection. In essence, this chapter addresses the questions of what interactive decisions teachers make and how they make these decisions. By asking teachers to identify and talk about those unanticipated decisions, by analysing the features of classroom discourse, this chapter goes some way to uncovering the nature of pedagogical decision-making.

INTERACTIVE DECISION-MAKING

Teachers' decision-making is a complex phenomenon, a cognitive, affective and pedagogical process. Understanding interactive decisions has two aspects. First, teaching is about making 'informed choices' (Stevick 1982: 2), a dynamic decision-making process in which teachers consider both macro-context about the curriculum, teaching and learning, teachers' roles, content or methodology, and micro-context concerning classroom dynamics and what learners bring to the process of teaching in every lesson (Li 2013). Second, decision-making is a basic teaching skill, which is involved in every aspect of a teacher's professional life.

Teachers may plan their lessons but do not necessarily follow the plan strictly in their interactions with students. Whenever teachers encounter a complex situation, they make an interactive or 'online' decision. Research suggests that when teachers make interactive decisions, they tend to fine-tune the original plan rather than making substantial changes (Joyce 1978–9) because the purpose of the interactive decision is to maintain a smooth flow of classroom activity (Duffy 1982; Shavelson 1983). Therefore, assumptions have been made that one of the reasons for interactive decision-making is to simplify the complexity of the task or activity in situ (e.g. Shavelson 1983). In the literature, two related lines of research have addressed questions of what cues inform teachers' interactive decisions: content of teachers' interactive thoughts, and antecedents of teachers' interactive decisions (Borko and Shavelson 1990). Related to the latter aspect of the research, McMahon (1995) concluded that expert teachers' interactive decision-making had antecedents, and the majority of these were related to the anticipated problems by the teacher.

The empirical research on interactive decisions so far lies in two major areas: research providing context-specific descriptions of teachers' interactive teaching through process-tracing procedure (Johnson 1992b; Bailey 1996), and research investigating factors influencing teachers' interactive decisions, and investigating the relationship between teachers' interactive thoughts and decisions, teachers' behaviour, and student outcomes (Clark and Peterson 1986). The results from this research shed lights on the nature of the interactive decision and its related factors. However, little is known about the kind of decision-making process that a teacher engages in to simplify the task or maintain the smooth flow of the activity. Various questions have been asked in relation to teachers' interactive decisions, such as:

> To what extent can teachers identify alternative acts? Can they estimate accurately the probability that each state of nature characterizes the learner? Can they estimate the probable outcomes of a particular teaching act under a particular state of nature? (Shavelson 1976: 386)

> How does a teacher define a teaching situation, and how does the teacher's definition of the situation affect his or her behavior? (Clark 1980: 42)

Like any decisions which a person makes, interactive decision-making is a complex process in which teachers utilise their perceived and believed appropriateness, relevance, importance and effectiveness in achieving their pedagogical goals. What makes interactive decision-making complex is that teachers need to make a decision in a very short period of time in accordance with their pedagogical objectives of the moment. Gaining insights into issues like this is thus critical in developing effective pedagogy, in understanding language teaching and learning, and in developing language teachers. There are different ways to tap into the 'why' and 'how' of teachers' interactive decisions. One useful way to do this is to use a technique called stimulated recall, where teachers watch a video-recording of their teaching and discuss it with a peer or colleague.

In an early study, Marland (1977, cited in Clark 1980) used an open-ended approach to stimulated recall to research teachers' decision-making. In that study, the teachers controlled the video-tape recorder and were asked to stop the tape where they wished and to report on their 'thoughts, feelings, moment-to-moment reactions, conscious choices, alternatives considered and reasons for choices' (Clark 1980: 44). From their comments, it was then possible to draw themes from the teachers' account to see how and why teachers make a particular decision. However, data treated in this way might not reveal the complete story of the decision-making that the teacher makes. Woods (1996: 49) claims that the central core of understanding teachers' decision-making is what we observe in the classroom: decisions being carried out as classroom actions and events. He further argues that *what* knowledge is activated and *how* it is used by teachers in making decisions about their day-to-day and moment-to-moment activities is crucial to our understanding of what teaching is (ibid.: 68). Thus, in considering interactive decision-making and its dynamic, unpredictable and interactive nature, I use the combination of classroom interaction data and the video-based reflections as a way to gain insights into the issue.

UNPACKING INTERACTIVE DECISIONS

Identifying interactive decisions, however, is not an easy task. In general, they can be accessed through the detailed scrutiny of classroom interaction, where the natural and smooth flow of the interaction is interrupted or where a swift topic change takes place. Interactive decisions can also be accessed through video-based reflections from the teacher. Although the majority of interactive decisions are made as a result of unexpected classroom events, there also exist other reasons why interactive decisions are made. In the complete dataset of pre-service teachers and in-service teachers, many interactive decisions were identified and it is apparent that teachers make interactive decisions when: (1) they receive unexpected contributions from learners, including contributions solicited by teachers and learner initiations; (2) they underestimate or overrate the difficulty level of the task; (3) there are immediate relevant learning opportunities that the teacher would like to utilise; and (4) the teachers claim insufficient knowledge. Each of these is now further explored through analysed transcripts of data.

UNEXPECTED LEARNER CONTRIBUTIONS

Teachers are not only expected to teach what they have planned, they are required to make constant interactive decisions in light of the constantly changing nature of classroom dynamics and in view of what learners bring to the classroom. If each learner contribution is regarded as a potential learning opportunity, we need to closely look at how teachers manage these learning opportunities to create space for learning (Walsh and Li 2013). In terms of what is meant by an *unexpected* contribution, the literature suggests different definitions. Expected answers thus can range from a sole correct answer to pedagogically relevant ones although not envisioned by the teacher (Fagan 2012). There are four types of unexpected contributions identified in the present dataset:

- unexpected and dispreferred contributions
- contributions which are outside the pedagogical focus of the lesson
- challenges from learners
- students' display of target knowledge

Unexpected and dispreferred contributions

Teachers use questions to elicit information from students to address their pedagogical goals (e.g. raising students' interest, eliciting the topic). In most cases, teachers try to get students to display their knowledge and understanding and have expected answers in mind. However, learners' contributions might not be exactly what the teacher expects and may contain incorrect information. The following extract illustrates an unexpected answer from a student which was considered by the teacher to be incorrect.

Extract 6.1

```
1    Liu   ((showing a picture of night with stars in sky)) ok on
2          summer nights (.) looking at the sky (.) what can you
3          see (0.8)
4    SS    stars/stars=
5    Liu   =stars (.) shining stars glittering stars (('glittering
6          stars' appearing on the slide)) and also what else?=
7    S1    =[moon =
8    S2     [sun
9    Liu   =((pointing to the slide)) ok stars glittering [stars
10   S1                                                   [moon
11   Liu   ((showing moon)) ok moon=
12   S3    =[UFO=
13   S2     [sun
14   Liu   =£UFO£ (.) have you ever seen UFO? (.) ok so an- now
15         look at the changing moon (( pointing to the screen))
16         very beautiful moon ok(.) look at the moon can you maybe
17         think fact (0.3) and fantasy(0.4)
18   SS    yeah/yeah/yes=
```

In this extract, Liu provides a picture of a summer night on the screen with glittering stars in the sky, eliciting a response (lines 1–3), to which students provide in unison (line 4). Liu acknowledges receipt of the information by echoing the students' responses (line 5). Repeating the students' contributions also serves as confirmation here. Liu initiates another question (line 6) to further develop the topic: what else can you see on summer nights, which generates two immediate responses from two individual students (lines 7 and 8). Liu refers to the slide to repeat his elaboration of the students' contribution while the first student also repeats her answer, overlapping Liu's turn (line 10). Liu acknowledges the student's information and from Liu's reaction of showing slides, it is obvious 'moon' is an expected answer. Liu's receipt of the information is followed by a latched turn from the second and the third student, each providing a second pair part to Liu's question in line 6, although the second student is repeating his earlier attempt. Here both contributions are considered as unexpected and perhaps incorrect and Liu's orientation to both contributions as unexpected is illustrated in two ways. First, there is a lack of feedback on or acknowledgment of student 2's turn as Liu glosses over student 2's two attempts (lines 8 and 13), signalling a dispreferred response to the turn of student 2. Glossing over learner contributions is referred to as a strategy taken by the teacher when unexpected learner contributions arise in either teacher- or learner-initiated sequences of talk (Fagan 2012). Second, Liu echoes student 3's turn with a smiley voice and a hurriedly asked counter-question, which conveys a negative assertion (have you ever seen UFO?). The counter-question (CQ) strategy (Markee, 1995, 2004) is used here to regain control of the classroom agenda and move the lesson forward (lines 14–17).

Glossing over unexpected learner contributions also happens when receiving acceptable responses that do not match what is anticipated (Fagan2012) or receiving inappropriate/incorrect responses. In the latter case, the teacher signals that the responses are problematic but does not specify the issue. Other strategies might be used to deal with the unexpected response, and in the following extract Jane illustrates different ways of responding to an unexpected and incorrect response from a student. This extract spans three minutes, over sixty lines, which will be discussed as Extracts 6.2a and 6.2b.

Extract 6.2a (13.34_14.53)

```
1    J    so can you give me something about the situation n↑ow
2         (0.8) in US↓A (.) in US↓A (.) how about the situations
3         of black peoples (.) do you know something about (.)
4         them ↓it
5         (2.8)
6    T    ((Ted raises his hand))
7    J    ↓ok=
8    T    =I think the change is not is not very (.) very big
9         because I think=
10   J    =not very ↓big (.) o↑k=
11   T    =I think the black people are also face discrimination
```

```
12          (.) discrimination °now° =
13     J    =mmmh (.)↑ok (.) ok mmmmh (.)
14     T    although the American government have already solve the
15          problem (.) but it didn't [come true
16     J                               [hhh (.) it didn't come ↑true
17          >ok↓<=
18     T    =>in my opinion< I think um hmm (1.0)the world is
19          peaceful (0.8) the world is a big family (0.3) I hope
20          our world is peaceful and [healthy >and< our human being
21     J                              [okay:
22     T    is much better (.) thank you=
23     J    =ok thank you very much (.) thank you (.) yes (.) we
24          all all of us just hope that we can live at peace they
25          can live in peace (.) an-just now she men- he mentioned
26          that er it didn't change a lot (.) didn't change a lot
27          (.) but do you think that the black man can receive
28          education n↓ow in Ameri↑can? (.) can receive any
29          education now? (2.9) do you think (.) do you know that.
30          black black people in America can receive any education
```

In this class, the teacher has presented a situation in which students are invited to compare the lives of black people living in America in the past and today. After Jane's multi-turned solicitation attempts to the whole class (1–5), in which she notices Ted raising his hand (line 6), she selects him for the next turn in the sequence. 'Ok' here is used to indicate a shared understanding between Jane and Ted that the next turn is allocated to Ted (line 7). Ted takes the turn and produces a second pair part (lines 8–9). This response is not anticipated by Jane and indeed is a surprise to her, which is evidenced by the interruption of Ted's turn in line 10. At this point, Jane echoes Ted's turn and the falling pitch suggests surprise but she still accepts what Ted offered, noting 'ok' with a rising pitch to indicate mild acceptance. Providing a vague acceptance token here could be considered as one way of glossing over the learner's contribution. Then Ted takes over the turn and carries on with his contribution (lines 11–12) and again Jane interrupts Ted's turn and does 'glossing over' by providing a hesitation marker together with an acknowledgement token (=mmmh (.) ↑ok (.) ok mmmmh). Ted carries on controlling the floor in lines 14–15. Overall, Jane is expressing her uncertainty about Ted's contribution and clearly Ted's turn is unexpected. This time Jane overlaps the last part of Ted's turn in line 16. Jane provides a hesitation marker followed by an echo of Ted's contribution with a rising tone, indicating uncertainty, then a hurriedly spoken acknowledgement token 'ok' in line 17 to close the exchange. However, Ted increases the speed of his talking to hold the floor to carry on his turn (lines 18–22), during which time Jane attempts to close down the space for Ted by using the turn closure token 'okay' (line 21).

At this point, it is clear that Ted has produced possibly relevant but unexpected and incorrect turns, which Jane is trying to close by interrupting, overlapping and closing the turn. Again, Jane is trying (unsuccessfully) to gloss over Ted's contribution on this occasion as she sees it as incorrect. In her feedback, Jane is trying to deal with the unexpected contribution. In lines 23–30, Jane first acknowledges and appreciates Ted's participation, and then agrees to his last point that human beings should live in peace (lines 23–5). Then Jane recaps the main point of what Ted said in lines 25–6 and challenges his view by taking education as an example to pose a question as a counter-argument for the whole class to respond to (27–30). The exchange carries on (6.2b) and Jane uses interactional strategies to deal with the unexpected contribution from Ted and to make a transition.

Extract 6.2b (continues from 6.2a) (14.53_16.41)

```
31        (3.0) Carol?
32   C    ((Carol is standing up))
33   J    ((to Carol)) do you think that black people in America
34        now can receive any education?=
35   C    =yes=
36   J    =yes (.) ok (.) so do you think that it is change a
37        little? (.)than before=
38   C    =yeah=
39   J    =[yes
40   C     [it change a lot=
41   J    =it change a lot (.) oh (.) what kind of work do you
42        know about changes?
43   C    (1.5) mmmh (0.5) the right (1.2)
44   J    human rights
45   C    >oh yeah< um and- (0.5)again lot of right than before=
46   J    =yeah (.) lot of rights than before=
47   C    =um [such as they=
48   J        [such as?
49   C    =they get on the bus an- they (0.4)only can in the front
50        part (.) and they (3.7) I just (0.3) that's all=
51   J    =that's all (.) ok thank you (.) thank you (.) she said
52        that it change a lot cause they can get on the bus an-
53        any seat they can take (.) any seat they can take but (.)
54        er in before that the black people only can sit (.)in
55        the limited seats that they are just separated from the
56        white people (0.4) from white people (.)>ok< ((operating
57        the computer to move to the next slide)) so I think that
58        the situation in America has improved (.) and the black
59        people now have same rights as white people (2.2) has
60        the same right as white people (1.2) ok (.) let's go on
```

After a longish pause (line 31), Jane nominates Carol to respond, putting Carol on a 'platform format' (Goffman 1983), and rephrases her question to Carol (lines 33–4). Carol provides an immediate preferred response (line 35), which Jane accepts and then follows up with a further question, this time directly challenging Ted's opinion that 'it didn't change much' (lines 36-7). Again, Carol provides a preferred second pair part, confirming it has changed (line 38), which Jane again receives with a positive assessment (line 39). This is overlapping with Carol's next turn in which Carol offers her view that it has changed a lot (line 40). In line 41, Jane echoes Carol's turn as a preferred agreement and then initiates a new question, seeking for further elaboration from Carol (lines 41-2). The longish gap here indicates that Carol perhaps is unwilling to participate and is put on the spot for a 'forced platform performance' (Rampton 2006: 7). Then after a hesitation marker and a brief pause, Carol attempts a relevant answer, this time very brief (line 43). This is followed by another longish pause, indicating again the effect of 'forced platform performance' on Carol, who perhaps finds it difficult to participate further. Jane then reformulates Carol's contribution making it explicit as 'human rights' (line 44), which serves as a springboard for Carol, who takes over the cue, agreeing, and emphasising that 'lot of rights than before'. Jane confirms Carol's idea and echoes Carol's turn to perhaps 'oil the wheel' to assist the flow of Carol's turn (line 46).

In lines 47 and 48, Carol and Jane are doing interactional work together to get Carol to complete her turn. Carol clearly is having problems in articulating the idea and produces a fragmented and unfinished turn in lines 49 and 50. Note that Carol displays her difficulty also in having a long pause and hurriedly finished turn (line 50). Rather than helping Carol further to elaborate the idea, Jane now elaborates Carol's idea and moves on the lesson (lines 51-60). In this rather long teacher turn, Jane first echoes Carol's contribution of closing the turn and appreciates her contribution. Then Jane develops Carol's fragmented talk to elaborate on the idea on behalf of Carol (lines 51-6). Jane now is ready to move on the lesson, as evidence by her operating the computer, and before she concludes this long exchange (line 60) she provides a summary of what she thinks about the situation of black people in America now (lines 57-60).

In this rather long exchange, Jane encounters an unexpected and incorrect response from a student and she uses different practices to deal with this. First of all, she uses different interactional strategies to gloss over Ted's contribution, including interrupting, overlapping and closing the turn. Having failed in these attempts, Jane challenges Ted's opinion indirectly by taking education as an example and involving another student. Although the second student, Carol, provides a very limited and fragmented contribution, Jane successfully uses the point made by Carol to disagree with Ted. Finally, Jane explicitly expresses her opinion – which is the opposite of Ted's contribution. Although Jane didn't directly point out the inaccuracy of Ted's contribution, she uses various interactional resources to display her assessment. So in this case, when glossing over a learner's contribution fails, Jane also utilises other methods, such as challenging a learner's contribution by using counter-example, and by inviting contributions from other students, and by directly offering the relevant contribution.

When students produce a turn which is relevant, but in some way unexpected or unacceptable, teachers must deal with this contribution by making an appropriate online decision. This is illustrated in Extract 6.3 below when the teacher, Zhou, tries different ways to have the student produce the expected answer. In the extract, Zhou asks the whole class to retell the story 'The Necklace' by saying one sentence each.

Extract 6.3 (30.32_32.18)

```
1   Zh  ((hand gesture to nominate a student))
2   J   (5.0)Jeanne said that he had (.) she had sold the
3       necklace=
4   Zh  =she::she had [sold what what does sold ((confused look))=
5   S                 [sold?
6   J   =(sold) ((in Chinese))
7   Zh  (3.0) ((hand gesture to sit down)) £she had sold£ the
8       necklace (.) go on ((hand gesture to nominate another
9       Student))
10  SS  ((16.0 students all saying different things))
11  S1  [the story is finished (.)
12  S2  [the necklace was £sold£
13  Zh  ((walking back to John))now from um from ((pointing to
14      the student before John)) he doesn't mean that well
15      he means Jeanne Jeanne sorry Mathedile told her the
16      story (1.0) go on
17      <Mathilde told her told Jeanne her story>
18      ((hand gesture inviting John))
19  J   told her story?=
20  Zh  =yes Mathilde=
21  J   =Math↓ilde (.)
22  Zh  Mathilde ((nodding head))
23  J   um the Jeanne=
24  T   =£no the Jeanne£=
25  SS  ((students laughing))
26  J   Jeanne um told Mathilde um (3.0) the necklace didn't
27      wasn't um real (.)
28  Zh  ((eyebrows are raised))
29      so it's over
30      [((the teacher and students laughs))
31  S3  [the story is over?
32  Zh  he just wanted to <end the story> quickly
33      um (.) I don't think so (0.8) sit down (.) think think
34      about it first (.) go on ((hand gesture inviting a
35      different student)) Mathilde is telling Jeanne the
36      story
```

Just before this extract, one student has pointed out in his turn that Mathilde is telling Jeanne the story. Zhou accepts this and nominates a different student to carry on the story (line 1). This nomination puts the student, John, on a 'forced platform performance' (Rampton 2006: 7) as the student seems reluctant to participate. The unwillingness is displayed through hesitation devices in the form of a rather long gap before his turn (line 2) and a false start: Jeanne said that he had. The false start and unwillingness to participate could be due to the fact that the student did not follow the teacher's instruction as he is quite unsure about the task. Zhou, in particular, explains the activity at a slow speed (line 17) and John seeks confirmation from the teacher (lines 19 and 21). When John produces another false start (line 23), Zhou has to provide direct corrective feedback (line 24).

Now back to the beginning of the extract: expected to produce a relevant turn to carry on the story, John makes his first attempt after a five-second-long pause (lines 2 and 3). Receiving this response, Zhou displays his confusion in his feedback and body language (line 4). In the meantime, confusion is expressed from a different student (line 5). Clearly, John's contribution is not acceptable to both the teacher and the student. John interprets their response as a clarification request and he repeats the word 'sold', this time in his first language (L1), to clarify what he means (line 6). The long pause (3.0 seconds) before Zhou's turn indicates that this answer is not acceptable, but Zhou is happy to let this unexpected and unacceptable answer go and allow other students to continue the story. Again, the unacceptance is displayed in Zhou's echo of John's contribution – he said it with a laugh (line 7), indicating less seriousness.

Then Zhou indicates for the student to sit down and nominates a different student to carry on the story (lines 8 and 9). Following this is a sixteen-second discussion among students before two students take turns simultaneously (lines 10 and 11). Both students' responses indicate that it is impossible to carry on the story and hence act as stimulus for Zhou to rethink his earlier decision to invite a different student to continue the story. At this point, Zhou walks back to John and explains to John what the student before him meant (lines 13–16). It is clear that Zhou is ready to ask John to make a second attempt to produce a relevant and acceptable turn so that the activity can carry on (line 16). Here, we can see that Zhou does interactive work to help John to produce the relevant turn. First, Zhou clarifies the contribution from the student before John (lines 14–16). Second, Zhou reformulates the contribution from the student before John to make sure that John understands what he is supposed to follow (line 17). In lines 19–22, John and Zhou do interactive work to clarify the storyline and John makes his second attempt again with a false start (line 23); this time Zhou provides corrective feedback in a friendly and joking way (line 24). John makes the third attempt (lines 26–7), again an unacceptable turn. The frowned eyebrows indicate a surprise (Ekman 1979) and unacceptance. In line 29, Zhou provides feedback on John's contribution to indicate that this is not what they expect although the contribution is relevant, as indicated by the laugh from both students and the teacher (line 30) and a surprise from another student (line 31). To deal with this unacceptable turn, Zhou first of all jokes about it to ease the tension in class, and perhaps to reduce the embarrassment for John (line 32), and then disagrees with John (line 33), provides advice (lines 33–4) and invites a different student to make another attempt (line 35).

In this extract, it is clear that it is not only John's unacceptable answer but also the reaction from the other students to John's unacceptable answer that influences Zhou's online decision-making. It is clear that in this extract, carrying on the activity and making it happen smoothly is important for the teacher. In other words, following his plan is critical to ensure the smooth flow of the lesson.

Outside the pedagogical focus of the lesson

Teachers also make interactive decisions in situations where a contribution from a student is irrelevant and outside the pedagogical focus of the lesson. Extract 6.4 illustrates a situation when a perceived irrelevant learner turn, which is outside the pedagogical focus of the lesson, occurs. Extract 6.4 is a continuation of Extract 6.1.

Extract 6.4

```
19   Liu   =what fantasies have you thought? (0.5) Zhang=
20   Z     =um Chang'e and her little rabbit (.)
21         ((students laughing))
22   Liu   chang'e and her rabbit (0.2) so there are Chinese
23         fantasies right? the moon (.) relating to the moon right?=
24   Z     =yes=
25   S4    =is that why [we eat mooncakes? ((tilts head to Liu))
26   SS                 [laughing
27   Liu   (0.3) ok↓ay ((eye gaze with student 4 and hands moving
28         up and down)) (0.3)
29         ((looking at the whole class)) now back to the topic (.)
30         fact and fantasy (0.2) anyone knows the difference of
31         fact and fantasy? (0.4)
```

Liu continues to progress the lesson by eliciting thoughts from students on fantasies about the moon (line 19). After a brief pause, Liu nominates a student, putting Zhang (the student) on a 'platform format' (Goffman 1983). Zhang immediately produces a relevant second pair part, a topic of a Chinese folk story about a beautiful woman and her rabbits living on the moon. This turn generates interest among students as evidenced by laughing. Here, laughing also is an indicator of acknowledging the receipt of the information. Liu repeats Zhang's contribution as a receipt of information and, after a brief pause, follows up with a confirmation request (lines 22 and 23). Zhang confirms (line 24). However, another student initiates a new turn here (line 25), possibly as a follow-up to what is being discussed. The student asks a question which is perceived as an unexpected learner contribution and out of pedagogical focus. Liu's orientation to student 4's turn as unexpected and out of pedagogical focus is displayed in the following ways. First, there is a brief gap prior to Liu's turn, signalling a dispreferred response to the turn of student 4 (Fagan 2012). Additionally, Liu uses a discourse marker 'okay', which is typically used at the end of a sequence (Schegloff and Sacks 1973; Beach 1993) to indicate that the topic is finished and the sequence is closed. Further, there is a gesture from Liu to indicate to the student to abandon the topic (lines 27–8). Then there is a slight gap of 0.3 seconds before Liu re-engages with the whole class. This brief pause again indicates that the discussion is closed. That his gaze moves away from student 4 to the whole class indicates that student 4's turn (question) is now dealt with and he is ready to move on with the lesson. The use of giving instructions here to get back to the topic is also an indicator of the dispreferred learner-initiation, which is perceived as off-topic and outside the pedagogical focus at that point in time.

Again, in dealing with this unexpected learner-initiation, Liu once more uses the strategy of glossing over the learner's turn by not addressing the learner's question. Bypassing a student's topic initiation was also reported in the literature as a strategy for a teacher to keep focused on the pedagogical goal and lesson plan (e.g. He, 2004).

Challenges from students

Unexpected student contributions also include challenges from students, although this is not widely observed because in a classroom, where roles are asymmetrical, both students and the teacher have their defined roles, with power normally residing with the teacher. This is especially so in an EFL classroom because students' language proficiency is limited. However, there are occasions when students pose questions which are interpreted as challenges by the teacher. In a situation in which the teacher's authority and power are challenged, the teacher uses different ways to tackle the unexpected event, including glossing it over, using a counter-question, assuming the role of authority and swiftly changing the topic. In Extract 6.5, Amy demonstrates the use of combined strategies in dealing with an unexpected initiation and challenge from a learner.

Extract 6.5

```
1   A      so do you understand what fantasy is now?=
2   SS     =yes (in unison) /°no° (.)
3   A      okay (.) [now let's
4   Joe    [is vampire fantasy or fact?
5   A      [(0.7) ↓vam↑pire (.) ((Amy's eyebrows are raised))
6   SS     [((laughing))
7   Joe    ((nodding his head))
8   A      okay (.) vampire (0.3)
9          ((turn to the class)) be quiet (.)
10         nothing to laugh about ok? (.) just a question
11         it's not polite to laugh when someone asks a question
12         (0.3) how do you feel when you ask a question and we
13         laugh (0.2) is it nice? (0.3) no (.) so don't
14         laugh (.) it shows no respect (.)
15         um so fantasy is what? (.)
16         now who can tell me the definition of fantasy (1.7)
17         we discussed just now (0.8)
18  S      °something not real°=
19  A      =yes something not real but based on fact
20         ((turning to Joe))
21         so is vampire fantasy or fact?
22  Joe    ((looking at the student sitting next to him)) (11.0)
```

23		°I don't know°
24	A	hm: you don't know (.) .hhh okay

In Extract 6.5, a challenge from a student, Joe, is observed in line 4. Amy's orientation to Joe's unexpected challenge can be interpreted in four ways. First, Amy checks students' understanding of the difference between fact and fantasy (line 1) and after receiving a preferred agreement from students (line 2), Amy moves the lesson forward (line 3). The use of the discourse marker 'okay' here indicates the closure of the topic (line 3). After a brief pause, Amy initiates a new turn (line 3) which Joe interrupts, as evidenced by the overlapping talk (line 4). Joe's interruption is a learner-initiated turn after Amy tries to move on, which makes this initiation an unexpected turn (Bilmes 1997). Second, there is a slight gap before Amy's response (line 5), again signalling an unexpected turn from Joe. Third, Amy's body language displays her surprise at Joe's turn (line 5) as the use of eyebrows is commonly used to illustrate surprise at the immediate prior turn (Ekman 1979). Finally, Amy's falling and rising tone displays her surprise when she echoes the key word 'vampire' from Joe's question (line 5), which Joe interprets as a confirmation request and provides an affirmative response by using his body language (line 7). Amy's surprise at Joe's turn is also echoed by the reaction of the laugh from the class (line 6).

Now let's turn to the strategies Amy uses to deal with this unexpected challenge. In line 8, Amy first acknowledges Joe's confirmation and then, after a brief pause, she turns to the class to tell them to be quiet (line 9), which can be interpreted as a temporary focus shift. Amy's focus is shifted from Joe's challenge to the classroom behaviour problem, which seems to be more important for her to deal with at that moment as she spends quite a bit of time lecturing students on their behaviour (lines 9–14). This behaviour perhaps is perceived as intolerant but it is obvious that the swift topic shift is the outcome of receiving an unexpected challenge from Joe. Then Amy recollects the question posed by Joe and addresses it indirectly. First, Amy asks a further question on the definition of 'fantasy' and seeks a volunteer to provide the definition (line 16). After a rather long pause, which indicates the dispreferred response from students, Amy then reminds the students that they had just discussed the meaning of 'fantasy', to hint for a preferred response from memory from the students (line 17). After a slight gap, again signalling lack of participation, a student delivers a desired second pair part in a low voice (line 18). A low voice is often used to illustrate uncertainty and in this case it shows that perhaps the students are not sure about the meaning of fantasy, despite their display of affirmation earlier (line 2). In line 19, Amy confirms the student's turn and then elaborates the idea. In line 20, Amy turns to Joe and throws the question back to him (line 21). At this point, Amy has been doing interactional work with the class to recall the meaning of 'fantasy' in order to enable the class (and Joe) to make a judgement on whether a vampire is fantasy or fact. However, Joe displays non-understanding (line 22), which is a dispreferred turn. Here, the body language of turning to his classmate suggests an attempt to avoid the question and perhaps also suggests help-seeking. Then after a long pause (line 22), without receiving any help, Joe delivers a definite dispreferred turn to claim insufficient knowledge (Koshik 2002) (line 23). Again the low voice is used to indicate his uncertainty. After a slight hesitation marker, Amy accepts the insufficient knowledge claim and then closes the turn by using the discourse marker 'okay'. Leaving the question with the student and accepting a claim of insufficient knowledge in this incident suggests that Joe's question is indeed a challenge for Amy. In dealing with this unexpected challenge, Amy uses different strategies, including switching the topic and giving the question back to the students (or leaving the question unaddressed).

Challenges from students may sometimes be displayed as a question to the teacher, but may be interpreted by the teacher as a challenge. The following extract is one such example.

Extract 6.6

```
1    T    now let's see the first one (.) draw a line to show
2         its frequency (.) then write its Chinese ↑meaning [oh
3    S                                                      [if
4         I can't draw the frequency?
5    T    (0.3) hmmm:::if you can't draw a graph to express the
6         frequency (0.9)you can use a number to indicate that (.)
7         you can use Chinese to explain the differences to the
8         class (.) if you can't explain very well (.) then draw
9         (21.7) (the teacher is checking students' work)
10        draw the difference (.) don't open your book or notes
11        (.) just think (0.7) ↑remember 'what's the difference?'
```

In Extract 6.6, the teacher sets a task for the students and one of them displays difficulty in completing the task (lines 3–4). This challenge is unusual as normally in Chinese classrooms students follow the instruction from the teacher without question. However, in this instance, when the teacher gives instructions to the students to draw a line to show the differences of adverbs for frequency, the student interrupts with a hypothetical question (lines 3–4). This is interpreted by the teacher as a dispreferred and unexpected response from a student, as evidenced by a slight gap before her turn and the hesitation in responding the student's question (line 5). Then the teacher echoes the student's question and after a longish pause, she makes alternative suggestions (lines 6–8). It's interesting to note that after a brief pause, the teacher reiterates her original instruction: draw (line 8), suggesting that she prefers students to use this approach to illustrate the differences between the adverbs. This is further verified by her repeated instruction after a very long pause (line 9) where she explicitly asks students to draw the difference. The teacher then finishes her turn by instructing students not to refer to their book or notes, but just to think and try to remember (lines 10–11). She is also helping students to recall what they've learnt (line 11). When the student poses the question, it would be natural for the teacher to 'permit' the students to choose their way to illustrate the difference. However, the teacher decides to convince students to follow her way. The long teacher turn in this case is rather authoritative (lines 5–11). It is clear from this teacher's interactive decision-making that following the plan is crucial and there is little flexibility for the teacher to consider alternative ways to complete the task, although she proposes several in the first instance. So following the plan to make the lesson flow smoothly is a priority for this teacher and she uses different strategies here to deal with the unexpected challenge from a student, including proposing alternatives, reiterating and emphasising the original task, and using authoritative talk.

Students' display of target knowledge
Although it is common for teachers to consider student knowledge when they plan a lesson, it is difficult for teachers to know how much students already know about the target language. Occasionally, students demonstrate target knowledge at a different level to that anticipated by the teacher, which causes the teacher to adjust his/her approach. Interactive decision are made by a teacher who discovers that the students have a better than anticipated understanding of the target language. The strategies adopted by teachers include checking with students to make sure they really know the taught materials (knowledge) and moving on to the next activity. Extract 6.7 is an example of this kind of interactive decision made by teachers.

Extract 6.7 (TinT18.19_19.02)

```
1    T    stop somebody from doing something
2         ((8.0 writing 'stop sb from doing sth' on the board
3         stop somebody from doing something))
4         ((translation))
5         other similar words? (0.4)
6    S1   keep=
7         =ok keep somebody from doing something ((writing on the
8         board))=
9    S2   =[prevent somebody from doing something
10   S3   [prohibit
11   T    (0.3) [prevent (.) prohibit
12   S1         [°restrain°
13        ((checking her lesson plan))ok (.) you got it all
14        does everyone know? yes? ((gesture for raising hands))
15   SS   ((students raising their hands))
16   T    ok (.) I won't explain these then
17        um now let's look at the next paragraph
```

In Extract 6.7 the teacher is going through a reading with students and highlights key vocabulary and its usage. In dealing with the key vocabulary and phrases, first, she introduces the phrase (line 1), and then writes the phrase on the board (line 2), and then provides a translation (line 4). For this teacher, pointing out the language, repeating it and translating it helps the learners notice the language and thereby facilitates grammar learning. After introducing the phrase, she expands the grammatical rule to other verbs by eliciting information from the students (line 5). Student 1 provides a relevant answer (line 6) and the teacher acknowledges and accepts it by reformulating the student's turn and writing the phrase on the board (lines 7 and 8). Immediately following this, two students' turns overlap with each other, proving another two verbs which follow the same pattern of use as 'stop' (lines 9 and 10). The teacher acknowledges this by echoing (line 11) and the slight pause before her turn indicates that the students' turns are unexpected. Her echo is overlapped by a new turn from the first student, proposing a different relevant response (line 12). At this point, as the teacher checks her lesson plan it is clear that the students have displayed the knowledge that the teacher planned to teach. The discourse marker in line 13 indicates the closure of the activity and the time to make an interactive decision. First, the teacher praises the students for displaying the target knowledge (you got it all), and then she checks with the whole class to make sure that everyone knows (line 14). After receiving confirmation from the students (line 15), the teacher abandons her plan of providing more explanations (line 16) and moves on to the next paragraph. It is clear that, for this teacher, classroom activities are quite flexible and she changes the activity and sequence according to the students' responses.

TASK OR ACTIVITY

The second type of factor contributing to interactive decision-making is the nature of the task or activity. Clearly, the use of a task/activity is the main focus in language classrooms because tasks provide a supportive methodological framework (Willis 1996). Indeed, the role of activity and task is even more important because an authentic and appropriate task/activity could enhance engagement and facilitate participation, thereby contributing to learning. However, selecting an appropriate activity always presents a problem for many EFL teachers. For one thing, it is difficult for language teachers to design a task in which the target language is used for a communicative purpose in order to achieve an outcome. For another, it is more difficult to design an interesting, engaging and appropriate task for learners based on communicative, socio-cultural and cognitive awareness (Clark 1987). Research suggests that activity types correlate to interactive language use in real-world or classroom situations (e.g. Prabhu 1987). This said, researchers also hold different views regarding the most helpful activity in facilitating L2 learning (e.g. Pica and Doughty 1985; Ellis 2003). Various activities have been proposed as effective in facilitating language learning in some aspects, and one of the key influential factors that decide their effectiveness is the students. This is also the reason why teachers find it difficult to foresee how well the planned activity will go in their classroom and how students will react. Thus, the activity itself contributes to changing the plan or making interactive decisions. Extract 6.8 illustrates how a difficult activity contributes to the teacher's decision-making.

Extract 6.8 (19.31_20.59)

```
1   T    have you got the answers?
2   SS   ((2.0 silence, some students shaking head))
```

INTERACTIVE DECISION-MAKING AND TEACHER COGNITION 151

```
3   T   no?(.) ok now (.) maybe we will listen to it again but
4       before that you can share your answers with your
5       partner (.) ((gesture for exchanging)) share what
6       you have already got with your partner
7       ((10.0 students discussing))
8       now first make sure you don't look at the textbook
9       ((57.0 students discussing))
10      ok now let's listen to it again
```

In Extract 6.8 the students are performing a listening comprehension activity. They have already been given a chance to listen to the material three times and now the teacher checks whether students have completed the activity (line 1). A 2.0-second silence (line 2) indicates a dispreferred answer in this case, because the students haven't filled in the gap. The teacher then first checks with the students (line 3) and, after a brief pause, she suggests listening to it again (line 3). Because the students have already listened to the material three times and display difficulty in completing the exercise, the teacher suggests at this point that they share their answers with their peers to reduce the difficulty of the exercise (lines 4–6). It is clear that this strategy is helpful from the students' discussion (line 7). Probably noticing students referring to the textbook, the teacher reminds students that they should not look at the textbook. The peer activity lasts about a minute and the teacher decides that the students need to listen to the material again. In this extract, it is clear that the teacher has to make a decision based on the difficulty of the material.

In the classroom, teachers do not just present materials and lecture to students, they need to engage students to participate and collaborate. The literature suggests various practices teachers might use to engage and motivate students in order to facilitate learning, including using authentic, interesting materials, designing relevant tasks, creating a friendly and relaxing environment, and using technology and multimedia, and so on. Any lack of interest or motivation from students is an obstacle to learning and it is observed that teachers make online decisions to help to engage students, using whatever is available to them. The following extract (6.9) illustrates how the teacher makes an interactive decision to deal with students' boredom.

Extract 6.9

```
1   T   item 27 (.) which one? (17.0)
2       ((noticing several students are falling asleep))
3   T   now I can see you are tired (.) are you tired?=
4   SS  =ye::s=
5   T   =I am tired too (.) £it's Friday afternoon£ (.)
6       maybe it's time to relax a bit (.)
7       do you want to play a game?
8   SS  yes ((with enthusiasm))(.)
9   T   ok now let's play the when where and what game ok?
10      now I need three volunteers (.) ((selecting students))
```

```
11      you when um you where((walking around)) (2.3) an-you
12      what (.) now begin (.)
13  S1  last Sunday=
14  S2  =Julia (.) >teacher you forget who<=
15  T   =sorry £I am too tired£ ((head down))
16  SS  ((laughing))
```

In Extract 6.9, the teacher is performing exercises with students. She checks answers for item 27 and fails to get a response from students, as indicated by a rather long pause (line 1). Then she notices the students' body language, suggesting that they are tired and bored (line 2). At this point, the teacher could continue to demand answers from the students and follow her lesson plan but, instead, she makes an interactive decision in response to the situation. First, she confirms with the students that they are tired (line 3) and after an affirmative response she acknowledges and shows empathy (line 5), joking that it's due to it being Friday afternoon. In dealing with this situation, the teacher makes a suggestion to play a language game (line 7), which the students welcome (line 8). She now moves away from the original task to a game (lines 9–12). It's worth noting that when playing the game a student spots that the teacher forgets one element of it (line 14), for which the teacher apologises then jokes with students again that she is too tired. This extract highlights four important aspects of pedagogical thinking. First, there is a degree of flexibility with this teacher. For her, getting the students engaged is more important than finishing the task. Second, the teacher has sufficient knowledge in motivating and engaging students. Third, the teacher demonstrates her understanding of her role as teacher; i.e. she is not merely an instructor or knowledge provider but a member of the community she is establishing with students. She jokes with the students, shows empathy and admits mistakes. Finally, she accepts the student's criticism and there is no evidence that she is the authoritarian in the classroom. The atmosphere she creates in this classroom seems to be egalitarian, relaxed, honest and friendly.

Potential learning opportunity
Teaching requires improvisation and being able to improvise based on a situation is one key characteristic of expertise. In the data, there is a type of interactive decision-making which arises when teachers believe they should teach to the moment, because such moments are perceived as potential learning opportunities. The following extract highlights how teachers make interactive decisions to follow up a cue from a student in order to maximise student participation and to enhance the learning strategy or metacognitive strategies.

Teachers are expected to manage the delivery of target knowledge to students but also, more importantly, to manage what learners bring to the classroom interactions. Any follow-up to a learner's contribution, to subsequently develop it in the next stage of the lesson, allows dialogic interaction between interlocutors (e.g. Cullen 2002). Extract 6.10 is an example of this, when the teacher (Sue) follows up a student's contribution in order to maximise student participation by allowing more time to explore a particular topic (Walsh and Li 2013).

Extract 6.10 (8.5_11.20) (Reprinted here – see also Extract 5.10)

```
1   T    so just now we are talking about all kinds of gifts
2        bought from shops (.) if we want to buy something from
3        shops what maybe <the most important thing that we
4        need>=
5   SS   =money=
6   T    =money ok (.) so we need money (.) and as Amy just
7        mentioned that daming's mother always buy expensive
8        clothes (.)what if daming doesn't have that much money?
9        and <he still wants to buy some presents for his
10       mother> what can you do (3.1) you? ((hand gesture))
11       (2.8)
12  S1   maybe er daming can borrow some money from her um
13       from his father er maybe s and um=
14  T    =still use parents' [money]
15  S1                       [um when daming have got um (0.6)
16       lot of moneies and he can give it back to his father=
17  T    =maybe one day he can return the money °ok° zhouwan (.)
18  S2   um I have another rea another way he can make the
19       clothes for your mother (.) I think it's very cheap and
20       also you can draw clothes (.) you know (.) I know a very
21       cheap way (.) on the website you can buy a clothes you
22       can draw it you draw a picture you like=
23  T    =very creative ideas (1.0) ((hand gesture to another
24       student)) more ideas?=
25  S3   =eh we can pick up some photos and er (2.0) fand erf
26       sell it and then we can earn some money=
27  T    =you can earn some money yourself (.) that's a good
28       choice (2.0)
29  S4   um I think er (1.0) daming can do some housework for
30       his parents and then he will get the money and buy the
31       clothes=
32  T    =((nodding her head)) earn the money himself (1.0) Ann=
33  S5   =um I think maybe just give his mother something he owns
34       because for the parents er anything from the child is
35       special=
36  T    =that's your idea (.)any more different ideas?
37       (3.0)
38  S6   um I think like pretty clothes don't have to be
39       expensive he could just look around and buy something
40       he could afford but his mother would like.
41  T    any more different ideas? (.)
42  S7   well I think if daming decided to buy his mother
43       a dress (.) he can start saving money um before his
```

```
44         mother's birthday and that I think the money will be
45         enough to buy one=
46    T    =very good (.) you have very creative ideas
```

In Extract 6.10, the teacher is discussing the topic of buying presents for different people and she picks up one contribution from a student in order to develop the lesson further. Earlier, the class was discussing buying all kinds of gifts from shops and one student (Amy) mentioned buying expensive clothes. Sue sees the opportunity of developing this topic further to allow students more opportunity to practise the language by solving a real-life issue: money. She then changes her lesson plan and includes a discussion with students, which spans over three minutes.

After Sue has elicited the topic from the students (lines 1–4), she presents the real-life issue of money (lines 5–10). Then she invites the first contribution from a student (line 10). Although in this case the teacher selects the speaker and there is a long pause (line 11) before the student's turn, it is not interpreted as unwillingness as the student produces a relevant and longish turn after the pause. The long pause here is an indication of a space that the student uses to develop her thoughts and perhaps rehearse them before speaking in public (Li 2011). After the student makes the first attempt (lines 12–13), Sue interrupts to challenge the idea (line 14). It is interesting to note that the student takes over the floor and overlaps Sue in line 15 to respond to Sue's challenge (lines 15–16). It is clear that the pedagogical goal of this moment is to maximise the opportunity for students to participate. The teacher minimises her role as a knowledge provider but acts as a facilitator to engage the students in the discussion, as is evidenced by particular long turns from students and the facilitating role that the teacher plays in encouraging contributions, for example through inviting different opinions in different ways (lines 17, 23–4, 32, 36 and 41). The encouragement for participation also is displayed in the student's self-selection (line 29).

There are a number of things worth noting in this extract. First, teaching to the moment is important for Sue and she displays flexibility in her planning. Flexibility is one characteristic of expertise. Second, Sue does not exercise her authority overtly in her interactional work with the students, suggesting that she values the students' contributions and sees that the opportunity to maximise students' participation is important. Third, the feedback is not evaluative by its nature and the teacher uses different feedback strategies, for example challenging the learner (line 14), reformulating the learner's contribution (line 17), providing positive feedback (lines 23, 27–8, 32, 46), summarising the learner's contribution (line 27, 32), and acknowledging the contribution (line 36). More importantly, the teacher does not place herself in a position to judge the contribution of the learner, rather she displays an open attitude. Fourth, there is no corrective feedback and clearly the meaning is the focus rather than the form. Finally, the learner turns are all long and well developed, and the teacher demonstrates interactional competence in jointly constructing the conversation with students. The interactional work is closer to a natural conversation.

Insufficient knowledge

In another lesson, Yuan, a very experienced teacher, displays insufficient knowledge and has to make a swift decision to deal with the situation. In Extract 6.11, a student is contributing information about Charles Dickens and his novel, *A Christmas Carol*.

Extract 6.11 The great writer Charles Dickens

```
1   S   the great writer er=
2   Y   =the great writer (.)oh (.)who?
3   S   ((2 unintelligible))
4   Y   hhhh (.) this kind of thing happens(.)Charles Dickens
5       right? Charles Dickens (.)yes (.)what are you going to say?
6   S   the Christmas (.)
7   Y   the Christmas carol right? (.) well I understand for some
8       new words you don't know how to pronounce (.) you need to
9       pay attention to pronunciation using dictionary to see how
10      to can pronounce for some words (.)I am not sure (.)for
11      example 那叫什么 (((what's that called))Chinese
12  S   ((2 unintelligible))
13  Y   xie ji sheng((mistletoe))... are you sure? xie! xie xie Chinese
14      I mean Chinese pronunciation
15  S   Xie
16  Y   are you sure? xie ji sheng 是吗((right?)) (.) 还是还是念别的((
17      or it's pronounced as something else?)) ((looking at one
18      student's book))有人说念 ((some people pronounce it)) xie 反正
19      ((anyway))Chinese (.)right? a kind of plant thanks you (.)
20      NAME mentioned some information very important even the great
21      writer Charles Dickens and he loves Christmas so much right?
22      Ok (1.2)and er by the way do you happen to know any other
23      besides Christmas carols any other written by this great
24      writer? (1.2)
25      yes! for example? 著作((works))
26      (6.0)
27      who can you remember who can think of any book written by
28      this great writer? you have to know something right?
29      Charles Dickens so famous a writer!
30      (2.3)
31      oh what is Chinese? Dickens!!! Dickens
```

Extract 6.11 suggests that teachers sometimes make interactive decisions due to insufficient knowledge, specifically a lack of cultural knowledge (Li 2013). The sequence shows how the teacher's utterances in conversation set up a sequential trajectory in which the teacher directs the conversation to a different focus so that the student finds less and less opportunity to discuss the topic, *A Christmas Carol*, without explicitly asking. It is in this interactional or micro-context that the conversational move of topic shifts becomes analysable as a means for avoiding the topic brought up by the student.

In this sequence, a student offers the topic 'great writer' as a try-marked example relating to Christmas, which is interrupted by the teacher in order to direct the conversation to the focus of 'who' the great writer is (line 2). It is typical authoritative discourse where the teacher controls the interaction. In this extract, the teacher produces the extended turn (lines 7–11) and positions the student(s) as a listener. Even when Yuan asks questions in this sequence, there is no real expectation of an answer (line 2), and indeed he answers his own questions sometimes (e.g. line 4). It is interesting that Yuan dictates which micro-context they are in by swiftly changing the topic from the great writer Charles Dickens and *A Christmas Carol* to the pronunciation problems that students experience, and by moving away from the topic initiated by the student (line 9). Then he gives an example of a word that he does not know how to pronounce in Chinese and emphasises the importance of checking pronunciation using a dictionary. It seems that Yuan is avoiding further discussion of *A Christmas Carol*. This authoritative sequence continues and Yuan moves back to the topic initiated by the student, *A Christmas Carol* and Charles Dickens, but changes the focus of the exchange. At lines 20–21, Yuan appears to invite an opinion, but before the appropriate turn is delivered Yuan closes the exchange and is ready to move on (line 22). After a silence (line 22), Yuan changes the positioning of the respondents in a new first pair part, this time projecting as conditionally relevant a second pair part containing an example of works by Charles Dickens (lines 22–4). After another longish pause (line 24) Yuan clarifies what is projected as a relevant answer by code-switching (line 25), extended wait time (lines 26 and 30), referential questions (lines 27–8), assertive encouragement (line 28), giving clues (line 29), and eventually seeking a translation of the author's name (line 31).

This extract shows how the teacher closes down the conversation space to shape the interaction into a more teacher-led discourse where he clearly assumes the roles of knowledge provider and instructor. Research suggests that teachers could encourage sequence continuation when a learner initiates a topic that is unfamiliar to the teacher (e.g. Richards 2006; Hawkins 2007; Fagan 2012). This sequence suggests that when teachers are in an uncomfortable and threatening situation, they revert to the authoritative role to make sure the lesson development is controlled.

SUMMARY

Interactive decisions or online decision-making is an important element in guiding a lesson to achieve its pedagogical goals and effectiveness for learning. However, little research focuses on teachers' interactive decision-making, which might be due to the difficulty in gaining insights into the moment-by-moment decisions made in classrooms. This chapter, focusing on why and how teachers make interactive decisions, investigates the micro-decisions that teachers make on a moment-by-moment basis.

A number of explanations have been identified in relation to those occasions where teachers make interactive decisions. The most important explanation is when a teacher receives an unexpected learner contribution, which includes unexpected and dispreferred contributions from learners, contributions outside the pedagogical focus of the lesson, challenges from learners, and when students display the target knowledge. Another common factor contributing to teachers' interactive decision-making is the task or activity. This includes the level of difficulty of the task or activity and students' reaction to the task or activity. A third strand of interactive decision-making is made when the teacher recognises a potential learning opportunity and teaches to the moment. In most cases, this refers to maximising students' participation by allowing more time on a topic. Learning opportunities also include the moment that teachers are able to enhance learners' learning strategy or metacognitive strategies in learning. The final category of factors contributing to teachers' interactive decision-making is teachers' insufficient knowledge, especially cultural knowledge. The moment-by-moment analysis of teachers' decision-making suggests that learner attributes – including their needs, understanding, involvement, perception, knowledge and behaviour – account for the large portion of a teacher's decision-making. Teachers' own knowledge also contributes to the decision-making in the classroom.

In terms of how teachers make interactive decisions, a detailed analysis revealed that teachers employ different interactional strategies to respond to the situation:

- glossing over unexpected learning contributions – either ignoring the learner's contribution or briefly acknowledging it;
- asking counter-questions without expecting answers from students;
- inviting other contributions;
- challenging indirectly;
- offering a relevant contribution;
- inviting a second attempt;
- swiftly shifting topic;
- lecturing students on their behaviour;
- sticking to the original plan;
- checking students' knowledge;
- abandoning the activity (changing the procedure) to progress the lesson;
- repeating the task;
- motivating or engaging students by games;
- promoting students' involvement by spending more time on the activity
- introducing a new topic;
- and resuming the role of authority or engaging in authoritative talk.

There are many other strategies that teachers might utilise in making interactive decisions and a detailed account enables both teachers and researchers to gain insights into their distributed cognition of the moment. That is, how they employ what they think, believe and know in making a decision without conscious planning. Teachers make decisions all the time and a good decision is one which contributes to successful learning. In this chapter, I have argued that a detailed study of teachers' interactive decision-making is useful in understanding effective instruction, hence promoting learning. In summary, there are many factors accounting for teachers' decision-making, but in the classroom a particular micro-context, that is the outcome of the interaction between the teacher and students, is a far more important factor than any other factors. By studying micro-contexts we not only understand why and how teachers make interactive decisions, but we also discover how teachers can improve their teaching and facilitate more learning opportunities.

PART C: APPLICATIONS

7

UNDERSTANDING PEDAGOGY

INTRODUCTION

This chapter discusses the practical implications of researching teacher cognition through social interaction as a means to understanding pedagogy. There are many aspects of pedagogy that we could consider, but the discussion offered in this chapter focuses on the main themes which emerged in earlier chapters. Suggestions are made regarding how individual teachers might develop their own pedagogy by analysing what they know, do and believe in their professional contexts.

Kern suggests that both insiders (e.g. learners, teachers, teacher-trainers, material developers, researchers and specialised agencies) and outsiders (e.g. learners' peers and parents, administrators and policy-makers) all bring their unique sets of beliefs and attitudes to bear in situations and decisions related to language learning and teaching (1995: 71). The roles of stakeholders and relevant parties are, therefore, important in understanding pedagogy. From a teacher's perspective, a focus on cognition-in-interaction, through the use of, for example, CA, provides opportunities for reflection and professional development, culminating in changes to practice. As pointed out in Chapter 2, the majority of research on teacher cognition uses reported data (e.g. questionnaires, interviews and metaphors), and the merit of a discursive psychological approach lies in its emic perspective of participants' own understanding of teaching and learning.

There are three specific associated reasons for making this claim. First, researchers have already highlighted the value of CA in the study of language learning (see, for example, Markee 2000; Brouwer and Wagner 2004; Kasper 2004, 2009; Huth 2006), while, at the same time, various studies have been conducted through CA to explore the dynamics and structure of the classroom (e.g. Seedhouse 2004). I would argue that CA has significant value in understanding and improving pedagogy (see Wong and Waring 2010). Second, although studying teachers' broad life stories and contexts provides useful insights into their attitudes towards teaching and learning, it is almost impossible and unrealistic to encompass every aspect of a teacher's life in the research through interviews or other research methods, and thus the description might be biased or segmental. Third, from a discursive psychological perspective, teacher cognition displays itself in talk as a fluid and constantly changing phenomenon. As a consequence of this observation, the focus of studying teacher cognition is not to compare what teachers do and say, but rather to examine their display of understanding in talk. Teachers are able to improve their pedagogy and classroom practice by closely studying the following areas through understanding teacher cognition via the lens of interaction:

- What is teaching and learning?
- What pedagogical position is adopted?
- How are instructions and feedback given?
- How are interactive decisions made?

UNDERSTANDING TEACHING AND LEARNING

Understanding teacher cognition enables us to understand the deep-rooted theories of teaching and learning. This is important because we not only understand teachers' thinking from their perspectives, but also we can gain possible insights into how the complex systems of teaching and learning interact in achieving pedagogical goals. The premise is that if we are to understand the nature of teaching and learning, we need to understand what teaching and learning is from teachers' perspectives. Teachers' understanding about teaching and learning influences how they plan to teach and what they do in teaching. Equally, their classroom practice displays teachers' knowledge and thinking about teaching and learning. In essence, and on one level, every teacher's understanding about their pedagogy is located on a continuum from teacher- to learner-centred. Teachers adjust their position on this continuum according to the local context, or, rather, micro-contexts. Similarly, every teacher's understanding about learning can be placed on a continuum with knowledge transmission at one extreme and discovery-based approaches at the other. As argued throughout this book, such understanding and beliefs are dynamic, fluid and context-specific; thus, we see that teachers sometimes have contradictory understandings and conflicts between what they say on one occasion and how they may behave on another. As discussed in Chapters 4 and 5, a teacher who understands learning as acquiring knowledge displays a language-focused interactional structure. This might involve knowledge memorisation and recall. On the other hand, a teacher who believes in a more communicative approach, emphasising communication both as the goal and means of learning a language, displays meaning-focused interaction with learners. However, I have no intention of generalising this as a formula – I merely offer it as a general observation that emerged from the data.

Research has highlighted the close relationship between interaction and language learning (e.g. Allwright 1984; Ellis 1992; Breen 1998; Walsh 2006). Here, I am suggesting that there is a strong relationship between teacher talk and their cognitions – what teachers think learning is and how they go about facilitating learning is displayed in their professional talk. That is, there is a strong link between teacher cognition about teaching and learning, and their professional discourse. Therefore, in facilitating learning and creating a space for learning we must understand teachers' beliefs and knowledge about language learning, as it is the teacher who controls the development of a lesson, opportunities for learning, and when and how they obstruct or construct these opportunities (Walsh 2002).

Teachers bring a body of knowledge and understandings about how language can be and is learnt, and how to teach and what teaching is about (Harmer 2003). It might sound absurd to ask what teachers teach, but it is true that we need to understand what teachers think what they teach in order to understand how they go about teaching. Language can be viewed differently in different contexts and according to the different needs learners have. As illustrated in the data, for some learners learning a language is acquiring blocks of language components, such as grammar, vocabulary and pronunciation, and therefore learning involves a massive effort of memorising, with emphasis placed on accuracy. For others, a language enables them to access other materials and learning content and it is a method, a tool and a channel. Within this perspective, learning involves using the language, and a focus is placed on meaning. There are also users and learners who consider language as a social practice and they use language to express themselves and communicate thoughts and ideas. Learning thus is a way to participate and collaborate. It is a means of achieving shared understanding and creating collective knowledge and cognition. However, these views do not exist separately and learners and teachers do not follow just one perspective (see Seedhouse et al. 2010 for different perspectives on 'language' and 'learning'). Very often, perhaps more so in EFL contexts than in any other language contexts, we see learners who need to master the language as a system, use the language as a tool and treat the language as a social practice. Thus, it is theoretically and practically inappropriate to treat teacher cognition as a fixed assumption and investigate which view the teacher holds about teaching and learning. As illustrated in this book, we see teachers display sophisticated understandings about teaching and learning language in their own professional contexts and these beliefs and understanding are fluid, and thus understanding teachers' thinking about teaching and learning of the moment, together with the pedagogical goal, is more appropriate. That is, when we talk about teachers' beliefs/knowledge about teaching and learning, we need to consider the macro-context as well as the micro-context, together with the teacher's pedagogical goal of the moment.

UNDERSTANDING PEDAGOGICAL KNOWLEDGE AND TEACHING METHODS

Research in teacher cognition has strong implications on the understanding of teachers' pedagogical considerations and teaching methods in their classrooms. In researching TESOL (Teaching English to Speakers of Other Languages) pedagogy and teaching effectiveness, the idea of a contrast between a focus on form and accuracy and a focus on meaning and fluency is an important area, which has become a common confusion and a widely accepted dilemma for teachers (e.g. Brumfit 1984; Seedhouse 2004). For this reason, there is much debate about whether CLT works and what role grammar plays in EFL contexts. I will take these two areas to illustrate how researching teacher cognition can help us develop in-depth understanding of teaching methodology and methods.

TESOL methodology has been changing over the years and the attention to strive for the best or most effective method has shifted to teachers' understanding about teaching methods. As noted by Kumaravadivelu (1994, 2003, 2006), we are now in the '*Postmethod era*' and perhaps it is not relevant to ask questions concerning the most effective method. In fact, in classrooms, teachers do not and cannot follow the principles of one teaching method but make active decisions on which method or methods serve the pedagogical goal of the lesson, or even of a task. In this sense, teachers are flexible and have autonomy to decide what the most effective method is for their lessons, and the effective method is contextualised within the teaching and learning agenda. Therefore, teachers' own understanding and conceptions of teaching methods are critical in helping teachers to select and operate effective methods for their lessons.

In the literature on teacher cognition, much attention has been given to teachers' conceptions and perceptions of CLT, despite the fact that task-based language teaching (TBLT) is a more recent development in pedagogical thinking and teaching methodology. CLT is:

> a theory of language teaching that starts from a communicative model of language and language use, and that seeks to translate this into a design for an instructional system, for materials, for teacher and learner roles and behaviours, and for classroom activities and techniques. (Richards and Rodgers 2001: 158)

It is now recognised as a set of principles which encourages communicative competence rather than a particular teaching method. Klapper (2003: 33) indicates that '... CLT adopts a "post-method" view of language pedagogy . . ., [and this] explains why there is no easily recognisable pedagogical framework, no single agreed version of CLT . . .'. Richards and Rodgers (2001) identify five principles underlying CLT, including:

- Learners learn a language through using it to communicate.
- Authentic and meaningful communication should be the goal of classroom activities.
- Fluency is an important dimension of communication.
- Communication involves the integration of different language skills.
- Learning is a process of creative construction and involves trial and error. (Ibid.: 172)

Clearly CLT is viewed by researchers as a method which advocates authentic language use, fluency and the importance of context in language learning. Teachers' understanding and beliefs about CLT have been widely researched; it is through these studies that we are able to see how a particular pedagogical principle is interpreted and appropriated by teachers, taking their local context into consideration (Gorsuch 2000, 2001; Sakui 2004, 2007; Taguchi 2005; Nishino 2011). Sato and Kleinsasser's study (1999), for example, concluded that the teachers in their study believed that CLT is possible despite being evolving and time-consuming; nevertheless, communicative activities are rarely observed in their classroom practices. In a different context, Nepal, Adhikari (2007) finds that CLT allows Nepalese secondary teachers and students to play an active role in the teaching and learning processes. In China, Liao (2004) suggested that CLT could be used in Chinese classrooms, and observed several communicative features in the participating teacher's classroom, such as the teaching of functional language, pair/group work and communicative activities. The teacher also demonstrates expertise in dealing with situational constraints, such as the large class size. This research certainly sheds light on teachers' understanding and beliefs about CLT and clearly has implications in understanding pedagogical principles in those contexts. What DP can offer here is to examine CLT or any teaching methodology in an actual context in which teachers work, thereby giving teachers some insights into their local context and a space in which they can pin down the identifiable features of the teaching methodology (e.g. CLT). That is, by investigating teacher cognition we are able to gain insights into the principles of teaching underlying teachers' planning, designing activities and evaluating materials, and help teachers to link their principles to the teaching 'action' and objectives. Such practice will raise teachers' awareness about appropriate teaching methodology for their local context.

A second popular but debatable area is about the role of linguistic knowledge. In many EFL classrooms, it is clear that accuracy of vocabulary and grammar has become the centre of the lesson. As stated in Chapter 1, one of the major themes of teacher cognition revolves around grammar and there are two associated reasons. First, research into grammar learning has a long history and has always been an important aspect of language learning (see the comprehensive review in Ellis 2008), and its importance and relevance remain key even though the focus of language learning has switched to communication. Second, research supports the role of grammar instruction in facilitating language learning (Nassaji and Fotos 2011), although it is still not clear how grammar should be approached. For example, researchers are constantly debating whether grammar is best taught integratively or as a separate component of the foreign language learning syllabus. One possible way to approach this question is through investigating teachers' and learners' beliefs and practices. For example, Borg and Burns reported that the majority of their participants (84% of an international sample of 176 teachers) disagreed that 'grammar should be taught separately' from other skills (2008: 466). However, in classroom practices, EFL teachers continue to value explicit grammar work (Sakui 2004, 2007; Sato and Kleinsasser 2004; Nishino 2011; Underwood 2012). Although there is no definite answer to the question of how to teach grammar, the teacher cognition research sheds light on how teachers value and conduct grammar work in their contexts. Further, if we believe participation and engagement is learning, teachers' understanding and conceptions about teaching grammar/vocabulary in action will help teachers develop their own methodology in teaching these areas.

In understanding appropriate pedagogy, Kumaravadivelu proposes that we have moved from a state of awareness towards a state of awakening. He writes:

> we have been awakened to the necessity of making methods-based pedagogies more sensitive to local exigencies, awakened to the opportunity afforded by postmethod pedagogies to hep practicing teachers develop their own theory of practice, awakened to the multiplicity of learner identities, awakened to the

complexity of teacher beliefs, and awakened to the vitality of macrostructures – social, cultural, political, and historical – that shape and reshape the microstructures of our pedagogic enterprise'. (2006: 81)

I would concur with Kumaravadivelu that appropriate methodology should ensure continuity and congruity with local knowledge, and we need not only to understand but develop pedagogy in the teachers' local context, which is similar to what Bax (2003) terms a 'Context Approach' to language teaching. Studying teacher cognition provides such opportunities to examine the context and pedagogy together from teachers' perspective, which is perhaps the most important perspective in order to achieve effective pedagogy as teachers are the ones who make decisions according to what's going in their classrooms. Specifically, the discursive psychological perspective adopted in this book offers a method with which to explore teachers' pedagogical understanding and stances in micro-contexts.

UNDERSTANDING INSTRUCTIONAL PRACTICE

Understanding teacher cognition has implications for improving instructional practice, and therefore in achieving effective teaching and learning. In understanding instructional practice, there are several key elements worth considering, including the overall classroom interaction structure practices, turn-taking and feedback practices. Equally, these three areas are important in unpacking and understanding teachers' instructional decisions and thinking. Previously, I have discussed the importance of researching teacher cognition through interaction in enhancing understanding of pedagogy. Similarly, researching teacher cognition-in-interaction helps both researchers and teachers understand and improve instructional practice, classroom interactions, classroom participation and feedback. I will unpack each of these three elements in more detail.

CLASSROOM INTERACTION STRUCTURE

In the following section, I will explore how research in teacher cognition through DP can shed light on improving classroom interaction structure. In particular, I propose alternative interaction structures so that teachers can engage students in dialogical and collaborative learning.

A discursive psychological perspective of teacher cognition provides researchers and teachers with a practice-based approach to examine the teachers' thinking and decision-making in situ. As I outlined in the section above, by analysing teacher cognition through DP, we can gain insights into how teachers understand teaching and learning, and make instructional decisions. One useful way to help teachers improve their instructional practice is to raise teachers' awareness of the kind of interaction they engage in with students.

Classroom interactions during whole-group activities often occur within the context of the Initiation-Response-Feedback (IRF) sequence and the three-part exchange has been long criticised for impeding student participation and, thus, learning (e.g. Tharp and Gallimore 1988; Nystrand 1997) while other researchers believe that teachers can promote student engagement and participation by utilising their turns more effectively (Nassaji and Wells 2000; Hall and Walsh 2002; Toth 2011).

In the data presented and discussed in previous chapters, it is fair to say that when teachers see learning as knowledge acquisition and themselves as knowledge provider, the majority of classroom discourse still follows this three-part exchange where the teacher dominates and orchestrates the direction of the interaction (Breen 1998). That is, the teacher asks the question/initiates the topic, sometimes invites a speaker, and then students provides a response, which the teacher evaluates. In this exchange, it is clear that the teacher takes on a more authoritative role, whereas students adopt a passive receiver role. This relationship is recognised and accepted by both parties as the norm, as displayed in the overall interactional structure. Although the teacher is recognised as knowledge provider and authority, there is evidence that teachers do have awareness of other roles they can and perhaps should play in the classroom. They also recognise the active role the learners might be able to play. However, if we look at this from a DP perspective and examine the assumptions displayed in discourse, it is clear that teachers largely assume the traditional dominant role. There are two issues worth exploring here. First, if teachers have an awareness of the different roles they might adopt, a close review of their interactions with students might enable them to 'take a back seat' from time to time, giving students more space and promoting more opportunities for students to take turns. This could be done by breaking the rigid three-part exchange by allowing students to initiate the talk, give feedback or provide opportunities for self-correction. Second, by engaging in detailed analysis of interactional structures, teachers are able to notice their roles in promoting learning. This awareness-raising further develops opportunities for teachers to change and grow. The very long teacher turn and brief learner turns suggest it is the teacher who derives the power to direct the conversation, and the power that teachers wield as an institutional authority has a major influence on the discourse (Zuengler 2011), particularly when teachers' pedagogical agenda focuses on knowledge transmission and memorisation.

Rigid three-part exchanges usually start with a display or closed question, to which the teacher already knows the answer. The majority of these questions serve the function of eliciting information from students and checking students' knowledge and understanding, and the ultimate goal is to reinforce knowledge acquisition or check learning. Much research suggests that more open, referential questions are always more likely to create space for conversation and learning opportunities (Li 2011; Walsh and Li 2013). The logical consequence of this is that if teachers can consider the alternatives in asking questions or simply using more referential questions, it would give students more space to produce relevant and long turns. Referential questions are more personal and meaningful to students, as individual opinions and perspectives are respected and sought. Therefore, these classrooms have more features that can be interpreted as participants' personal involvement with the context and with each other. In such an environment, it is more likely for students to think and integrate different subject knowledge to reason with their interlocutors, using the language as a cultural tool. Referential questions have the potential to lead to extended learner turns and generate multiple turn-taking and -giving among participants so that negotiation, co-construction, interaction and problem-solving can be possible. This is in stark contrast to display questions which typically seek short responses which may close down the conversation. There is no doubt that teachers who only use display questions are likely to restrict or even hinder learning opportunities (c.f. Walsh 2002; Li 2011). When teachers change the way they use questions, perhaps they are developing awareness and cognition to use language for authentic purposes – collaboration and discussion – rather than for memorising linguistic rules and knowledge. That is, using a range of question types demonstrates a finer-grained understanding of language and what language learning is about; by deliberately using more open questions, teachers may enhance their cognition of interactional competence and promote a more participatory learning approach.

As discussed above, IRF still dominates the language classroom, especially in the foreign language context where language is treated more as a subject rather than a means of communication or social practice. The problem with excessive use of IRF lies in its potential to limit student participation. As we already know, in every IRF exchange, the teacher has two moves and the learner has one, which is very brief in most cases. Apart from deliberately changing the 'I' move as outlined above, IRF can be modified in various ways in order to facilitate participation, knowledge co-construction and sharing.

ITRF

ITRF (Initiation-Thinking space-Response-Feedback) is a modified IRF cycle which has thinking space after initiation. That is, after initiation the teacher could create a thinking space to give the learners thinking time to develop learner initiatives and manage the dialogue with the teacher and their peers (Li 2011). 'Thinking space' can be used to provide rehearsal time, but in essence it is more than providing a space to rehearse the response. It is a space in which learners are given opportunities to engage in critical, creative and reflective thinking. As observed in many classrooms, teachers tend to fill in the space by echoing or paraphrasing their questions. However, this might not be a good practice pedagogically as students need time to comprehend and process the question before they respond. That is, students need some time to gather their thoughts together and perhaps practise in private before they speak publicly; when students are using a foreign language, it inevitably takes them longer time to do so. Li (2011) observes that in foreign language classrooms where thinking skills are promoted there is a 'silence' feature, and she calls for teachers to reconsider silence from students and resist the temptation to 'fill the silence' or give out the answers. Therefore, asking referential questions, increasing wait time and reducing teacher echo could be a useful means of securing learner contributions. I specifically emphasise the thinking space here for three important reasons. First, essentially language is a psychological tool, a 'tool for thought', and 'a means for engaging in social and cognitive activity' (Ahmed 1994: 158). Second, language classrooms can be seen as social learning communities and discourse communities (Hall and Verplaetse 2000), where learners and the teacher interact to create a space for thinking, sharing and learning. It is the interactions in classrooms that enhance language learning as a social enterprise, jointly constructed and intrinsically linked to learners' repeated and regular participation in activities (Consolo 2006). Third, language in language classrooms is not only the subject matter – lexis, structure and phonology – but a tool with which to achieve meaning co-construction, where a degree of thinking skill is required; for instance, being critical, open to other ideas, collaborative, imaginative and independent in learning activities.

IDRF

In education, a number of studies have investigated ways of enhancing communication and promoting dialogue in classrooms. Wegerif (2006), for example, proposes 'dialogic spaces' in which different perspectives co-exist and inter-animate each other. In practice, the dialogic spaces can be created after the teacher's initiation, when the learners are given time to discuss and interact as a small group and the IRF structure can be modified as Initiation-Dialogic space-Response-Feedback (IDRF). Li (2011) proposed this as a preferred practice in language classrooms: teachers give students opportunities to discuss answers in small groups before presenting those answers to the class. There are two assumptions underlying this proposal. First, learning is considered to be a process of achieving shared understanding and constructing meaning jointly; dialogue is central to this process. Second, learning takes place through and in interaction (Ellis 1998). By discussing within a group, students are able to share ideas and take each other's perspective into consideration to construct group cognition. The learning process therefore takes places as group cognition development within the community. Of course, for some learners, especially those who are not very confident speaking publically, this also provides the students with rehearsal time and space (Schmitt 2000).

A spiral IRF

A third form of modified IRF is a spiral IRF, which is a series of verbal exchanges during which the teacher 'tunes in' to the students' present state of ability or understanding. (Panselinas and Komis 2009 also talk about spiral IDRF with a peer discussion before response.) A spiral IRF encourages participation and negotiation (see Chapter 5). In a spiral IRF, when the teacher's feedback (F) initiates a new initiation (I), students' participation and involvement are enhanced, and a new learning cycle is created. Thus, a spiral IRF exchange assists in developing the possibility of sharing opinions and creating a learning context – a spiral IRF is desirable in creating and developing space to allow extended learner turns (Li 2011).

Because the type of questions and classroom interaction structures are closely related to teachers' underlying thinking, therefore examining teachers' cognition-in-interaction can help teachers understand how their pedagogical thinking is reflected in the kind of questions they ask and the interaction in which they engage with students.

TURN-TAKING

If we accept that the view of 'learning as doing' is at least as relevant as the view of 'learning as having' (Sfard 1998), then learner participation and engagement is equally as important as acquiring linguistic knowledge. Thus, understanding the mechanisms by which learners take a turn-at-talk is an important aspect in understanding and improving instructional practice. As we understand, any lesson is a series of complex, dynamic and interrelated micro-contexts and the prime responsibility for establishing and shaping the interaction lies with the teacher, who has an important role to play in shaping learner contributions (Jarvis and Robinson 1997). Students take cues from the teacher through whom they direct most of their responses. Teachers should pay particular attention to the turn-taking system, which involves how and when to take the floor, intervene, give feedback and transit class (Hellermann, 2008). The previous chapters (see Chapters 4, 5 and 6) suggest that classroom discourse reveals the pedagogical goals of the teacher at a given moment. That is, by studying teacher cognition through and in classroom interaction, we are able to gain insights into what teachers think at a given moment in order to realise their pedagogical goal. More importantly, the interactional strategies employed by learners and the teacher give us insights into how knowledge is co-constructed between the teacher and learners, and what learning is from the perspectives of both parties. That is, by looking at how turns are both given and taken, we discover how meaning is jointly achieved and how learning takes place.

Turning-taking is particularly important in understanding the relationship between the teacher and learners. Teachers' beliefs about 'self-as-teacher' are interpreted in the interaction with learners, and equally learners' roles in learning activities are displayed in the interaction. That is, the role of the teacher and learners is displayed in the interaction through the interactional work that both parties do. If we take a closer look at what is in the interaction, it is clear to us that teachers dominate the class in terms of what to say, who says it and whether what's been said is relevant or not. In other words, it is clear that teachers not only raise the topic, but also allocate turns to students. Normally, this is observed as 'individual selection' (Mehan 1979), which results in either preferred response or the student being put on a 'forced platform performance' (Rampton 2006: 7). The turn allocation displays the right to speak whereas the follow-up feedback is an evaluation of the relevance of the contribution. Because both students and the teacher recognise the authoritative power the teacher has in the classroom, the relationship is displayed in the language and discourse as described by Benwell and Stokoe, '[w]ho we are to each other, then, is accomplished, ascribed, disputed, resisted, managed and negotiated in discourse' (2006: 4). Of course, in many EFL contexts, as described in this book, the role of learners is managed and prescribed by the teacher, and less negotiated. It is important to realise this as, in order to create a learning environment for learners to use the resources available to engage in the learning process, it is essential for learners to take a more active role or for the teachers to create a space for learners to participate.

We have known for a while that a classroom is a place where learners and the teacher jointly construct meanings through conversation. Despite the fact that teachers have more turns in classrooms as a result of the more dominant IRF exchange, learners should take an active role in order to gain participation. One possible way to enhance learner participation, or let learners take a more active role, is floor management where learners are allocated turns to make contributions. Again, the responsibility mainly lies with the teacher as we have to recognise the important role the teacher plays in structuring the classroom talk. If the teachers consider their role as facilitator or organiser rather than knowledge provider and performance judge, then perhaps they could give students more turns by inviting multiple contributions to one initiation, by creating a space for students to follow up with each other, by expanding learner contributions to increase the scope of the dialogue, by offering follow-ups rather than evaluative feedback, and by helping students to produce more complex turns. The above-mentioned strategies can be summarised as an appropriate use of interactional strategies of clarification request, modification, seeking elaboration and providing feedback on content (see Walsh 2011).

FEEDBACK

As illustrated in the dataset, acknowledging students' contributions and providing evaluation on their contributions dominates the third turn. Research suggests that if the teachers' feedback is simply acknowledgement or strict evaluation, it could potentially close down the space for student participation. Indeed, the acknowledgement of learners' contributions, such as ok, oh, yes (Mehan 1979), or the repetition of learners' contributions, and strict evaluations (such as very good) are indicators of closing the topic (Waring 2008; Wong and Waring 2009). In researching teacher cognition-in-interaction, we see not only how teachers could facilitate learning by encouraging learner participation but also how teachers might create space for learners to learn in the third turn when teachers provide feedback or evaluation. This position is well supported by several relevant theoretical positions, including socio-cultural perspectives on learning (Vygotsky 1978; Lantolf 2006).

The construct of affordances proposed by van Lier (2000, 2004) is also relevant here, as the relationship between learners and particular features in their environment which have relevance to the learning process. The affordance is situated in the ecological approach to learning which emphasises its emergent nature and attempts to explain learning in terms of the verbal and non-verbal processes in which learners engage. That is, rather than trying to understand learning as a cognitive process, which take place in the head, we should view learning as a meaning-making process which is co-constructed between interlocutors. In the latter view, interactions lie at the heart of the meaning co-construction. Essentially, by gaining closer understanding of how the expert (teachers) provide the novice (learners) with assistance, we are gaining a closer understanding of the role of the teacher in learning and how learning takes place. Teachers' third move or feedback move therefore is the space where teachers can assist learners by shaping learners' contributions. In the dataset, we can see different interactional strategies are adopted by teachers to shape and scaffold learner contributions.

Scaffolding has been viewed as an important classroom practice through which teachers provide support and guidance to learners. It is important to note that an ability to shape learner contributions goes way beyond practices such as repair and scaffolding. Shaping explicitly refers to the ability of the teacher to assist the learner's contribution in the form of expanding, clarifying or summarising a student contribution. That is, rather than giving positive or corrective feedback a teacher could summarise a student's contribution to make it accurate and relevant to the whole class. Teachers could also expand learners' contributions or help learners to expand or clarify their contributions by doing interactional work, such as a challenge and clarification request.

A related area that teachers could also improve is the ability to encourage and facilitate self-correction when the main focus is on accuracy. As noted in the dataset and also the literature, teachers very often provide direct feedback on student contributions. Although direct feedback is more accurate and time-efficient, it might not provide learners with the best learning opportunity. Instead, teachers could help students to self-correct in order to raise their awareness of accuracy.

UNDERSTANDING INTERACTIVE DECISION-MAKING

One critical aspect of teacher cognition is interactive decision-making, which I argue can be understood through the perspective of DP. Teachers are active decision-makers who make decisions before, while and after teaching. The pre-teaching decision-making allows teachers to project future events, and post-teaching reflections enable teachers to evaluate and monitor their plan in order to adjust for future lessons. This process exists on a continuous basis (Woods 1996), and much attention has been given to this area. However, teachers' interactive decisions are equally, if not more, important (see Chapter 6). Woods observed different things happening in two classrooms and claimed that '[B]y looking at the ways in which teachers' classroom verbalizations are related to their plans, we can establish a link between planning in verbal behaviours and planning in the broader sense of accomplishing educational objectives' (ibid.: 55–6). The reasons why interactive decisions are so important in studying teacher cognition lie in two aspects. First, any lesson is developmental in nature because teachers have to adjust their plans according to interactions with students, unexpected events, task difficulty levels and the pedagogical goal of the moment. In this decision-making, teachers have to draw on the repertoire and knowledge they have developed over years through both theoretical study and practical work to make an online decision immediately. It thus requires teachers to have high competence in interaction to be able to make the manoeuvre so that the lesson develops towards the desired direction. Second, an ability to make a good judgement and interactive decisions lies in the heart of teacher expertise. It is true that studies describing what expert teachers do and say contribute to our understanding of the complexity of expertise in teaching, but studies examining how teachers make interactive decisions can further our knowledge about how teachers display and use expertise in dealing with demanding tasks. For any teacher, if we are able to see how they make interactive decisions over a period of time, we might be able to observe how 'expertise is gained and developed' in action. Therefore, one way to help teachers develop expertise is to increase teachers' competence in making good decisions, which further contributes to successful learning. Here, I will focus on models for interactive decision-making that can be explored and understood based on the analysis I presented in an earlier chapter (Chapter 6), and I will follow some of the ideas presented here with more practical suggestions in the next chapter.

As observed in Chapter 6, interactive decisions are made in a range of situations, prompted by a number of reasons, and teachers make decisions in various ways. Theories of action (Argyris and Schön 1974) can be used to provide a theoretical basis for understanding interactive decision-making. Theories of action are the 'mechanisms' by which human beings link their thoughts with their actions, which indicate that humans as agents act/respond to their environment and plan their further actions in relation to what they learn from the present situation. In a real-life situation, what humans as agents do is '[they] learn a repertoire of concepts, schemas, and strategies, and they learn programs for drawing from their repertoire to design representations and action for unique situations' (Argyris et al. 1985: 81). Theories of action involve two contrasting theories, namely theories-in-use and espoused theories. The distinction made between the two contrasting theories of action is between those theories that are implicit in what people do, and those that people talk about in terms of what they believe or intend to do in a certain situation. Simply put, what people talk about is their espoused theories, which they give allegiance to and communicate to others. People do have awareness of what their intentions are and what outcomes they want to achieve, and they can even articulate explicitly what they plan to implement to achieve these goals. However, when examining people's behaviours it is suggested that theories-in-use actually govern their actions, which tend to be tacit structures. Theories-in-use are responsible for what teachers do in teaching or, in other words, what teachers draw on to make interactive decisions. Their relation to action, in the words of Argyris and Schön, 'is like the relation of grammar-in-use to speech; they contain assumptions about self, others and environment – these assumptions constitute a microcosm of science in everyday life' (1974: 30). These two theories may or may not match, and the individual may or may not be aware of it. Argyris (1980) makes the case that effectiveness results from developing congruence between theories-in-use and espoused theories. In other words, if these two theories are compatible in one case, this leads to a better understanding of intentions, actions and consequences. However, when there is a gap between these two theories, seeking a connection creates a dynamic for reflection and dialogue. Argyris and Schön (1978) further suggest two responses to this mismatch, and these can be seen in the notion of single- and double-loop learning. In the field of teacher education, studying both espoused theories and theories-in-use is necessary and essential, as Thompson puts it:

> Any serious attempt to characterize a teacher's conception of the discipline he or she teaches should not be limited to an analysis of the teacher's professed views. It should also include an examination of the instruction setting, the practices characteristic of that teacher, and the relationship between the teacher's professed views and actual practice. (1992: 134)

In other words, if teachers are to learn and develop, it is important to examine the relationship between their espoused theories and their theories-in-use, and to understand the relationship between these two theories. This happens when teachers look closely at how they act (effectively or ineffectively) in the classroom and compare what they intend to do to achieve effectiveness.

Another useful model which can be used to understand interactive decision-making is the notion of reflective teaching (Schön 1987), which highlights the importance of reflecting for the purpose of making sense of teachers' problem-solving and decision-making. In particular, the process of reflection-in-action is relevant here, which 'is a reflective conversation with the materials of a situation' (ibid.: 16). It is concerned with what teachers are doing in the classroom while they are doing it. That is, reflection-in-action occurs in the midst of acting (El-Dib 2007; Urzúa and Vásquez 2008), and gives teachers opportunities to reshape what they are doing while they are working on it based on the interaction in situ. Reflection-in-action is not necessarily conscious and teachers are not necessarily aware of the kind of decisions they make. Research suggests that teachers may just improvise, drawing upon experiences they have acquired. However, when we closely look at the decisions teachers make, expert or novice, we gain a better understanding of what and how unexpected events or perceived influential moments are dealt with. In previous chapters (see Chapter 6), we have seen teachers gloss over learners' contributions when they are considered to be outside their pedagogical goal, or irrelevant or dispreferred. We have also seen examples of the teacher deviating from the lesson plan to allow the students to develop their turns and the unexpected topics.

From the above, we can learn two things. First, teachers often give their pedagogical goals priority and when the pedagogical goals are jeopardised teachers use a variety of strategies to reinstate their original goal. It is therefore crucial to consider the pedagogical goal of each activity and predict the potential unexpected contributions and knowledge brought by the students. Second, it is perhaps important to make teachers aware of the kinds of actions they can take in making interactive decisions in order to create learning opportunities. For example, as identified in Chapter 6, resuming the role of authority, glossing over the learner's contribution, letting the learner take the lead and developing the learner's contribution further are different options available for teachers to take. How teachers use the interactional strategies to execute these actions to create learning opportunities is what expertise is. Expert teachers can make the distinction between the immediate and long-term learning opportunities, and then take the relevant actions to fulfil their objectives. That is, by analysing teachers' reflection-in-action behaviours, or their interactive decisions, we can gain a grounded perspective of the notion of 'expertise' in a local context (Gatbonton 1999).

SUMMARY

In this chapter, I have assembled evidence and arguments from previous chapters to present a case for researching teacher cognition in understanding (and potentially improving) pedagogy. There is a clear link between studying teacher cognition and understanding pedagogy through a study of interaction, especially from an emic approach where an up-close perspective is offered. In this chapter, the relationship between cognition and pedagogy has been considered from a range of perspectives. First of all, the relevance of researching teacher cognition through a discursive psychological perspective on the understanding of teaching and learning is offered. Language can be viewed on a continuum from linguistic knowledge to social practice, hence teaching and learning are displayed as mastering the knowledge through structured practice and memorisation to authentic communication and engagement in a social context. Equally, researching teacher cognition offers a fine-grained understanding of pedagogical knowledge and teaching methods. EFL teachers in particular search for an effective and appropriate teaching methodology to address the various needs of the EFL learner, and there is a balance to achieve between a CLT and a grammar-oriented approach. A closer understanding of what teachers know and do in their local context benefits a grounded approach to a context-specific teaching methodology. An emic approach to teacher cognition benefits understanding instructional practice, focusing on how teachers go about teaching to address their pedagogical goal. In considering three key elements – namely overall classroom interaction structure, turn-taking and feedback – useful approaches for instructional practice are proposed, such as modified IRFs, turning-taking and -giving, and interactional strategies in feedback. Finally, this chapter considers the relevance of researching teacher cognition to understanding interactive decision-making. It is clear that good interactive decision-making requires expertise, and the detailed account of when, why and how teachers make interactive decision-making not only sheds light on the decision-making process but also displays the complex system in which teachers engage in reflection-in-action.

8

LANGUAGE TEACHER EDUCATION

Researchers in SLTE have already taken teacher cognition as a source of experientially-based professional 'know-how' which serves as a focus for both initial teacher education and reflective practice (Freeman and Richards 1996; Farrell 2013). This chapter builds on the analyses in the previous chapters to discuss the applications of researching teacher cognition for teacher learning. From a constructivist perspective, teacher learning is a process of 'organizing and reorganizing, structuring and restructuring a teacher's understanding of practice. Teachers are viewed as learners who actively construct knowledge by interpreting events on the basis of existing knowledge, beliefs, and dispositions' (Uhlenbeck et al. 2002: 243). Teacher learning is, therefore, an interactive, reflective and experiential process. In this process, interaction with peers and experts (e.g. tutors) and negotiation in the community are important features. Much research on teacher learning in the literature of teacher cognition and teacher education focuses on teacher knowledge; in contrast, this chapter places emphasis on knowing. As a starting point, perhaps it is important to distinguish between knowing and knowledge. Knowing is a process of inquiry while knowledge constitutes the stable outcomes of inquiry (Boyles 2006). Kumaravadivelu calls for more attention to the process, knowing, rather than the product, knowledge, in teacher education, 'as knowing is deemed to have greater significance than knowledge' (2012: 20).

In order to understand teacher learning through the study of teacher cognition, the first step is to revisit the concept of teacher cognition. As argued and illustrated in the previous chapter, from a discursive psychological perspective, teacher cognition is teachers' understanding, knowing, positioning, conceptualising and stance-taking that are publicly displayed in action. This is teacher cognition-in-interaction, which is defined and displayed by the participants orienting practically in an ongoing interaction. Thus, cognition is fluid and changing, it exists in situ and is shaped by the understanding of the prior turns, and shapes the development of the next turn. With this in mind, the merit of studying teacher cognition for teacher education is not to change the misconceptions teachers might have and change their cognition for a better one, rather it lies in the possibility of seeing, understanding and developing teachers from their own perspectives. The rest of the chapter is divided into two sections: a review of the themes emerging from the previous chapters, and future directions and challenges for teacher cognition and education. In arguing the critical but underestimated role of teacher cognition, this chapter also makes practical suggestions as to how to enhance teacher learning and development in EFL contexts.

PART 1: UNDERSTANDING TEACHER LEARNING THROUGH TEACHER COGNITION

In this section, I focus on understanding teacher learning through teacher cognition, drawing on themes emerging from the book and relating them to the existing literature on teacher cognition and education. I place particular emphasis on teacher learning which can take place at any time and in any place, and make references to teacher education and development respectively.

Traditionally, SLTE has been centred on the learning of second languages to develop competent language teachers, rather than on teachers as learners of teaching (Freeman and Johnson 1998). The focus of such an approach also looks at developing teachers' content knowledge and how content is learnt. Although the theoretical understanding of teacher learning has recently shifted from developing language teachers' knowledge, it is still clear that both teacher educators and trainee teachers focus on knowledge. Therefore, we see that much of research in teacher cognition focuses on teacher knowledge, such as content knowledge, subject knowledge, pedagogical knowledge and personal knowledge. These areas are investigated in the manner that knowledge is treated as a concrete product which we are able to observe and examine.

TEACHERS' LANGUAGE AWARENESS

As illustrated in this book, any conception of language plays a key role in teachers' decisions on material choice, activity design and interaction patterns. We see at least three different conceptions of language displayed in the EFL classroom. The first and predominant conception is language as a system. In many EFL classrooms, language learning focuses on grammar and vocabulary, and in the pre-service teacher's talk this view comes out strongly. On the one hand, we see that teacher education now is moving away from a knowledge-based paradigm, and on the other hand, teachers (both pre-service and in-service) place emphasis on the acquisition of knowledge. This leads to the assumption that they as teachers also need to acquire sufficient subject knowledge. There seems to be a contradiction between the theoretical thinking of teacher education and practical teachers' needs and professional activities. There are at least two important reasons accounting for the conception of language as knowledge and teacher learning as a process of acquiring subject knowledge. First, in language classrooms, a teacher is still a knowledge source, and this is especially true in EFL contexts, where students do not have much language input or opportunities to practise the language outside the classroom. Hence, in this learning environment, the teacher is the most important source of language input and having sufficient knowledge is important for teachers to be in the position of being the knowledge source. Second, high-stakes tests which are mainly knowledge based shape the teaching and learning of English as a focus on form. The washback effect of high-stakes examinations has been reported in diverse contexts, such as Orafi and Borg (2009) in Libya, Choi (2008) in South Korea, and Underwood (2012) in Japan. This is to do with the macro-context of how language is interpreted in both national and local policies and curriculum. Therefore, 'policy changes in pedagogy not supported by changes in assessment may have little practical impact in the classroom' (Orafi and Borg 2009: 252).

This said, there is also a prevailing view of English being a tool, a resource, a channel to gain access to another culture and community and a power which can help people to gain opportunities in their work, study and personal lives. In fact, this view is becoming a norm in many EFL contexts despite the difficulty that teachers have in implementing this view in their teaching owing to local constraints such as the curriculum and examination system. English, as revealed in this book, certainly can be a power, especially for pre-service teachers, as it not only leads to a better job but to a better status and a better life potentially. In recent years, English has also attained significant value at a societal level where it may act as a gateway to studying abroad and securing a job or a power that brings respect to the teacher. It is this important status that enables teachers to focus on their own language development.

In this book, we also see a different conception of language, language as a social practice, where meaning is central and 'the expression of deeply embedded concepts that denote ways of feeling, seeing, and being in the world is focused' (Johnson 2009a: 46). It is also noted that teachers who conceptualise language as social practice also have experience of using language for social purposes. It seems that teachers' own experience with language contributes to their way of thinking of language.

It is clear that language knowledge is important for teachers, despite the different conceptions of what language is. Insufficient subject knowledge might exert a strong negative impact on teachers' confidence (Murdoch, 1994), which further influences the way they manage teaching, materials and access to language resources (Tsui 2003; Farrell and Richards 2007). In a classroom setting, teachers' subject knowledge certainly influences their instructional decisions (Andrews 2007; Borg 2011). So target language proficiency is an important factor of being a teacher, as teachers need to have an advanced level of language to provide explanations and rich language input and to respond to learners' questions spontaneously and knowledgeably (Richards et al. 2013: 244). As we have already observed in this book, insufficient knowledge also diverts the direction of the interaction, which hinders student participation, especially when learners initiate unfamiliar topics to teachers, or raise questions that are beyond teachers' knowledge capacity. From a language development perspective, teachers' language knowledge and proficiency level facilitates learners' language growth.

In essence, there are three issues we need to address in relation to raising teachers' subject knowledge awareness. First, despite the importance of subject knowledge in influencing instructional decisions and learners' language development, it is important to raise teachers' awareness of the nature of language. The argument is that if teachers are aware of the different conceptions of language, they are in a better position to guide students and to develop their competence in meeting learners' needs. That is, teachers can implement different approaches in teaching English as a system, as a communicative tool or as a social practice. Second, rather than focusing purely on developing teachers' own language competence, it is more sensible to develop their awareness of their language knowledge. That is, knowing what they know and what they do not know is more important than trying to improve their own language proficiency. Third, teachers and researchers might want to consider the role of metalanguage. In Chapter 4, we see teachers struggling to decide whether they should be presenting grammar using terminology. This raises a question of pedagogical consideration in teacher knowledge of metalanguage and the use of it in teaching. It is clear that knowledge of grammatical terminology enhances teachers' understanding of grammar rules, but does it enhance learning too?

PEDAGOGICAL THINKING

Of course, there is an opposite view that an adequate level of knowledge does not guarantee good teaching practice (Bartels 2005; Johnson 2009b). As pointed out throughout this book, pedagogical knowledge is equally if not more important than subject knowledge. There are two areas in particular which merit discussion. First, there is classroom management, including teaching procedures and how to make smooth transitions from one activity to another. For all teachers, including student teachers, novice teachers and expert teachers, effective classroom management is key to the creation of an environment for successful learning (LePage et al. 2005), including being able to create a cohesive lesson, transitioning smoothly from one stage of a lesson to another, and maintaining students' engagement and attention. In line with the existing literature (e.g. Burnard 1998; Silvestri 2001), in this book student and novice teachers often cite classroom management issues as their greatest challenge, whereas teachers who demonstrate expertise in this area clearly show ability in engaging students and managing learning well. It is this gaining and maintaining engagement that makes teaching effective (Acheson and Gall 2003; Nolan and Hoover 2008). One aspect of managing learners' engagement and the smooth transition of a lesson is about managing learners' behaviours and setting up classroom norms and rules. This kind of classroom management is well identified in novice teachers' classrooms, and the majority of which involves disciplining and managing behaviours. As discussed in previous chapters, the attention to students' behaviour suggests teachers' level of confidence and beliefs about misbehaviour (Arbuckle and Little 2004). The more time teachers spend on managing classroom behaviour, the less confident they are and the less able to tolerate unexpected behaviours in the classroom.

The second area relating to pedagogical consideration is what teaching methodology or methods teachers have adopted and what learning they are facilitating. As I have argued in Chapter 7 and throughout the book, it might not be legitimate that teachers try to fit in a specific teaching method as we are in the post-method era and teachers need to consider more of the local context in order to address the students' needs and learning styles. There is a tension between knowledge-based learning and participatory learning. I would argue that what teachers promote in their classroom should be relevant and appropriate for the context. This said, encouraging students' participation and engagement should be the key to effective learning.

CONTEXTUAL KNOWLEDGE

The importance of the context and its influence on teaching practice is well documented in the literature (e.g. Andrews 2003; Hayes 2009, 2010). Tsui (2003) proposes that teachers constantly construct and reconstruct their understandings of their work as teachers as a result of their interactions with the people in their context of work. Holliday (2005: 2) notes that '[I]t is people, not places, who have professions, prejudices and cultures', and the ideas and cultures that people bring to their interaction defines the nature of teaching and learning, the classroom order, the appropriate materials and language use in the classroom. For this reason, perhaps teacher education should place a strong emphasis on understanding the context and the influence of the local context on teaching practice. As we understand now, teachers develop their pedagogies within their professional contexts and through their interaction with the materials available to them, to their colleagues, to students and to influential parties (such as parents and school principals), and they engage in negotiation between macro-level educational policies and micro-level classroom realities.

There are several types of contextual knowledge that language teachers need to develop at both a macro- and a micro-level. At a macro-level, teachers need to understand language policy, the curriculum, the impact of testing, the ideology of learning, cultural norms and so on, and how these factors play out in their classroom practice. At the micro-level, the first and foremost issue is knowledge of their students. Mullock (2003) found that knowing and understanding students, their needs, and their strengths and weakness was considered a feature of a good teacher. His later study (Mullock 2006) suggests that knowing ones' students – their backgrounds, personalities, proficiency levels, strengths and weakness – and being able to adjust one's teaching to suit one's students is one of the most frequently mentioned knowledge issues identified by teachers. It is this contextual knowledge that teachers refer to in fine-tuning their pedagogical knowledge in classroom practice.

Context features in many studies in teacher cognition, as Borg highlights: '[T]he study of cognition and practice without an awareness of the contexts in which these occur will inevitably provide partial, if not flawed, characterisations of teachers and teaching' (2006: 106). Recognizing the critical role that context plays in teachers' decision-making and practice, it is legitimate to encourage teachers to engage in critical and reflective thinking about the contextual factors in relation to their practice and student learning. This can be done through detailed analysis of their thinking, lesson planning and teaching in a dialogic and collaborative manner. I will return to this later.

CLASSROOM INTERACTIONAL COMPETENCE

Walsh argues that the construct of CIC is vitally important for teaching and learning, telling us '[I]t puts interaction firmly at the centre of teaching and learning and argues that by improving their CIC, both teachers and learners will immediately improve learning and opportunities for learning' (2011: 158).

The importance of CIC lies not only in improving learning but also in improving teachers as professionals. There are two reasons to examine CIC with regard to teacher cognition. First of all, teachers' knowledge about CIC and how teachers develop CIC and how CIC can assist learning is key to improve teaching effectiveness. We can see that there is a clear need to develop teachers' interactional competence to enable learners to participate and contribute to the class. In order to do that, teachers need to understand the role of classroom interaction in learning, and also develop their CIC in facilitating a learner-centred approach. A discursive psychological approach to teacher cognition plays an important role in developing teachers' CIC. Through detailed analysis of what is going on in the classroom and by examining the pedagogical goals and interactional strategies that teachers utilise in facilitating learning, we can understand what CIC is from teachers' perspectives and how they implement interactional resources in different contexts. The content-specific moment-by-moment practitioner practice of CIC will enable us to understand further what CIC entails at a practical level, which can be transferred to the design of teacher education and development.

Second, there exists a strong relationship between CIC and expertise. As illustrated and discussed in Chapter 5, one of the key features of expertise is teachers' CIC. Because classroom interaction is central in understanding teacher cognition and CIC is a key feature of expertise, it is important to have CIC development as a key agenda in teacher education. As Walsh (2013) claims, CIC is about good decision-making, and by examining CIC we come closer to understanding expertise. That is, expertise is no longer an abstract concept but a practice teachers can identify in their actual teaching through examining their classroom interaction. In terms of developing teacher expertise, one useful way is to engage in a close examination of the moment where CIC is displayed and help teachers become conscious about utilising the interactional strategies outlined above in achieving their pedagogical goals, creating space for learner participation, and shaping learning.

THE ROLE OF EXPERIENCE (AND) EXPERTISE

Teachers' knowledge exists largely in very personalised terms, based on unique experiences, individual conceptions and their interaction with local context. As discussed in Chapter 1, personal practical knowledge is used to refer to a teacher's knowledge, to highlight the personalised and experience-based features. It becomes clear that experience plays a significant role in teachers' instructional choices, their thinking and their doing.

Learning and teaching experience plays a significant role in shaping teachers' conceptions and understandings. As we understand, much of teachers' theory is based on practical personal knowledge, which stems from their own experience of being a student, their teaching experience, and other experiences they engage with in the professional world. On the one hand, student teachers' past educational and school experiences play a significant role in shaping and developing their own conception of teaching, which exerts a strong influence on teachers' future professional lives. This learning experience serves as a filter for teachers to process new information. On the other hand, in the workplace teachers develop practitioner knowledge (Johnson

2009b) which can serve as a knowledge base for L2 teacher education. The practitioner knowledge links with practice in that it develops in response to issues emerging from the practice. That is, practitioner knowledge stems from the problems of practice and, as such, it is detailed, concrete and specific, and is highly context-related and non-transferrable in many cases. However, when this type of practitioner knowledge is made public and represented in a way that is accessible to others and open for inspection, verification and modification, it becomes legitimate knowledge for L2 teacher education. Then this knowledge is transferrable, concrete but also relevant to a specific context. There are three obvious reasons to examine the problems that come up in practice and make them relevant to teacher education. First, these problems/issues are generated in and emerge from teachers' lived experience and therefore they are authentic. Second, the problems are situated in a specific context, which might be shared by other teachers. And third, they highlight the interconnectedness of teachers' thinking in practice (Johnson 2006). Teachers' 'thinking' can be observed in and through practice.

Expertise can be conceptualised as a quality or as a process. It is distributed, which is displayed in the talk-in-interaction. It is also multiple, which means it is not a certain characteristic which only exists in expert teachers, but is an ability which both novice and expert teachers can have at a given moment. Berliner (1995) and Gatbonton (2008) assert the importance of comparing novice and experienced teachers because this has strong implications for teacher development. Therefore, it is important to examine closely the expertise displayed by teachers, using an up-close approach to map out what expertise is and how it is displayed in action. Chapter 6 has focused on the areas which have been neglected in the literature, such as how expertise is related to the contexts of work, what contributes to expertise and how expertise is displayed in teachers' dealings with subject-content knowledge (Tsui 2003). A comparison between expert and novice teachers suggests that expertise is closely related to experience and critical reflection. Expertise has a close relationship to experience as teachers develop their understanding, competence, practical knowledge and flexibility through practice, although experience does not necessarily lead to expertise (Ericsson et al. 1993) and some experienced teachers remain non-expert (Tsui 2003).

Nishimuro and Borg argue that critical reflection informed by propositional knowledge might promote productive pedagogy (2013: 45). The critical reflection, which can be interpreted as deliberate practice, also contributes to developing expertise. Deliberate practice, as Ericsson et al. argued, 'would allow for repeated experiences in which the individual can attend to the critical aspects of the situation and incrementally improve her or his performance in response to knowledge of results, feedback, or both from a teacher' (1993: 368). Therefore, it is within the rich experience of teaching that an individual can achieve expertise through purposeful and reflective engagement with the practice (Palmer et al. 2005). There is a clear role for studying teacher cognition through a discursive psychological perspective in facilitating and developing expertise. As illustrated in Chapters 4, 5 and 6, through engaging in an up-close analysis of moment-by-moment thinking a teacher can engage in critical reflection of their practice. From a teacher learning perspective, it is more meaningful to assist teachers to engage in such reflections and analysis in order to understand the relationship between their pedagogical goals and their decision-making. Such an approach will improve the level of performance of teachers and help them to make deliberate choices.

I would also like to highlight the role of personal experience in contributing to effective instruction. It seems a deliberate choice by teachers to use personal experience in teaching, in particular in introducing a topic, engaging students and relating to student contributions. Personal experience also is used to contextualise learning materials, to expand learning opportunities and to increase authenticity.

PART 2: IMPLICATIONS OF TEACHER COGNITION ON TEACHER LEARNING

ADDRESSING CHALLENGES FOR PRE-SERVICE AND IN-SERVICE TEACHER TRAINING

In the last twenty or so years, researchers in SLTE have attempted to adopt a perspective that seeks to reconceptualise the field and establish a research-based approach to language teacher education. In essence, teacher education has moved from the 'cognitive apprenticeship' to a socio-cultural perspective of teacher education (Atkinson 1997: 87). The direction of teacher education has shifted from a transmissive mode, addressing deficits in teacher knowledge with appropriate input from theory and research domains, to a transformational approach, where the objective is to support teachers to understand and enhance their practice, and to engage in professional learning (Burns 2009). That is, the focus of teacher education has shifted from developing trainee teachers' classroom skills and techniques to enabling trainee teachers to develop their own theories and become aware of their own learning-to-teach processes. The meaning of mediation and strategies for scaffolding are introduced in SLTE, and different approaches to teacher education have emerged (e.g. see Johnson 2009a). Although the current theoretical perspective of teacher education has switched to the transformational approach to enhance teachers' professional learning, there exist challenges and issues that are widely acknowledged in teacher education.

The first issue concerns the complexity of teacher training. Researchers in teacher learning agree that it is complicated (Wilson et al. 2002) because it draws on different external and internal resources and it happens over time and is contextualised, unpredictable and often idiosyncratic (Darling-Hammond, 2006). Copland (2008) claims that initial English language teacher training courses can be exciting, confusing and traumatic at the same time for trainees. It is very common for teachers to feel confused because of the jargon and traumatised because of the assessed practical teaching, despite the excitement of embarking on a new learning experience. It is true that teacher education has become more challenging, and in order to understand how teachers learn and how their professional lives evolve it is important to focus on their cognition development and personal learning experience (Freeman and Richards 1996; Freeman and Johnson 1998).

As evidenced in the literature, much attention has been paid to the impact of teacher education on the development or change of student teacher cognition (Horwitz 1985; Peacock 2001; Li 2012). Wyatt (2009), Morton and Gray (2010) and Li (2012) suggest that formal instruction has a positive impact on teachers' practical knowledge growth. While it is clear from this evidence that efforts are being made to establish a link between teacher cognition and teacher education, it is as yet unclear how recognition of this importance translates into concrete action in teacher education programmes. Some research suggests that teacher educators should take into account the belief systems of pre-service teachers early in training as a means of correcting erroneous beliefs by maximising input (Peacock 2001; Lo 2005). I would argue that rather than focusing on changing teachers' beliefs as the goal of the teacher education, it is more important to determine how teacher cognition research can impact on teacher education. In fact, teacher cognition can have influence on almost every aspect of teacher education, from course design and delivery to assessment. For example Busch (2010) suggests that teacher cognition research can influence teacher training course design in terms of topic and assessment. He asserts that a formative, non-graded approach to the professional development of student teachers, perhaps as part of portfolios containing reflective commentary, is a useful alternative assessment. I would take this one step further to suggest that teacher education programmes should take a practice-based approach to allow teachers to have space and capacity in analysing and reflecting on their own understanding and pedagogical thinking, taking their knowledge, context and personal experience into account. The detailed analysis of their cognition-in-interaction will shed light on their understanding, knowing, conceptualising and stance-taking relating to teaching and learning.

The second challenge and issue in teacher education is the role of knowledge, especially subject and pedagogical knowledge (see Chapters 4 and 7). There is evidence in the literature that trainee teachers struggle with grasping the knowledge and focus on developing their knowledge. It is clear that trainee teachers need to develop their subject content knowledge as well as their pedagogical knowledge, which involves knowledge-based learning. On the other hand, as Edwards et al. (2002) and Johnson (2009a) note, student teachers are learning to teach in a climate marked by political, economic, cultural and philosophical uncertainty; therefore, 'the challenge is to avoid notions of a "knowledge-base" which are synonymous with simple fixed certainties, but to consider how teachers relate to the contestable and shifting knowledge available to them' (Edwards et al. 2002: 7). This challenge thus requires teacher education programmes to shift the focus from knowledge to developing students' ability to appropriate the knowledge available to them. It is true that students learn better when they participate, collaborate and construct their own ideas. However, simply asking trainee teachers to talk about their own understandings may be inadequate both in providing them with the subject knowledge they need to perform well as teachers and in enabling them to theorise their practice. Therefore, there is a tension between focusing on developing trainee teachers' subject and pedagogical knowledge and enhancing their professional learning by participation, reflection and collaboration.

The third challenge, which is closely related to the second, is that there is a lack of a shift in practice from the transmissive mode of teacher education to the transformational approach, as Burns (2009) warns. Because the immediate need of teacher trainees is for knowledge (in terms of both subject and pedagogical knowledge), together with the difficulty of developing teachers' ability to relate to the contestable and shifting knowledge available to them, teacher education, for the most part, remains a cognitive apprenticeship or a transmissive model, where teacher educators model or lecture trainee teachers. Studying teacher cognition through the lens of interaction is especially relevant for a transformational approach to teacher education, when teachers can articulate and analyse their thinking in a moment-by-moment manner.

ADDRESSING CHALLENGES FOR INFORMAL PROFESSIONAL DEVELOPMENT

Drawing on the broad literature of teacher learning in mainstream education, teacher professional learning is often characterised as ineffective, partly because professional learning is conceptualised in a simplistic way, which fails to consider how learning is embedded in professional lives and working conditions (Borko 2004; Timperley and Alton-Lee 2008). As pointed out by Darleen Opfer and Pedder (2011: 377), the majority of the writing on the topic (of teacher professional learning) continues to focus on 'specific activities processes, or programs in isolation from the complex teaching and learning environments in which teachers live', and they further emphasise that in order to explain teacher professional learning, one must 'consider what sort of local knowledge, problems, routines, and aspirations shape and are shaped by individual practices and beliefs (ibid.: 379). In examining the relevance of teacher cognition to teacher professional learning through informal ways, there are several issues worth considering.

The first issue concerns the conditions for successful and effective professional development. There are four important conditions necessary for successful professional development to happen. The first and perhaps the most important one is sufficient time – this includes both the time available to teachers and the length of the time that professional activities require. Time is strongly associated with the effectiveness of professional learning (Guskey 2000). The second condition is space – teachers' professional learning is more effective if it is school-based and integrated into their daily teaching, with the colleagues who share the same concerns, practices and understandings. That is, a local practice-based approach is more desirable than an abstract and distant approach. Teachers are more interested in ideas that can improve their teaching, rather than abstract specific prescriptive theories and techniques. The third condition concerns the approach to the professional learning – teachers' professional learning should reflect the way that they are required to teach students, or through loop input (Woodward 1986, 2003). That is, if teachers are expected to focus on developing communicative skills for students, then professional learning should provide them with an opportunity to experience the kind of learning that they are expected to practice. They do not just experience it, they learn the content this way. The final condition is about the nature of the professional learning. Collaborative professional development activities contribute to effective professional learning – teachers share the same interest working towards the same goal and support each other. In mainstream teacher education research, there is evidence that teachers' learning and innovation in practice is improved through teacher collaboration, which is usually termed as a professional community of practice (McLaughlin and Talbert 2001, 2006). McLaughlin and Talbert (2006: 9) concluded that:

> Researchers agree that teachers learn best when they are involved in activities that (a) focus on instruction and student learning specific to the settings in which they teacher; (b) are sustained and continuous, rather than episodic; (c) provide opportunities for teachers to collaborate with colleagues inside and outside the school; (d) reflect teachers' influence about what and how they learn; (e) help teachers develop theoretical understanding of the skills and knowledge they need to learn.

As such, this not only engages teachers in reflection but also develops what Lord calls 'critical colleagueship' (Lord 1994). Thus, creating conditions that facilitate teachers engaging in professional learning is perhaps the first issue facing both teachers and researchers.

The second issue is the continuity of professional development. Kiely and Davis (2010) suggest that continuity is always a central issue in professional development and they argue for a need to develop continuity between teachers' own experience-based analyses and frameworks from the literature. A discursive psychological perspective of teacher cognition gives teachers a tool to engage in professional development, with which they can link their practice in actual contexts to any potential theoretical input they can get. That is, teachers are able to engage in critical reflection on their knowing displayed in the classroom interaction to theorise their professional knowledge. These kinds of opportunities provide teachers with data-led reflective practice and link their actual work to theories. Such reflection therefore can be ongoing because it is from the teachers' own context and the teachers are able to engage with data-led reflections regularly.

The third issue within professional development is around the role of reflective practice. As suggested earlier, professional growth involves critical thinking and reflection. When teachers engage in critical reflection on their teaching, they are more likely to learn and develop. Reflection is 'deliberate thinking about action with a view to its improvement' (Hatten and Smith 1995: 34), and because of the complexity of teaching and the interactive decisions teachers have to make in teaching, reflection is a meaningful method to engage in teachers' deliberate thinking. However, reflective practice has been criticised as being vague, problematic and 'of unproven benefit' (Griffiths 2000). The problems with reflective practice are several and the most pressing one perhaps is that it is ambiguous and superficial (Mann and Walsh 2013). On the one hand, teachers are expected to reflect without a concrete basis, and, on the other, reflective practice in most professional development ends up by paying lip-service to it or even 'faking it' (Hobbs 2007). There is also a related issue regarding the difficulty of conducting reflective practice despite the existing model for reflections (e.g. Kolb's experiential learning model, 1984). In general, teachers do not know how to reflect and what tools are available for reflection (Walsh 2013).

Russell proposed that '[R]eflective practice should be taught – explicitly, directly, thoughtfully and patiently – using personal reflection-in-action to interpret and improve one's teaching of reflective practice to others' (2005: 203–4). Walsh proposed that teachers should engage in data-led reflective practice because 'most reports of reflective practice do not include any evidence of people actually *doing* reflection' (2013: 116) but 'the process of reflection itself requires evidence (in the form of data)' (ibid.: 117). That is, if teachers can improve their teaching through reflective practice, then one way to do so is to facilitate them in engaging in reflecting on their thinking and teaching. This has to be based on data (evidence) so that teachers have a concrete base to reflect upon, thereby making the data-led reflection deeper and longer-lasting. Currently, and in many contexts where reflective practice is encouraged (whether in pre-service and in-service teaching programmes or in informal professional development), teachers are adopting the individually introspective approach. Recognising the importance of collaboration in learning and the active role the learners play, Convery (1998) proposes a collaborative and social approach. In a similar vein, Johnson (2009a) proposes inquiry-based professional development and reviews models that promote collaboration and dialogue, including critical friends groups, peer coaching/mentoring, lesson study, cooperative development and teacher study groups, separately. Inquiry-based professional development encourages teachers to take the active role in identifying the issues and problems they encounter and to work out possible solutions with support from colleagues who come from the same practice and have obtained the local knowledge.

It is clear that inquiry-based professional development and a critical reflective approach is desirable in addressing teachers' professional needs. A collaborative and practitioner-driven approach with an explicit focus on exploring and analysing context-specific professional issues is effective. In their professional lives teachers experience a variety of encounters with the professional world which enable them to foster the refinement of craft skills, professional knowledge and experiential resources (Garton and Richards 2008). Simply put, in order to promote teacher professional learning, local knowledge, problems, routines and aspirations that shape and are shaped by individual practices and beliefs must be taken into consideration. These issues presented above are challenges but also opportunities for alternative approaches to teacher education. In embracing the idea of learning as a socially-constructed practice and the idea that people learn when they reflect and engage in dialogues, a dialogic reflective approach is beneficial for professional learning.

A COLLABORATIVE DIALOGIC REFLECTIVE PRACTICE (CDRP)

A reflective approach engages teachers in developing their personal theories of teaching, systematically examining their own decision processes and teaching practices, and developing critical thinking skills that lead to self-awareness and change (Richards 1998a). A reflective approach views (trainee) teachers as active agents of their learning-to-teach processes and provides the groundwork for continuous self-development (Vélez-Rendón 2002: 463). This often involves critical reflection and awareness raising. However, this does not mean that teachers will develop if they are simply given space for reflection. In the case of pre-service and in-service teacher education, it does not mean that teachers become aware of the relevance of theoretical input from the course to their own teaching. Taking the conditions for professional learning outlined above, a dialogic reflective approach can be effective. There are at least three conditions for an effective dialogic reflective approach. First, it requires ample opportunities for the teachers to acquire the relevant theoretical underpinnings of the profession and understand them. Understanding theories is different from reproducing them when required but is a stance that teachers can take in relation to their own teaching context. Second, teachers need sufficient analytical and reflective skills to connect between theory and practice. And third, teachers need to work in a collaborative community where they work and interact with critical colleagues. A CDRP rests on the belief that teachers learn together through dialogues in a trusting and supportive environment (see also Mann and Walsh 2013). It gives teachers opportunities to analyse and engage in high-leverage practices such as providing feedback and scaffolding. This kind of work enables teachers to engage in critical reflection on their own practice, and integrate theory with practice rather than disconnect the two (Grossman et al. 2009).

TOOLS FOR PROFESSIONAL LEARNING

There are different types of methods and tools that enable reflection. To ensure learning takes place, the reflective tools must be data led. Next, I will review three different methods that teachers can use for professional learning and that researchers can use for investigating teacher learning.

The post-observation feedback session

The post-observation feedback session is a common approach many teacher educators take to evaluate trainee teachers' teaching. Copland (2008) summarises the two main objectives of this kind of feedback session: (1) to provide an opportunity for participants to talk about what happened in the lesson, and (2) to provide trainees with feedback on the lesson. In essence, the feedback has dual foci, with one being to allow trainees to reflect on action and perhaps explain what they were thinking in that moment, and the other being evaluation of the trainees' teaching offered by the teacher educator. As noted in Chapter 4 and also in the literature (e.g. Copland 2008), one of the major areas that prospective teachers focus on is pedagogy, in particular effectiveness in teaching. Teachers display what they know and believe, and reflect what they do in their interaction with the teacher trainer. In this reflection, the majority of attention has been paid to *what* has been said rather than *how* it is said and what insights the interaction can offer in assisting teacher learning. So, if we can draw our attention to what is displayed in the interaction rather than what the interaction is, in the post-observation feedback session we become closer to understanding the thinking that a teacher engages at that moment.

Lesson-planning conference/team planning

Taking situated learning (Lave and Wenger 1991), and specifically Wenger's (1998) model of learning as participation in communities of practice, Morton and Gray (2010) focus on 'lesson planning conferences' (LPCs), in which a teacher educator and a group of student teachers worked on one student teacher's lesson plan. The lesson-planning conference is a dynamic recursive process in which problems of instruction emerge and solutions are suggested. Morton and Gray argue that shared lesson planning is a promising strategy for the construction of novice language teachers' personal practical knowledge, because in this process they do not just get input from the expert but also have space to realise and develop their own thinking. The lesson-planning conference places emphasis on knowing and can be seen as a 'discursive problem-solving' action that takes place in a socially-structured place (Edwards et al. 2002: 114). In this social place, novice and expert construct their understanding of teaching and learning through doing genuine productive work. The lesson-planning conference has a dual function – it serves as genuine practice in which teachers engage in schools when they prepare their lessons together and as an example of instruction. That is, the lesson-planning conference resembles the authentic professional life in which trainee teachers are expected to participate and to conduct their practice within the community. This dialogic reflective learning experience helps them to form the habit of continuous reflection with colleagues through dialogues. Equally, expert teachers or teacher educators provide models for successful teaching that could be used as scaffolding for novice teachers to develop their competence (Berliner 1995).

Video-based reflection

Breen (1991) suggests that one route to curriculum change in teacher training is through the promotion of teacher reflection, in particular by encouraging teachers to evaluate the 'actual classroom events'. The use of post-lesson reflection based on video-recordings not only raises students' awareness of what happens when they teach, but also provides them with a structure and concrete evidence to reflect on, develop and learn what they know, believe and do. Video-based reflection is one form of stimulated recall which teachers can use to examine their classroom practice. This could be used in different ways such as watching and analysing their interactive decisions within critical friends' groups or with peers. The teacher and their peers can engage in a reflective dialogue. It could occur in the format of critical friends' groups where their conversations are more structured by the protocols or remain open so that both parties can raise any questions and comment on aspects of their teaching. This provides teachers with 'the opportunity to verbalize their thinking, in a relatively free and open-ended manner' (Borg 2006: 210). The video-based reflection serves as the basis for teachers to reflect on and become aware of their decision-making and for researchers to see from the teachers' perspective their understanding, knowing and decision-making (Li 2013).

All the above-mentioned techniques are data led, and provide teachers with evidence that they reflect on. Further, because the data is teachers' own practice, they enable teachers to identify an agenda for development which is based on their needs.

Additionally, it is a dialogic reflective approach. That is, teachers are supported within a collaborative environment in which they can converse. The merit of having a dialogic reflective approach is that it provides the participants with opportunities to engage in a closer understanding of what they display in their understanding through interacting with others. This process enables the teachers to explore not only what they know and believe but how their knowing and believing is displayed in their doing. A traditional view of an ideal partner with whom trainee or novice teachers can engage in reflection is one who is experienced and knowledgeable and who can lead and support the teacher in their reflection and connection between theory and practice. Although it is true that teacher educators and expert teachers are able to provide scaffolding at both theoretical and practical levels, a collaborative process between teachers, in which they share experiences and jointly explore ways of developing, is more attractive. That is, teachers could use more peer dialogic reflection in assisting each other because the nature of collaboration promotes the development of insights and possibilities for innovative practice (Kiely and Davis 2010).

There are other types of methods to engage teachers in collaborative dialogic reflection, but the role of detailed analysis of moment-by-moment thinking and knowing is critical. Seedhouse (2008) argues that many of the complexities and subtleties of professional discourse may not be always evident during observation or video, but can be revealed by fine-grained CA. The discursive psychological perspective of teacher cognition using the principles of CA has merits in unveiling the moment-by-moment thinking, decision-making and understanding. The stance that teachers take can be seen from the fine-grained analysis of their instructional practices.

FUTURE DIRECTIONS

Darling-Hammond (2000) proposes that the quality of teacher education greatly influences student achievement, therefore it is vitally important for teacher educators to enhance the quality of teacher education. The issues in teacher education outlined above continue to be challenges for L2 teacher education but the future directions can be taken with multiple perspectives.

DEVELOPING TEACHERS' AWARENESS OF LANGUAGE AS SOCIAL PRACTICE

One of the challenges derived from this book is the place of teacher knowledge in teacher learning. To what extent should subject knowledge and pedagogical knowledge be taught? And how explicitly should it be taught? This is especially true for pre-service teacher education. Given the importance of knowledge in effective teaching, and the current trend of developing teachers' awareness of language rather than knowledge of language, there is a gap between the theoretical thinking of developing and educating teachers and the practical needs and concerns of teachers. One way forward is to focus on developing teachers' awareness of language as social practice (Johnson 2009a). Traditionally, language awareness focuses on 'developing a conscious understanding of, and the meta-linguistic terminology to explain, the structural and/or functional features of language' (ibid.: 47). For language teacher education to embrace a language as a social practice perspective the focus is shifted to teachers' ability to guide students not only to use the language appropriately in different situations but, more importantly, to develop an explicit awareness of the social and pragmatic norms which underlie appropriate use of the language. Although Johnson does not make explicit reference to interactional competence, her idea of language as social practice aligns nicely with the concept of interactional competence. In relation to language teacher education and development, it is clear that teachers need to develop awareness of language as social practice and interactional competence in order to develop students' skills in manipulating and utilising resources available in achieving communicative goals. That said, it does not mean that teachers should not develop knowledge about structural properties, rather having the meta-knowledge of linguistic properties will enable teachers to assist students to develop their interactional competence or focus on the meaning through understanding of the linguistic form and language function. As Johnson (2009a) claims, when language is conceptualised as social practice the focus of teaching is shifted towards helping learners develop the capacity to interpret and generate meanings relevant to languaculture (see Lantolf and Johnson 2007). From a teacher education perspective, in order to help teachers to embrace the concept of language as social practice, teachers need to become more conscious about how language conveys meanings in different contexts and this can be achieved through discourse analysis. Moreover, teachers must come to the understanding that language is not fixed and meaning is developed in situ as a consequence of interaction between participants.

TRANSFORMATIVE TEACHER EDUCATION

As noted earlier, the direction of teacher education has shifted from a transmissive mode, addressing deficits in teacher knowledge, to a transformational approach, empowering teachers to understand and enhance their practice and to engage in professional learning (Burns 2009). This shift in understanding of teacher learning remains at the theoretical level and there is a lack of practice in adopting the transformative approach in teacher education (ibid.). As outlined in this book, teacher learning needs to be centred on the process of knowing, which calls for future teacher education to be directed to enable teachers to know and engage in the process of knowing in their professional lives. The transformative approach to teacher education, which focuses on empowering teachers to develop their understanding, aligns with this direction. Exercising a transformative approach to teacher education can be approached by utilising the role of teacher cognition. As argued throughout the book, teacher cognition is not a fixed entity but involves thinking, knowing, understanding, conceptualising and stance-taking which is displayed in the professional encounters. Teacher cognition can be about anything in their professional context which shapes and is shaped by their lived experience. By exploring teacher cognition-in-interaction, teachers can be taught how to access their thinking, knowing, conceptualising and stance-taking, thus raising their own awareness of professional needs in learning. Implementing a transformative approach to teacher education needs to take into account the professional setting in which the teacher works. This is a meaningful way for teachers to understand what it means to be a teacher. The transformative approach therefore emphasises the understanding of the individual teacher in the specific setting. In practice, perhaps the focus needs to be placed on how theoretically effective pedagogy is relevant to the local context.

Johnson (2006) also argues the importance of taking into account the social, political, economic and cultural histories that are located in the contexts in which L2 teachers teach and learn. She proposes 'located' teacher education which takes into account local constraints. She further suggests that 'located' L2 teacher education 'begins by recognizing why L2 teachers do what they do within the social, historical, and cultural contexts within which they work and from there works to co-construct with L2 teachers locally appropriate responses to their professional development needs' (ibid.: 246). Recognising teachers' thinking in their context can be realised through researching teacher cognition. Of course, by examining teacher cognition teachers come to the understanding of how and why macro-structures, such as curriculum, policy and testing, impact their classroom practices. Similarly, the 'located' teacher education focuses on navigating and sustaining teacher expertise in their professional contexts and identity construction (see below), which in turn shapes the development of teacher cognition.

COGNITION AND IDENTITY

Closely related to language teacher cognition is the area of teacher identity. Miller highlights the relationship between cognition and identity, claiming that 'thinking, knowing, believing, and doing are enacted in classroom contexts in a way that cannot be separated from identity formation. What teachers know and do is part of their identity work, which is continuously performed and transformed through interaction in classroom' (2009: 175). When teachers conceptualise and conduct their professional work, they construct multiple identities which constantly shift across both space and time (Beijaard et al. 2004; Miller 2009). That is, teacher identities are shaped through social interactions that occur within the contexts in which teachers work (Miller Marsh 2003: 10), and identity shifts develop over time. Like teacher cognition, identity is developed through teachers' personal experience, shaped by contextual factors and influenced by professional values and standards. Because both macro- and micro-contexts contribute to the development of teacher cognition and identity, it is important to understand teacher identity in order to explore the power relations and teacher agency (Morgan and Clarke 2011). That is, the lived experience of teachers and the interaction with the context defines the nature of teacher identity as continuously co-constructed in situ, shaped by personal experience, cultural norms and societal values. In particular, teacher identity, similar to teacher cognition, is highly influenced by the school culture, institutional practices, curriculum, access to professional development, interaction with important others (such as colleagues and students) and any resources available to them. The close relationship between teacher cognition and identity is highlighted in understanding possible language teacher selves, defined as 'language teachers' cognitive representations of their ideal, ought-to and feared selves in relation to their work as language teachers' (Kubanyiova 2009: 315).

In the research on teacher cognition the most relevant work is around teacher cognition of self, or of being a good language teacher (e.g. Farrell 2011; Li 2012). Specifically, these researchers concern themselves with the roles of teachers in teaching and highlight the multiple roles teachers should play in facilitating learning – such as organizer, participant, resource, controller and assessor – despite the popularity of the concept of the teacher being the knowledge provider and authority in the classroom. There is a clear link between what teachers are and what teaching and learning is. When teaching and learning is viewed as knowledge transmission and acquisition, teachers are considered as knowledge provider, authority and evaluator. When teaching and learning is viewed as knowledge sharing and co-constructing, teachers are considered as facilitator and participant in activities.

Duff and Uchida (1997: 451) present key elements in understanding teacher identity, suggesting that 'language teachers and students in any setting naturally represent a wide array of social and cultural roles and identities'. It is a truism that language teachers display the ongoing construction and deconstruction of who they are and what they are in the social space. The school and the classroom are examples of social space where teachers construct their professional identity through interaction with their colleagues, students, materials and curriculum. One particular issue that is relevant to EFL teachers is the non-native speaker identity and the role of subject knowledge. Non-native teachers in becoming and being language teachers experience conflicts and challenges in defining themselves with regards being a knowledge provider. It is in many EFL contexts that teachers feel that they have responsibilities in providing students with sufficient language knowledge and input on the one hand, while, on the other, helping them to acquire interactional competence. Although these two areas are not necessarily in conflict with each other, for many non-native English speaking teachers, it is a challenge to strike a balance. The psychological self-image in becoming and being a teacher is a social process taking place in an institutional setting where the professional context shapes and is shaped by teachers' positioning and agency. Teachers need to understand that identity is a complex and multiple individual and social phenomenon, which has impact on pedagogy and instructional practice. Miller (2009) calls for more research in teacher identity, with regard to the nature of identity, and identity and pedagogy. Endorsing Gee's (1996) understanding of identity, Miller reinforces the concept of identity being multidimensional and multifaceted. A core part of understanding teacher identity is about agency and power relations. The power and agency that teachers have in the classroom will consequentially impact their instructional practice and pedagogy; in particular, agency empowers teachers to take an active role in changing practices and bring innovation into their teaching.

Varghese et al. (2005) propose the importance of the social and dialogic nature of identity and the need to focus on both 'identity-in-practice' and 'identity-in-discourse'. In this sense, identity is a product of social practice and is a social matter, while 'identity-in-discourse' emphasises that 'identity is constructed, maintained and negotiated to a significant extent through language and discourse (ibid.: 23).

Discourses 'are historically, culturally, politically generated patterns of thinking, speaking, acting, and interacting that are sanctioned by a particular group of people' (Miller Marsh 2003: 7). That is, the interactional work in which teachers engage in their professional contexts displays their thinking, actions and their individual and collective images of being teachers. Teacher identity does not just come out nothing, but occurs in relation to a global and local discourse that shapes the meanings of teacher and teaching. As Beauchamp and Thomas (2011: 7) point out, 'a teacher's experience can be one of not only active construction of an identity, but also of an imposed identity stemming from societal and cultural conceptions of teachers'.

The way in which language teachers use language in their professional contexts reflects the dialogical and representational possible self. As Olsen (2011: 262) suggests, identity arises from language as 'any self is defined, made, and continually remade by participation in language and language practices'. A representational view sees identity as represented by language use. So when teachers conduct their professional work, the language they use and how they use language in instruction is a window into their professional identities and possible selves. From the language and the interactional work they do with their students, we see a spectrum of the teacher being a learning facilitator and scaffolder, and knowledge provider and evaluator (see more in Morton and Gray, forthcoming).

Researching teacher identity has become majority part of teacher education, informing individual teachers' professional growth in an independent and critical way. Focusing on teacher identity formation when exploring teacher cognition not only enables teachers to better understand their thinking and actions in actual contexts, but also to realise possible selves in their professional contexts and the connections between self and the contextual factors. It is through understanding their own thinking, beliefs and behaviours that teachers can reach 'deep considerations of the self in relation to educational contexts' (Beauchamp and Thomas 2009: 185–6).

FINAL REMARKS

This book set out to investigate language teacher cognition through the lens of social interaction by using DP and CA as the methodology. Cognition is defined as cognition-in-interaction, referring to the ways in which teachers construct knowledge, understandings and propositions in interaction. Cognition therefore is publically displayed and socially shared, focusing on knowing, thinking, conceptualising, stance-taking and similar psychological processes. Unlike existing research in teacher cognition, talk (interaction) is not treated as a channel to gain teachers' understanding and beliefs; rather, it is viewed as a medium of action and a display of cognition.

Researching teacher cognition through social interaction thus has value in understanding teachers' planning, decision-making and beliefs. As I have argued throughout the book, teaching is based on interactive decision-making, therefore it is important to view teacher cognition in the moment-by-moment context and take the pedagogical goals of that moment into consideration. In fact, more work is necessary to research teacher cognition through interaction when teachers engage in professional practice. Only in this way can we achieve fine-grained, up-close descriptions of teacher cognition-in-interaction in their professional context, and understand how and why decisions are made, and explore opportunities to improve pedagogy and develop teachers.

Teacher cognition is a very important area for improving pedagogy, teacher learning and educational effectiveness. In researching teachers we must remember that teachers are active decision-makers who make interactive decisions in their local contexts. Therefore, it is vital to consider their cognition-in-interaction. DP offers a perspective to understand that cognition is fluid, developmental and context-shaping. Again, learning to teach or teaching to learn is not just about teaching techniques, but is a process of teachers developing their expertise and identity. It involves personal experience, subject knowledge, contextual knowledge and pedagogical knowledge. Professional learning therefore should be continuous, long term and situated in teachers' practice contexts. Such learning should address the needs of teachers through exploring teachers' knowing, understanding, conceptualising and stance-taking. It has become clear through the analysis of various aspects of teacher cognition in this book that cognition-in-interaction could well be used in professional development to enable teachers to conduct guided reflective practice, thereby improving pedagogy. I have also suggested ways to improve pedagogy and teacher learning in this book; however, the concept of 'best method' and 'good teaching' should be abandoned in favour of the diversity of the teacher and teaching contexts (Garton 2008). Teachers can be differently successful and effective. The key message here is that the aim of language teacher education is not to develop 'best' teachers but to 'empower' individual teachers by understanding their practice in 'live' contexts through understanding their own knowing and doing.

Although much work has been done in investigating teachers' beliefs and knowledge, language teacher cognition-in-interaction is only beginning to offer in-depth understandings of teachers' thinking and decision-making. There is still much more work to be done, especially in uncovering how teachers develop expertise, when and why they make interactive decision-making, and how teachers use their knowledge to develop learning opportunities.

APPENDIX: TRANSCRIPTION CONVENTIONS

ADAPTED FROM HUTCHBY AND WOOFFITT (2008)

(1.8)	Numbers enclosed in parentheses indicate a pause. The number represents the number of seconds' duration of the pause, to one decimal place.
(.)	A pause of less than 0.2 seconds.
=	An equal sign is used to show that there is no time lapse between the portions connected by the equal signs. This is used where a second speaker begins their utterance just at the moment when the first speaker finishes.
[ ]	Brackets around portions of utterances show that those portions overlap with a portion of another speaker's utterance.
.hh	This indicates an audible inhalation of air, for example a gasp. The more h's, the longer the in-breath.
((looking))	A description enclosed in a double bracket indicates a non-verbal activity or the transcriber's note.
an-	A dash indicates an abrupt cut-off, where the speaker stopped speaking suddenly.
sou::nd	A colon after a vowel or a word is used to show that the sound is extended. The number of colons shows the length of the extension.
?	A question mark indicates a rising intonation.
.	A period indicates that there is slightly falling intonation.
!	Exclamation marks are used to indicate an animated or emphatic tone.
(would)	When a word appears in parentheses it indicates that the transcriber has guessed as to what was said, because it was indecipherable on the tape. If the transcriber was unable to guess as to what was said, it is noted as unintelligible.
↑↓	Up or down arrows are used to indicate that there is sharply rising or falling intonation. The arrow is placed just before the syllable in which the change in intonation occurs.
Under	Underlines indicate speaker emphasis on the underlined portion of the word.
CAPS	Capital letters indicate that the speaker spoke the capitalised portion of the utterance at a higher volume than the speaker's normal volume.

°would°	This indicates an utterance that is much softer than the normal speech of the speaker. This symbol will appear at the beginning and at the end of the utterance in question.
> <, < >	'Greater than' and 'less than' signs indicate that the talk they surround was noticeably faster or slower than the surrounding talk.
£C'mon£	Sterling signs are used to indicate a smiley or jokey voice.
(T:00.23)	Data source.

REFERENCES

Abelson, R. (1979). Differences between belief systems and knowledge systems. *Cognitive Science*, 3, 355–366.
Acheson, K. A. and Gall, M. D. (2003). *Clinical supervision and teacher development: Preservice and inservice application*. Hoboken, NJ: John Wiley and Sons.
Adhikari, K. (2007). An investigation of Nepalese English teachers' perception of CLT and its implementation in Nepalese secondary schools. *Journal of NELTA*, 12(1 and 2), 1–7.
Ahmed, M. K. (1994). Speaking as cognitive regulation. A Vygotskian perspective on dialogic communication. In J. P. Lantolf and G. Appel (Eds) *Vygotskian approaches to second language research* (pp. 157–171). Norwood, NJ: Ablex Publishing Corporation.
Ajzen, I. (1988). *Attitude, personality and behaviour*. Chicago, IL: Dorsey Press.
Akyel, A. (1997). Experienced and student EFL teachers' instructional thoughts and actions. *Canadian Modern Language Review*, 53(4), 677–704.
Alanen, R. (2003). A sociocultural approach to young language learners' beliefs about language learning. In P. Kalaja and A. M. F. Barcelos (Eds) *Beliefs about SLA: New research approaches*. Dordrecht: Kluwer Academic Publishers.
Allen, L. (1996). The evaluation of a learner's beliefs about language learning. *Carleton' Papers in Applied Language Studies*, 13, 67–80.
Allwright, R. L. (1984). The importance of interaction in classroom language learning. *Applied Linguistics*, 5, 156–171.
Andrews, S. (1999). Why do L2 teachers need to 'know about language'? Teacher metalinguistic awareness and input for learning. *Language and Education*, 13(3), 161–177.
Andrews, S. (2003). 'Just like instant noodles': L2 teachers and their beliefs about grammar pedagogy. *Teachers and Teaching*, 9(4), 351–375.
Andrews, S. (2006). The evolution of teachers' language awareness. *Language Awareness*, 15, 1–19.
Andrews, S. (2007). *Teacher language awareness*. Cambridge: Cambridge University Press.
Andrews, S. and McNeil, A. (2005). Knowledge about language and the 'good language teacher'. In N. Bartels (Ed.), *Applied linguistics and language teacher education* (pp. 159–178). New York: Springer.
Arbuckle, C. and Little, E. (2004). Teachers' perceptions and management of disruptive classroom behaviour during the middle years (years five to nine). *Australian Journal of Educational & Developmental Psychology*, 4, 59–70.
Argyris, C. (1980). *Inner contradictions of rigorous research*. New York: Academic Press.
Argyris, C. and Schön, D. A. (1974). *Theory in practice: increasing professional effectiveness*. San Francisco, CA: Jossey-Bass.
Argyris, C. and Schön, D. (1978). *Organisational learning: a theory of action perspective*. Reading, MA: Addison-Wesley.

Argyris, C., Putnam, R. and McLain Smith, D. (1985). *Action science: concepts, methods, and skills for research and intervention*. San Francisco, CA: Jossey-Bass.

Atkinson, D. (1997). A critical approach to critical thinking in TESOL. *TESOL Quarterly*, 31(1), 71–89.

Bailey, K. M. (1996). The best laid plans: teachers' in-class decisions to depart from their lesson plans. In K. M. Bailey and D. Nunan (Eds) *Voices from the language classroom: qualitative research in second language education* (pp. 15–40). Cambridge: Cambridge University Press.

Bailey, K. M., Curtis, A. and Nunan, D. (2001). *Pursuing professional development: the self as source*. Boston, MA: Heinle and Heinle.

Bailey, K. M., Bergthold, B., Braunstein, B., Jagodzinski Fleischman, N., Holbrook, M. P., Tuman, J., Waissbluth, X. and Zambo, L. J. (1996). The language learners' autobiography: examining the 'apprenticeship of observation'. In D. Freeman and J. C. Richards (Eds) *Teacher learning in language teaching* (pp. 11–29). New York: Cambridge University Press.

Ball, D. L., Lubienski, S. and Mewborn, D. S. (2001). Research on teaching mathematics: the unsolved problem of teachers' mathematical knowledge. In V. Richardson (Ed.) *Handbook of research on teaching* (pp. 433–456). Washington, DC: American Educational Research Association.

Bandura, A. (1986). *Social foundations of thought and action: a social cognitive theory*. Englewood Cliffs, NJ: Prentice-Hall.

Barcelos, A. M. F. (2000). Understanding teachers' and students' language learning beliefs in experience: a Deweyan approach (John Dewey). Unpublished doctoral dissertation. The University of Alabama, Tuscaloosa.

Barcelos, A. M. F. (2003). Researching beliefs about SLA: a critical review. In P. Kalaja and A. M. F. Barcelos (Eds) *Beliefs about SLA: new research approaches* (pp. 7–33). Dordrecht: Kluwer Academic Publishers.

Barnard, R. and Burns. A. (Eds) (2012). *Researching language teacher cognition and practice: international case studies*. Clevedon, UK: Multilingual Matters.

Bartels, N. (2005). Researching applied linguistics in language teacher education. In N. Bartels (Ed.) *Applied linguistics and language teacher education* (pp. 1–26). New York: Springer.

Barwell, R. (2003). Discursive psychology and mathematics education: possibilities and challenges. *Zentralblatt für Didaktik der Mathematik*, 35(5), 201–207.

Barwell, R. (2006). Using discursive psychology in research in mathematics classrooms: what can be seen and what is obscured? In D. Hewitt (Ed.) *Proceedings of the British Society for Research into Learning Mathematics* 26(2). Accessed 27 October 2014 at http://www.bsrlm.org.uk/IPs/ip26-2/BSRLM-IP-26-2-2.pdf

Basturkmen, H. (2012). Review of research into the correspondence between language teachers' stated beliefs and practices. *System*, 40(2), 282–295.

Basturkmen, H., Loewen, S. and Ellis, R. (2004). Teachers' stated beliefs about incidental focus on form and their classroom practices. *Applied Linguistics*, 25(2), 243–272.

Bax, S. (2003) The end of CLT: a context approach to language teaching. *ELT Journal*, 57(3), 278–287.

Beach, W. A. (1993). Transitional regularities for 'causal' 'okay' usages. *Journal of Pragmatics*, 19, 25–52.

Beauchamp, C. and Thomas, L. (2009). Understanding teacher identity: an overview of issues in the literature and implications for teacher education. *Cambridge Journal of Education*, 39(2), 175–189.

Beauchamp, C. and Thomas, L. (2011). New teachers' identity shifts at the boundary of teacher education and initial practice. *International Journal of Educational Research*, 50(1), 6–13.

Beijaard, D., Meijer, P. and Verloop, N. (2004). Reconsidering research on teachers' professional identity. *Teaching and Teacher Education*, 20, 107-128.

Ben-Peretz, M. (2011). Teacher knowledge: what is it? How do we uncover it? What are its implications for schooling? *Teaching and Teacher Education*, 27, 3-9.

Benwell, B. and Stokoe, E. (2006). *Discourse and identity*. Edinburgh, UK: Edinburgh University Press.

Bereiter, C. and Scardamalia, M. (1993). *Surpassing ourselves - an inquiry into the nature and implications of expertise*. Illinois: Open Court.

Berliner, D. C. (1994). The wonder of exemplary performances. In J. N. Margieri and C. C. Block (Eds) *Creating powerful thinking in teacher and students' diverse perspectives* (pp. 161-186). Fort Worth, TX: Harcourt Brace College.

Berliner, D. C. (1995). The development of pedagogical expertise. In P. K. Siu and P. T. K. Tam (Eds) *Quality in education: insights from different perspectives* (pp. 1-14). Hong Kong: Hong Kong Educational Research Association.

Berliner, D. C. (2001). Learning about and learning from expert teachers. *International Journal of Educational Research*, 35, 463-482.

Bernat, E. and Gvozdenko, I. (2005). Beliefs about language learning: current knowledge, pedagogical implications, and new research directions. *TESL-EJ*, 9(1), 1-21.

Bilmes, J. (1997). Being interrupted. *Language in Society*, 26, 507-531.

Borg, M. (2001). Teachers' beliefs. *ELT Journal*, 55(2), 186-188.

Borg, M. (2005). A case study of the development in pedagogic thinking of a pre-service teacher. *TESL-EJ*, 9, 1-30.

Borg, M. G. and Falzon, J. M. (1998). Secondary school teachers' perception of students' undesirable behaviors. *British Journal of Educational Psychology*, 68, 67-79.

Borg, S. (2003a). Teacher cognition in grammar teaching: a literature review. *Language Awareness*, 12(2), 96-108.

Borg, S. (2003b). Teacher cognition in language teaching: a review of research on what language teachers think, know, believe, and do. *Language Teaching*, 36(2), 81-109.

Borg, S. (2006). *Teacher cognition and language education: research and practice*. London: Continuum.

Borg, S. (2009). English language teachers' conceptions of research. *Applied Linguistics*, 30(3), 355-388.

Borg, S. (2011). The impact of in-service teacher education on language teachers' beliefs. *System*, 39(3), 370-380.

Borg, S. (2012). Current approaches to language teacher cognition research: a methodological analysis. In R. Barnard and A. Burns (Eds) *Researching language teacher cognition and practice: international case studies* (pp. 11-29). Clevedon, UK: Multilingual Matters.

Borg, S. and Burns, A. (2008). Integrating grammar in adult TESOL classrooms. *Applied Linguistics*, 29(3), 456-482.

Borko, H. (2004). Professional development and teacher learning: mapping the terrain. *Educational Researcher*, 33, 3-15.

Borko, H. and Shavelson, R. J. (1990). Teacher decision making. In B. F. Jones and L. Idol (Eds) *Dimensions of thinking and cognitive instruction* (pp. 311-346). Hillsdale, NJ: Lawrence Erlbaum Associates.

Boyles, D. R. (2006). Dewey's epistemology: an argument for warranted assertions, knowing and meaningful classroom practice. *Educational Theory*, 56(1), 57-68.

Brannan, D. and Bleistein, T. (2012). Novice ESOL teachers' perceptions of social support networks. *TESOL Quarterly*, 46(3), 519-541.

Brazil, D. (1997). *The communicative value of intonation in English*. Cambridge: Cambridge University Press.
Breen, M. P. (1991). Understanding the language teacher. In R. Phillipson, E. Kellerman, L. Selinker, M. Sharwood Smith and M. Swain (Eds), *Foreign/second language pedagogy research* (pp. 213–233). Clevedon, UK: Multilingual Matters.
Breen, M. P. (1998). Navigating the discourse: on what is learned in the language classroom. In W. A. Renandya and G. M. Jacobs (Eds) *Learners and Language Learning. Anthology Series 39*, Singapore: SEAMO Regional Language Center.
Breen, M. P., Hird, B., Milton, M., Oliver, R. and Thwaite, A. (2001). Making sense of language teaching: teachers' principles and classroom practices. *Applied Linguistics*, 22(4), 470–501.
Brick, J. (1991). *China: a handbook in intercultural communication*. Sydney: Macquarie University.
Britzman, D. (2003). *Practice makes practice: a critical study of learning to teach, revised edition*. Albany, NY: State University of New York Press.
Brophy, J. and Good, T. L. (1986). Teacher behavior and student achievement. In M. C. Wittrock (Ed.) *Handbook of research on teaching* (3rd edition) (pp. 328–375). New York: Macmillan.
Brouwer, C. E. and Wagner, J. (2004). Developmental issues in second language conversation. *Journal of Applied Linguistics*, 1(1), 29–47.
Brown, J. and McGannon, J. (1998). What do I know about language learning? The story of the beginning teacher. *23rd ALAA Congress*. Accessed 17 February 2006 at http://www.cltr.uq.edu.au/alsaa/proceed/bro-mcgan.html
Brumfit, C. (1984). *Communicative methodology in language teaching*. Cambridge: Cambridge University Press.
Bryan, L. A. (2003). Nestedness of beliefs: examining a prospective elementary teacher's belief system about science teaching and learning. *Journal of Research in Science Teaching*, 40(9), 835–868.
Budd Rowe, M. (1986). Wait time: slowing down may be a way of speeding up! *Journal of Teacher Education*, 37, 43–50.
Bullough, Jr. R. V., Knowles, J. G. and Grow, N. A. (1992). *Emerging as a teacher*. London: Routledge.
Burnard, S. (1998). *Developing children's behaviour in the classroom: a practical guide for teachers and students*. London: Falmer Press.
Burns, A. (2009). Action research in second language teacher education. In A. Burns and J. Richards (Eds) *The Cambridge guide to second language eeacher Education* (pp. 289–297). Cambridge: Cambridge University Press.
Burns, A. and Knox, J. (2005). Realisation(s): systemic-functional linguistics and the language classroom. In N. Bartels (Ed.) *Applied linguistics and language teacher education* (pp. 235– 259). New York: Springer.
Busch, D. (2010). Pre-service teacher beliefs about language learning: the second language acquisition course as an agent for change. *Language Teaching Research*, 14(3), 318–337.
Calderhead, J. (1995). Teachers as clinicians. In L. W. Anderson (Ed.) *International Encyclopedia of Teaching and Teacher Education* (2nd edition) (pp. 9–11).Oxford: Pergamon.
Calderhead, J. (1996). Teachers: beliefs and knowledge. In D. C. Berliner and R. C. Calfee (Eds) *Handbook of educational psychology* (pp. 709–725). New York: Macmillan.
Chan, J. K. S. (1999). Student teachers' beliefs – what have they brought to the initial teacher training. Accessed 12 December 2006 at http://eric.ed.gov/ERICWebPortal/Home
Chawhan, L. and Oliver, R. (2000). What beliefs do ESL students hold about language learning? *TESOL in Context*, 10(1), 20–26.

Choi, C. (2008). The impact of EFL testing on EFL education in Korea. *Language Testing*, 25, 39–62.
Clandinin, D. J. (1985). Personal practical knowledge: a study of teachers' classroom images. *Curriculum Inquiry*, 15(4), 361–385.
Clandinin, D. J. and Connelly, F. M. (1986). Rhythms in teaching: the narrative study of teachers' personal practical knowledge of classrooms. *Teaching and Teacher Education*, 2(4), 377–387.
Clandinin, D. J. and Connelly, F. M. (1987). Teachers' personal knowledge: what counts as personal in studies of the personal. *Journal of Curriculum Studies*, 19(6), 487–500.
Clandinin, D. J. and Connelly, M. (2000). *Narrative inquiry: experience and story in qualitative research*. San Francisco, CA: Jossey-Bass.
Clandinin, D. J., Downey, C. A. and Huber, J. (2009). Attending to changing landscapes: shaping the interwoven identities of teachers and teacher educators. *Asia-Pacific Journal of Teacher Education*, 37(2), 141–154.
Clark, C. M. (1980). Choice of a model for research on teacher thinking. *Journal of Curriculum Studies*, 12(1), 41–47.
Clark, C. M. and Peterson, P. L. (1986). Teachers' thought processes. In M. C. Wittrock (Ed.) *Handbook of research on teaching* (3rd edition) (pp. 255–296). New York: Macmillan.
Clark, C. M. and Yinger, R. (1987). Teacher planning. In J. Calderhead (Ed.) *Exploring teachers' thinking*, (pp. 84–103). London: Cassell Publications.
Clark, J. (1987). *Curriculum renewal in school foreign language learning*. Oxford: Oxford University Press.
Clarke, M. (2008). *Language teacher identities: co-constructing discourse and community*. Clevedon, UK: Multilingual Matters.
Cohen, A. D. and Fass, L. (2001). Oral language instruction: teacher and learner beliefs and the reality in EFL classes at a Colombian university. *Journal of Language and Culture*, 6, 43–62.
Cohen, L., Manion, L. and Morrison, K. R. B (2000). *Research methods in education* (5th edition). London: Routledge.
Cole, M. and Wertsch, J. V. (1996). Beyond the individual-social antinomy in discussions of Piaget and Vygotsky. *Human Development*, 39, 250–256.
Connelly, F. M. and Clandinin, D. J. (1985). Personal practical knowledge and the modes of knowledge: relevance for teaching and learning. In E. Eisner (Ed.) *Learning and teaching in the ways of knowing. Yearbook of the national society for the study of education*, 84 (pp. 174–198). Chicago, IL: University of Chicago Press.
Connelly, F. M. and Clandinin, F. M. (1988). *Teachers as curriculum planners: narratives of experience*. New York: Teachers College Press.
Connelly, F. M. and Clandinin, D. J. (1995). Teachers' professional knowledge landscapes: secret, sacret, and cover stories. In D. J. Clandinin and F. M. Connelly (Eds) *Teachers' professional knowledge landscapes* (pp. 3–15). New York: Teachers College Press.
Connelly, F. M., Clandinin, D. J. and He, M. F. (1997). Teacher's personal practical knowledge on the professional knowledge landscape. *Teaching and Teacher Education*, 13(7), 665–674.
Consolo, D. (2006). Classroom oral interaction in foreign language lessons and implications for teacher development. *Linguagem & Ensino*, 9(2), 33–55. Accessed 21 November 2009 at http://rle.ucpel.tche.br/php/edicoes/v9n2/02Consolo.pdf
Convery, A. (1998). A teacher's response to 'reflection-in-action'. *Cambridge Journal of Education*, 28(2), 197–205.
Cook, V. (2007). The nature of the L2 user. In L. Roberts, A. Gruel, S. Tatar and L. Marti (Eds) *EUROSLA Yearbook*, 7, (pp. 205–220). Amsterdam, the Netherlands: John Benjamins.

Cook, V. (2008). *Second language learning and language teaching* (4th edition). London: Hodder Education.

Cook, V. (2010). Prolegomena to second language learning. In P. Seedhouse, S. Walsh and C. Jenks (Eds) *Conceptualising 'learning' in applied linguistics* (pp. 6–22). Basingstoke, UK: Palgrave Macmillan.

Copland, F. (2008). Deconstrucing the discourse: understanding the feedback event. In S. Garton and K. Richards (Eds) *Professional encounters in TESOL: discourses of teachers in teaching* (pp. 1–5). Basingstoke, UK: Palgrave.

Cullen, R. (2002). Supportive teacher talk: the importance of the F-move. *ELT Journal*, 56(2), 117–127.

Cundale, N. (2001). Do we practice what we preach? Stated beliefs about communicative language teaching and classroom questioning strategies. *Language Teacher*, 25(5), 4–9.

Danielewicz, J. (2001). *Teaching selves: identity, pedagogy and teacher education*. Albany, NY: SUNY.

Darleen Opfer, V. and Pedder, D. (2011). Conceptualizing teacher professional learning. *Review of Educational Research*, 81(3), 376–407.

Darling-Hammond, L. (2000). *Teacher quality and student achievement. Educational Policy Analysis Archives*, 8(1). Accessed 21 September 2016 at *http://epaa.asu.edu/ojs/article/view/392/515*

Darling-Hammond, L. (2006). *Powerful teacher education: lessons from exemplary programs*. San Francisco, CA: Jossey-Bass.

Davis, A. (2003). Teachers' and students' beliefs regarding aspects of language learning. *Evaluation and Research in Education*, 17(4), 207–222.

Decker, D. M., Dona, D. P. and Christenson, S. L. (2007). Behaviorally at-risk African American students: the importance of student-teacher relationships for student outcomes. *Journal of School Psychology*, 45(1), 83–109.

Demetriou, H., Wilson, E. and Winterbottom, M. (2009). The role of emotion in teaching: are there differences between male and female newly qualified teachers' approaches to teaching? *Educational Studies*, 35(4), 449–473.

Denscombe, M. (1998). *The good research guide for small-scale social research projects*. Buckingham, UK: Open University Press.

Dewey, J. (1933). *How we think. A restatement of the relation of the reflective thinking to the educative process* (revised edition). Boston, MA: D.C. Heath.

Donaghue, H. (2003). An instrument to elicit teachers' beliefs and assumptions. *ELT Journal*, 57(4), 344–351.

Dreyfus, H. L. and Dreyfus S. E. (1986). *Mind over machine*. New York: Free Press.

Duff, P. and Uchida, Y. (1997). The negotiation of teachers' sociocultural identities and practices in postsecondary EFL classrooms. *TESOL Quarterly*, 31(3), 451–461.

Duffy, G. (1982). Response to Borko, Shavelson and Stern: There's more to instructional decision-making in reading than the 'empty classroom'. *Reading Research Quarterly*, 17(2), 295–299.

Duffy, G. and Metheny, W. (1979). *Measuring teacher's beliefs about reading*. Research Series No. 41. East Lansing, MI: Institute for Research on Teaching.

Edwards, D. (1997). *Discourse and cognition*. London: Sage.

Edwards, D. (2005). Discursive psychology. In K. Fitch and R. Sanders (Eds) *Handbook of language and social interaction* (pp. 257–273). Mahwah, NJ: Erlbaum.

Edwards, D. and Potter, J. (1992). *Discursive psychology*. London: Sage.

Edwards, D. and Potter, J. (1993). Language and causation: a discourse analytical approach to description and attribution. *Psychological Review*, 100, 23–41.

Edwards, A., Gilroy, P. and Hartley, D. (2002). *Re-thinking teacher education: collaborating for uncertainty*. London: Routledge/Falmer.

Eisenhart, M. A., Shrum, J. L., Harding, J. R. and Cuthbert, A. M. (1988). Teacher beliefs: definitions, findings and directions. *Educational Policy*, 2(1), 51–70.

Ekman, P. (1979). About brows: emotional and conversational signals. In M. von Cranach, K. Foppa, W. Lepenies and D. Ploog (Eds) *Human ethology* (pp. 169–248). Cambridge: Cambridge University Press.

Elbaz, F. (1981). The teacher's 'practical knowledge': report of a case study. *Curriculum Inquiry*, 11(1), 43–71.

Elbaz, F. (1983). *Teacher thinking: a study of practical knowledge*. London: Croom Helm.

El-Dib, M. A. B. (2007). Levels of reflection in action research: an overview and an assessment tool. *Teaching and Teacher Education*, 23(1), 24–35.

Ellis, R. (1992). Learning to communicate in the classroom. *Studies in Second Language Acquisition*, 14(1), 1–23.

Ellis, R. (1998). Discourse control and the acquisition-rich classroom. In W. A. Renandya and G. M. Jacobs (Eds) *Learners and language learning. Anthology* (pp. 145–171). Singapore: SEAMO Regional Language Centre.

Ellis, R. (2000). Task-based research and language pedagogy. *Language Teaching Research*, 49, 193–220.

Ellis, R. (2003). *Task-based language learning and teaching*. Oxford: Oxford University Press.

Ellis, R. (2008). Investigating grammatical difficulty in second language learning: implications for second language acquisition research and language testing. *International Journal of Applied Linguistics*, 8(1), 4–22.

Ericsson, K. A., Krampe, R. Th. and Tesch-Romer, C. (1993). The role of deliberate practice in the acquisition of expert performance. *Psychological Review*, 100, 363–406.

Ernest, P. (1989). The knowledge, beliefs and attitudes of the mathematics teacher: a model. *Journal of Education for Teaching*, 15, 13–34.

Fagan, D. S. (2012). 'Dealing with' unexpected learner contributions in whole-group activities: an examination of novice language teacher discursive practices. *Classroom Discourse*, 3, 107–128.

Farrell, T. S. C. (1999). The reflective assignment: unlocking pre-service English teachers' beliefs on grammar teaching. *RELC Journal*, 30(2), 1–17.

Farrell, T. S. C. (2001). English language teacher socialisation during the practicum. *Prospect*, 16(1), 49–62.

Farrell, T. S. C. (2011). Exploring the professional role identities of experienced ESL teachers through reflective practice. *System*, 39(1), 54–62.

Farrell, T. S. C. (2013). *Reflective practice in ESL teacher development groups: from practices to principles*. Basingstoke: Palgrave Macmillan.

Farrell, T. S. C. and Lim, P. C. P. (2005). Conceptions of grammar teaching: a case study of teachers' beliefs and classroom practices. *TESL-EJ*, 9(2), 1–13.

Farrell, T. S. C. and Richards, J. (2007). Teachers' language proficiency. In T. S. Farrell (Ed.) *Reflective language teaching: from research to practice* (pp. 55–66). London: Continnum.

Fenstermacher, G. D. (1979). A philosophical consideration of recent research on teacher effectiveness. In L. S. Shulman (Ed.) *Review of research in education*, 6 (pp. 157–185). Itasca, IL: Peacock.

Fishbein, M. and Ajzen, I. (1975). *Beliefs, ittitude, Intention, and behaviour: an introduction to theory and research*. Reading, MA: Addison-Wesley.

Foley, M. and Hart, A. (1992). Expert-novice differences and knowledge elicitation. In

R. R. Hoffman (Ed.) *The psychology of expertise: cognitive research and empirical AI* (pp. 233–344). New York: Springer Verlag.

Foss, D. H. and Kleinsasser, R. C. (1996). Preservice elementary teachers' views of pedagogical and mathematical content knowledge. *Teaching and Teacher Education*, 12(4), 429–442.

Foss, D. H. and Kleinsasser, R. C. (2001). Contrasting research perspectives: what the evidence yields. *Teachers and Teaching: Theory and Practice*, 7(3), 272–295.

Freeman, D. (1992). Language teacher education, emerging discourse, and change in classroom practice. In J. Flowerdew, M. Brock and S. Hsica (Eds) *Perspectives on second language teacher development* (pp. 1–21). Hong Kong: City Polytechnic of Hong Kong.

Freeman, D. and Johnson, K. (1998). Reconceptualizing the knowledge-base of language teacher education. *TESOL Quarterly*, 32, 397–417.

Freeman, D. and Richards, J. (1996). (Eds) *Teacher learning in language teaching*. Cambridge: Cambridge University Press.

Garton, S. (2008). Teacher beliefs and interaction in the language classroom. In S. Garton and K. Richards (Eds) *Professional encounters in TESOL: discourses of teachers in teaching* (pp. 67–86). London: Palgrave.

Garton S. and Richards, K. (2008). Introduction. In S. Garton and K. Richards (Eds) *Professional encounters in TESOL: discourses of teachers in teaching*. London: Palgrave.

Gass, S. M. and Mackey, A. (2006). Input, interaction and output: an overview. *AILA Review*, 19, 3–17.

Gatbonton, E. (1999). Investigating experienced ESL teachers' pedagogical knowledge. *Modern Language Journal*, 83(1), 35–50.

Gatbonton, E. (2008). Looking beyond teachers' classroom behaviour: novice and experienced ESL teachers' pedagogical knowledge. *Language Teaching Research*, 12(2), 161–182.

Gee, J. P. (1996). *Social linguistics and literacies: ideologies in discourses* (2nd edition). London: Taylor & Francis.

Gellert, U. (2001). Research on attitudes in mathematics education: a discursive perspective. In M. van den Heuvel-Panhuizen (Ed.), *Proceedings of the 25th meeting of the International Group for the Psychology of Mathematics Education* 3 (PME-XXV) (pp. 33–40). Utrecht: Utrecht University.

Glaser, R. (1987). Thoughts on expertise. In C. Schooler and W. Schaie (Eds), *Cognitive functioning and social structure over the lifecourse* (pp. 81–94). Norwood, NJ: Ablex.

Goffman, E. (1983). The interaction order: American Sociological Association, 1982 presidential address. *American Sociological Review*, 48, 1–17.

Golombek, P. R. (1998). A study of language teachers' personal practical knowledge. *TESOL Quarterly*, 32(3), 447–464.

Gorsuch, G. J. (2000). EFL educational policies and educational cultures: Influences on teachers' approval of communicative activities. *TESOL Quarterly*, 34(4), 675–710.

Gorsuch, G. (2001). Japanese EFL teachers' perceptions of communicative, audiolingual and yakudoku activities: the plan versus the reality. *Education Policy Analysis*, 9(10). Accessed 5 January 2014 at http://epaa.asu.edu/epaa/v9n10.html

Griffiths, V. (2000). The reflective dimension in teacher education. *International Journal of Educational Research*, 33, 539–555.

Grossman, P. M., Wilson, S. M. and Shulman, L. S. (1989). Teachers of substance: subject matter knowledge for teaching. In M. C. Reynolds (Ed.) *Knowledge base for the beginning teacher* (pp. 23–36). Oxford: Pergamon.

Grossman, P., Hammerness, K. and McDonald, M. (2009). Redefining teaching, re-imagining teacher education. *Teachers and Teaching*, 15(2), 273–289.

Guskey, T. R. (2000). *Evaluating professional development*. Thousand Oaks, CA: Corwin Press.

Hall, G. (2011). *Exploring English language teaching: language in action*. London: Routledge.
Hall, J. K. and Verplaetse, L. S. (Eds) (2000). *Second and foreign language learning through classroom interaction*. Mahwah, NJ: Lawrence Erlbaum.
Hall, J. K. and Walsh, M. (2002). Teacher-student interaction and learning. *Annual Review of Applied Linguistics*, 22, 186-203.
Hargreaves, A. (2000). Four ages of professionalism and professional learning. *Teachers and Teaching: Theory and Practice*, 6(2), 151-182.
Hargreaves, A. (2005). Educational change takes ages: life, career and generational factors in teachers' emotional responses to educational change. *Teaching and Teacher Education*, 21, 967-983.
Harmer, J. (2003). Popular culture, methods and context. *ELT Journal*, 57(3), 288-294.
Harré, R. and Gillett, G. (1994). *The discursive mind*. London: Sage.
Harvey, O. (1986). Beliefs systems and attitudes toward the death penalty and other punishments. *Journal of Personality*, 54, 659-675.
Hatten, N. and Smith, D. (1995). Reflection in teacher education: towards definition and implementation, *Teaching and Teacher Education*, 12(1), 33-49.
Hawkins, B. (2007). Open-endedness, the instructional conversation and the activity system: how might they come together? In R. Alahen and S. Pöyhönen (Eds) *Language in action: Vygotsky and Leontievian legacy today* (pp. 245-279). Newcastle, UK: Cambridge Scholars Publishing.
Hayes, D. (2009). Non-native English-speaking teachers, context and English language teaching. *System*, 37, 1-11.
Hayes, D. (2010). 'Education is all about opportunities, isn't it?' A biographical perspective on learning and teaching English in Sri Lanka. *Harvard Educational Review*, 80, 517-540.
He, A. W. (2004). CA for SLA: arguments from the Chinese language classroom. *The Modern Language Journal*, 88, 568-582.
Hellermann, J. (2003). The interactive work of prosody in the IRF Exchange: teacher repetition in feedback moves. *Language in Society*, 32(1), 79-104.
Hellermann, J. (2008). *Social actions for classroom language learning*. Clevedon, UK: Multilingual Matters.
Hepburn, A. and Wiggins, S. (2005). Developments in discursive psychology. *Discourse & Society*, 16, 595-601.
Heritage, J. (1998). Oh-prefaced responses to inquiry. *Language in Society*, 27, 291-334.
Hitchcock, G. and Hughes, D. (1995). *Research and the teacher* (2nd edition). London: Routledge.
Hobbs, V. (2007). Faking it or hating it: can reflective practice be forced? *Reflective Practice*, 8, 405-417.
Hogan, T., Rabinowitz, M. and Craven, J. A. (2003). Representation in teaching: inferences from research of expert and novice teachers. *Educational Psychologist*, 38, 235-247.
Holliday, A. R. (1994). *Appropriate methodology and social context*. Cambridge: Cambridge University Press.
Holliday. A. R. (2005). *The struggle to teach English as an international language*. Oxford: Oxford University Press.
Horwitz, E. K. (1985). Using student beliefs about language learning and teaching in the foreign language methods course. *Foreign Language Annals*, 18, 333-340.
Horwitz, E. K. (1987). Surveying student beliefs about language teaming. In A.L. Wenden and J. Robin (Eds) *Learner strategies in language learning* (pp. 119-132). London: Prentice Hall.
Howatt, A. P. R. (1984). *A history of English language teaching*. Oxford: Oxford University Press.

Hutchby, I. and Wooffitt, R. (2008). *Conversation analysis* (2nd edition). Cambridge: Polity Press.

Huth, T. (2006). Negotiating structure and culture: L2 learners' realization of L2 compliment-response sequences in talk-in-interaction. *Journal of Pragmatics*, 38, 2025–2050.

Jarvis, J. and Robinson, M. (1979). Analysing educational discourse: an exploratory study of teacher response and support to pupils' learning. *Applied Linguistics*, 18, 212–228.

Johnson, K. E. (1992a). The relationship between teachers' beliefs and practices during literacy instruction for non-native speakers of English. *Journal of Reading Behavior*, 24(1), 83–108.

Johnson, K. E. (1992b). Learning to teach: instructional actions and decisions of preservice ESOL teachers. *TESOL Quarterly*, 26, 507–535.

Johnson, K. E. (1994). The emerging beliefs and instructional practices of preservice English as a second language teachers. *Teaching and Teacher Education*, 10(4), 439–452.

Johnson, K. E. (2006). The sociocultural turn and its challenges for L2 teacher education. *TESOL Quarterly*, 40(1), 235–257.

Johnson, K. E. (2009a). *Second language teacher education: a sociocultural perspective*. New York and London: Routledge.

Johnson, K. E. (2009b). Trends in second language teacher education. In A. Burns and J. C. Richards (Eds) *The Cambridge guide to second language teacher education* (pp. 20–29). Cambridge: Cambridge University Press.

Johnson, K. E. and Golombek, P. R. (Eds) (2002). *Teachers' narrative inquiry as professional development*. New York: Cambridge University Press.

Joyce, B. (1978–1979). Toward a theory of information processing in teaching. *Educational Research Quarterly*, 3, 66–76.

Kalaja, P. (1995). Student beliefs (or metacognitive knowledge) about SLA reconsidered. *International Journal of Applied Linguistics*, 5(2), 191–204.

Kalaja, P. (2003). Research on students' beliefs about SLA within a discursive approach. In P. Kalaja and A. M. F. Barcelos (Eds) *Beliefs about SLA: new research approaches* (pp. 87–108). Dordrecht: Kluwer Academic Publishers.

Kang, Y. and Cheng, X. (2013). Teacher learning in the workplace: A study of the relationship between a novice EFL teacher's classroom practices and cognition development *Language Teaching Research*, 18, 169–186.

Kasper, G. (2004). Participant orientations in German conversation-for-learning. *The Modern Language Journal*, 88, 551–567.

Kasper, G. (2009). Locating cognition in second language interaction and learning: inside the skull or in public view? *International Review of Applied Linguistics*, 47, 11–36.

Kelly, G. A. (1955). *The psychology of personal constructs: a theory of personality* (Vols 1 and 2). New York: W. W. Norton.

Kennedy, C. and Kennedy, J. (1996). Teacher attitudes and change implementation. *System*, 24(3), 351–360.

Kennedy, J. and C. Kennedy (1998). Levels, linkages, and networks in cross-cultural innovation. *System*, 26(4), 455–469.

Kern, R. G. (1995). Students' and teachers' beliefs about language learning. *Foreign Language Annals*, 28(1), 71–92.

Kiely, R. and Davis, M. (2010). From transmission to transformation: Teacher learning in English for speakers of other languages. *Language Teaching Research*, 14(3), 227–295.

Klapper, J. (2003). Taking communication to task? A critical review of recent trends in language teaching. *Language Learning Journal*, 27, 33–42.

Kokkinos, C. M., Panayiotou, G. and Davazoglou, A. M. (2004). Perceived seriousness of students' undesirable behaviors: the student teachers' perspective. *Educational Psychology*, 24, 109–120.

Kolb, D. A. (1984). *Experiential learning: experience as the source of learning and development* (Vol. 1). Englewood Cliffs, NJ: Prentice-Hall.

Koshik, I. (2002). Designedly incomplete utterances: a pedagogical practice for eliciting knowledge displays in error correction sequences. *Research on Language and Social Interaction*, 35, 277–309.

Kramsch, C. (2003). Metaphor and the subjective construction of beliefs. In P. Kalaja and A. M. F. Barcelos (Eds) *Beliefs about SLA: new aesearch Approaches* (pp. 109–128). AA Dordrecht, the Netherlands: Kluwer Academic Publishers.

Kubanyiova, M. (2009). Possible selves in language teacher development. In Z. Dörnyei and E. Ushioda (Eds) *Motivation, language identity and the L2 Self* (pp. 314–332). Clevedon, UK: Multilingual Matters.

Kumaravadivelu, B. (1994). The postmethod condition: (e)merging strategies for second/foreign language teaching. *TESOL Quarterly*, 28(1), 27–48.

Kumaravadivelu, B. (2003). *Beyond methods: macrostrategies for language teaching*. New Haven, CT: Yale University Press.

Kumaravadivelu, B. (2006). *Understanding language teaching: from method to postmethod*. Mahwah, NJ: Routledge.

Kumaravadivelu, B. (2012). *Language teacher education for a global society: a modular model for knowing, analyzing, recognizing, doing, and seeing*. New York: Routledge.

Kuntz, P. S. (1996). *Beliefs about language learning: the Horwitz model*. ERIC Document Reproduction Service, No. ED397649.

Lamb, M. (1995). The consequences of inset. *ELT Journal*, 49(1), 72–80.

Lantolf, J. P. (2006). Sociocultural theory and second language learning: state of the art. *Studies in Second Language Acquisition*, 28, 67–109.

Lantolf, J. and Johnson, K. E. (2007). Extending Firth & Wagner's ontological perspective to L2 classroom praxis and teacher education. *The Modern Language Journal*, 91(v), 875–890.

Larsen-Freeman, D. (2000). *Techniques and principles in language teaching* (2nd edition). New York: Oxford University Press.

Lave, J. and Wenger, E. (1991). *Situated learning. Legitimate peripheral participation*. Cambridge: Cambridge University Press.

Lee, O. and Yarger, S. J. (1996). Modes of inquiry in research on teacher education. In J. Sikula (Ed.), *Handbook of research on teacher education* (2nd edition) (pp. 14–37). New York: Simon and Schuster Macmillan.

Lee, Y. (2007). Third turn position in teacher talk: contingency and the work of teaching. *Journal of Pragmatics*, 39, 180–206.

LePage, P., Darling-Hammond, L., Akar, H., Gutierrez, C, Jenkins-Gunn, E., and Rosebrock, K. (2005). Classroom management. In L. Darling-Hammond and J. Bransford (Eds) *Preparing teachers for a changing world: what teachers should learn and be able to do* (pp. 327–357). San Francisco, CA: Jossey-Bass.

Lerner, G. H. (1995). Turn design and the organization of participation in instructional activities. *Discourse Processes*, 19(1), 111–131.

Li, L. (2008). EFL teachers' beliefs about ICT integration in Chinese secondary schools. Unpublished doctoral thesis. Queen's University, Belfast.

Li, L. (2011). Obstacles and opportunities for developing thinking through interaction in language classrooms. *Thinking Skills and Creativity*, 6(3), 146–158.

Li, L. (2012). Belief construction and development: two tales of non-native English speaking student teachers in a TESOL programme. *Novitas-ROYAL (Research on Youth and Language)*, 6(1), 33–58.

Li, L. (2013). The complexity of language teachers' beliefs and practice: one EFL teacher's theories. *Language Learning Journal*, 41(2), 175–191.

Li, L. (2014). Understanding language teachers' practice with educational technology: a case from China. *System*, 46, 105–119.

Li, L. and Walsh, S. (2011). 'Seeing is believing': looking at EFL teachers' beliefs through classroom interaction. *Classroom Discourse*, 2(1), 39–57.

Liao, X. (2004). Readers response: the need for communicative language teaching in China. *ELT Journal*, 58(3), 270–273.

Lightbown, P. M. and Spada, N. (1993). *How languages are learned*. Oxford: Oxford University Press.

Liu, Y. (2008). Teacher–student talk in Singapore Chinese language classrooms: a case study of initiation/response/follow-up (IRF). *Asia Pacific Journal of Education*, 28(1), 87–102.

Llurda, E. and Lasagabaster, D. (2010). Factors affecting teachers' beliefs about interculturalism. *International Journal of Applied Linguistics*, 20(3), 327–353.

Lo, Y.-H. G. (2005). Relevance of knowledge of second language acquisition: an in-depth case study of a non-native EFL teacher. In N. Bartels (Ed.) *Applied linguistics and language teacher education* (pp. 85–102). New York: Kluwer Academic.

Lord, B. (1994). Teachers' professional development: critical colleagueship and the role of professional communities, In Cobb, N. (Ed.) *The future of education; perspectives on national standards in education* (pp. 175–204). New York: College Entrance Board.

Lortie, D. (1975). *Schoolteacher: a sociological study*, Chicago, IL, The University of Chicago Press.

MacDonald, M., Badger, R. and White, G. (2001). Changing values: what are theories of language learning and teaching? *Teaching and Teacher Education*, 17, 949–963.

McDonough, J. and McDonough, S. (1997). *Research methods for English language teachers*. London: Arnold.

McLaughlin, M.W. and Talbert, J. (2001). *Professional communities and the work of high school teaching*. Chicago, IL: University of Chicago Press.

McLaughlin, M.W. and Talbert, J. (2006). *Building school-based teacher learning communities*. New York and London: Teachers College Press.

McMahon, L. A. (1995). A study of how teachers employ their teaching skills during interactive decision making. Doctoral dissertation, University of Lowell. *Dissertation Abstracts International*, 56, 2205.

Mangubhai, F., Marland, P., Dashwood, A. and Son, J.-B. (2004). Teaching a foreign language: one teacher's practical theory. *Teaching and Teacher Education*, 20(3), 291–311.

Mann, S. and Walsh, S. (2013). RP or 'RIP': a critical perspective on reflective practice. *Applied Linguistics Review*, 4(2), 291–315.

Markee, N. (1995). Teachers' answers to learners' questions: problematizing the issue of making meaning. *Issues in Applied Linguistics*, 6, 63–92.

Markee, N. (2000). *Conversation analysis*. Mahwah, NJ: Lawrence Erlbaum.

Markee, N. (2004). Zones of interactional transition in ESL slasses. *The Modern Language Journal*, 88, 583–596.

Marland, P. W. (1977). A study of teachers' interactive thoughts. Doctoral dissertation. The University of Alberta.

Mattheoudakis, M. (2007). Tracking changes in pre-service EFL teacher beliefs in Greece: a longitudinal study. *Teaching and Teacher Education*, 23(8), 1272–1288.

Mehan, H. (1979). *Learning lessons*. Cambridge, MA: Harvard University Press.

Miller, J. (2009). Teacher identity. In A. Burns and J. C. Richards (Eds) *The Cambridge guide to second language teacher education* (pp. 171–181). New York: Cambridge University Press.

Miller Marsh, M. (2003). *The social fashioning of teacher identities*. New York: Peter Lang Publishing.

Mok, W. E. (1994). Reflecting on reflections: a case study of experienced and inexperienced ESL teachers. *System*, 22(1), 93–111.

Moon, J. (2005). *Guide for busy academics no 4: learning through reflection*. York, UK: Higher Education Academy.

Morgan, B. and Clarke, M. (2011). Identity in second language teaching and learning. In E. Hinkel (Ed.) *Handbook of research in second language teaching and learning* (pp. 817–836). New York: Routledge.

Morton, T. (2012). Classroom talk, conceptual change and teacher reflection in bilingual science teaching. *Teaching and Teacher Education*, 28(1), 101–110.

Morton, T. and Gray, J. (2010). Personal practical knowledge and identity in lesson planning conferences on a pre-service TESOL course. *Language Teaching Research*, 14(3), 297–317.

Morton, T. and Gray, J. (forthcoming). *Social interaction and teacher identity*. Edinburgh: Edinburgh University Press.

Mullock, B. (2003). What makes a good teacher? The perspectives of postgraduate TESOL students. *Prospect*, 18(3), 3–24.

Mullock, B. (2006). The pedagogical knowledge base of four TESOL teachers. *The Modern Language Journal*, 90, 48–66.

Munby, H. (1982). The place of teachers' beliefs in research on teacher thinking and decision making, and an alternative methodology. *Instructional Science*, 11, 201–225.

Munby, H., Russell, T. and Martin, A. K. (2001). Teachers' knowledge and how it develops. In V. Richardson (Ed.) *Handbook of research on teaching* (4th edition) (pp. 877–904). Washington, DC: American Educational Research Association.

Murdoch, G. (1994). Language development provision in teacher training curricula. *ELT Journal*, 48(3), 253–259.

Nassaji, H. and Fotos, S. (2011). *Teaching grammar in second language classrooms: integrating form-focused instruction in communicative context*. New York: Routledge.

Nassaji, H. and Wells, G. (2000). What's the use of 'triadic dialogue'? An investigation of teacher learner interaction. *Applied Linguistics*, 21, 376–406.

Nespor, J. K. (1987). The role of beliefs in the practice of teaching. *Journal of Curriculum Studies*, 19, 317–328.

Ng, J. and Farrell, T. S. C. (2003). Do teachers' beliefs of grammar teaching match their classroom practices? A Singapore case study. In D. Deterding, A. Brown and E. L. Low (Eds) *English in Singapore: research on grammar* (pp. 128–137). Singapore: McGraw-Hill.

Nikitina, L. and Furuoka, F. (2006). Re-examining Horwitz's beliefs about Language learning inventory (BALLI) in the Malaysian context. *Electronic Journal of Foreign Language Teaching*, 3(2), 209–219.

Nisbett, R. E. and Ross, L. (1980). *Human interferences: strategies and shortcomings of social judgement*. Englewood Cliffs, NJ: Prentice-Hall.

Nishimuro, M. and Borg, S. (2013). Teacher cognition and grammar teaching in a Japanese high school. *JALT Journal*, 35(1), 29–50.

Nishino, T. (2011). Japanese high school teachers' beliefs and practices regarding communicative language teaching. *JALT Journal*, 33(2), 131–155.

Nolan, J. F. and Hoover, L. A. (2008). *Teacher supervision & evaluation: theory into practice*. Hoboken, NJ: John Wiley & Sons.

Norrick, Neil R. (1987). Functions of repetition in conversation. *Text*, 7, 245–264.

Nunan, D. (1992). The teacher as decision-maker. In J. Flowerdew, M. Brock and S. Hsia (Eds) *Perspectives on second language teacher education* (pp. 135–165). Hong Kong: City Polytechnic.

Nystrand, M. (1997). Dialogic instruction: when recitation becomes conversation. In M. Nystrand, A. Gamoran, R. Kachur and C. Prendergast (Eds) *Opening dialogue: understanding the dynamics of language and learning in the English classroom* (pp. 1–29). New York: Teachers College Press.

Olsen, B. (2011). 'I am large, I contain multitudes': teacher identity as a useful frame for research, practice, and diversity in teacher education. In A. Ball and C. Tyson (Eds) *Studying diversity in teacher education* (pp. 267–273). Washington, DC: Rowman & Littlefield Publishers.

Oppenheim, A. N. (1992). *Questionnaire design, interviewing and attitude measurement*. London and New York: Continuum.

Orafi, S. M. S. and Borg, S. (2009). Intentions and realities in implementing communicative curriculum reform. *System*, 37, 243–253.

Pajares, M. F. (1992). Teachers' beliefs and educational research: cleaning up a messy construct. *Review of Educational Research*, 62(3), 307–332.

Palmer, D. J., Stough, L. M., Burdenski, T. K. and Gonzales, M. (2005). Identifying teacher expertise: an examination of researchers' decision making. *Educational Psychologist*, 40(1), 13–25.

Panselinas, G. and Komis, V. (2009). 'Scaffolding' through talk in groupwork learning. *Thinking Skills and Creativity*, 4, 86–103.

Peacock, M. (1999). Beliefs about language learning and their relationship to proficiency. *International Journal of Applied Linguistics*, 9(2), 247–263.

Peacock, M. (2001). Pre-service ESL teachers' beliefs about second language learning: a longitudinal study. *System*, 29, 177–195.

Pica, T. and Doughty, C. (1985). The role of groupwork in classroom second language acquisition. *Studies Second Language Acquisition*, 7, 233–248.

Plomp, T., Ten Brummelhuis, A. and Rapmund, R. (1996). *Teaching and learning for the future*. Report of the Committee on Multimedia in Teacher Training (COMMITT) to the Netherlands Minister of Education. The Hague: Sdu.

Potter, J. (1997). Discourse analysis as a way of analysing naturally occurring talk. In D. Silverman (Ed.) *Qualitative research* (pp. 144–160). London: Sage.

Potter, J. (2003). Discursive psychology: between method and paradigm. *Discourse & Society*, 14, 783–794.

Potter, J. (2005). Making psychology relevant. *Discourse & Society*, 16, 739–747.

Potter, J. (2012a) Discourse analysis and discursive psychology. In H. Cooper (Editor-in-Chief) *APA handbook of research methods in psychology: Vol. 2. Quantitative, qualitative, neuropsychological, and biological* (pp. 111–130). Washington, DC: American Psychological Association Press.

Potter, J. (2012b). Re-reading discourse and social psychology: transforming social psychology. *British Journal of Social Psychology*, 51(3), 436–455.

Potter, J. and Edwards, D. (2001). Discursive social psychology. In W. P. Robinson and H. Giles (Eds) *The new handbook of language and social psychology* (pp. 103–118). London: John Wiley.

Potter, J. and Edwards, D. (2003). Rethinking cognition: on Coulter, discourse and mind. *Human Studies*, 26, 165–181.

Potter, J. and Hepburn, A. (2005). Qualitative interviews in psychology: problems and possibilities. *Qualitative research in psychology*, 2, 281–307.

Potter, J. and Hepburn, A. (2008). Discursive constructionism. In J. A. Holstein and J. F. Gubrium (Eds) *Handbook of constructionist research* (pp. 275-293). New York: Guildford.

Prabhu, N. S. (1987). *Second language pedagogy: a perspective.* Oxford: Oxford University Press.

Putnam, R. and Borko, H. (2000). What do new views of knowledge and thinking have to say about research on teacher learning. *Educational Researcher*, 29(1), 4-15.

Rampton, B. (2006). *Language in late modernity: interaction in an urban school.* Cambridge: Cambridge University Press.

Rich, Y. (1993). Stability and change in teacher expertise. *Teacher & Teacher Education*, 9(2), 137-146.

Richards, J. C. (1996). Teachers' maxims in language teaching. *TESOL Quarterly*, 30(2), 281-296.

Richards, J. C. (1998a). *Beyond training.* Cambridge: Cambridge University Press.

Richards, J. C. (1998b). Teacher beliefs and decision making. In J. C. Richards (Ed.) *Beyond training* (pp. 65-85). Cambridge: Cambridge University Press.

Richards, J. C. (2006). *Communicative language teaching today.* Cambridge: Cambridge University Press.

Richards, J. C. and Farrell, T. S. C. (2005). *Professional development for language teachers: strategies for teacher learning.* Cambridge: Cambridge University Press.

Richards, J. C. and Lockhart, C. (1994). *Reflective teaching in second language classrooms.* Cambridge: Cambridge University Press.

Richards, J. C. and Pennington, M. (1998). The first year of teaching. In J. C. Richards (Ed.) *Beyond training* (pp. 173-190). Cambridge: Cambridge University Press.

Richards, J. C. and Rodgers, T. S. (2001). *Approaches and methods in language teaching* (2nd edition). Cambridge: Cambridge University Press.

Richards, J. C., Tung, P. and Ng, P. (1992). The culture of the English language teacher: a Hong Kong example. *RELC Journal*, 23(1), 81-102.

Richards, J. C., Li, B. and Tang, A. (1998). Exploring pedagogical reasoning skills. In J. C. Richards (Ed.) *Beyond training* (pp. 86-102). Cambridge: Cambridge University Press.

Richards, J. C., Gallo, P. and Renandya, W. A. (2001). Exploring teachers' beliefs and the processes of change. *PAC Journal*, 1(1), 41-58.

Richards, H., Conway, C., Roskvist, A. and Harvey, S. (2013). Foreign language teachers' language proficiency and their language teaching practice. *The Language Learning Journal*, 41(2), 231-246.

Richards, K. (2006). 'Being the teacher': identity and classroom conversation. *Applied Linguistics*, 27, 51-77.

Richardson, V. (1996).The role of attitudes and beliefs in learning to teach. In Sikula, J. (Ed.) *Handbook of research on teacher education* (pp. 102-119). New York: Macmillan.

Riddell, D. (2001). *Teaching English as a foreign/second language.* London: Cox and Wyman.

Roth, W. (2008). The nature of scientific conceptions: a discursive psychological perspective. *Educational Research Review*, 3, 30-50.

Roth, W.-M. (2009). Realizing Vygotsky's program concerning language and thought: tracking knowing (ideas, conceptions, beliefs) in real time. *Language and Education*, 23, 295-311.

Ruohotie-Lyhty, M. (2011). Constructing practical knowledge of teaching: eleven newly qualified language teachers' discursive agency. *The Language Learning Journal*, 39(3), 365-379.

Russell, T. (2005). Can reflective practice be taught? *Reflective Practice*, 6(2), 199-204.

Sakui, K. (2004). Wearing two pairs of shoes: language teaching in japan. *ELT Journal*, 58(2), 155-163.

Sakui, K. (2007). Classroom management in Japanese EFL classrooms. *JALT Journal*, 29(1), 41-58.

Sato, K. and Kleinsasser, R. C. (1999). Communicative language teaching (CLT): practical understandings. *The Modern Language Journal*, 83(4), 494–517.

Sato, K. and Kleinsasser, R. C. (2004). Beliefs, practices, and interactions of teachers in a Japanese high school English department. *Teaching and Teacher Education*, 20(8), 797–816.

Schegloff, E. A. (1991). Conversation analysis and socially shared cognition. In L. Resnick, J. Levine and S. Teasley (Eds) *Perspectives on socially shared cognition* (pp. 150–171). Washington, DC: American Psychological Association.

Schegloff, E. A. (2007). *Sequence organization in interaction: a primer in conversation analysis*. Cambridge: Cambridge University Press.

Schegloff, E.A. and Sacks, H. (1973). Opening up closings. *Semiotica*, 7, 289–327.

Schegloff, E.A., I. Koshik, S. Jacoby and D. Olsher (2002). Conversation analysis and applied linguistics. *Annual Review of Applied Linguistics*, 22, 3–31.

Schmitt, N. (2000). *Vocabulary in language teaching*. Cambridge: Cambridge University Press.

Schön, D. A. (1983). *The reflective practitioner: how professionals think in action*. New York: Basic Books.

Schön, D. (1987). *Educating the reflective practitioner: toward a new design for teaching and learning in the professions*. San Francisco, CA: Jossey-Bass.

Seedhouse, P. (1997). The case of the missing 'NO': the relationship between pedagogy and interaction. *Language Learning*, 4(3), 547–583.

Seedhouse, P. (2004). *The interactional architecture of the language classroom: a conversation analysis perspective*. Malden, MA: Blackwell.

Seedhouse, P. (2005). Conversation analysis and language learning. *Language Teaching*, 38(4), 165–187.

Seedhouse, P. (2008). Learning to talk the talk: conversation analysis as a tool for induction of trainee teachers. In S. Garton and K. Richards (Eds) *Professional encounters in TESOL: discourses of teachers in teaching* (pp. 42–57). Basingstoke: Palgrave Macmillan.

Seedhouse, P. and Walsh, S. (2010). Learning a second language through classroom interaction. In P. Seedhouse, S. Walsh and J. Chris (Eds) *Conceptualising 'learning' in applied linguistics* (pp. 127–146). Basingstoke: Palgrave Macmillan.

Seedhouse, P., Walsh, S. and Chris, J. (Eds) (2010). *Conceptualising 'learning' in applied linguistics*. Basingstoke: Palgrave Macmillan.

Sert, O. (2015). *Social interaction and L2 classroom discourse*. Edinburgh: Edinburgh University Press.

Sfard, A. (1998). On two metaphors for learning and the dangers of choosing just one. *Educational Researcher*, 27(1), 4–13.

Shavelson, R. J. (1976). Teacher's decision making. In N. L. Gage (Ed.) *The psychology of teaching methods*. Chicago, IL: NSSE.

Shavelson, R. J. (1983). Review of research on teachers' pedagogical judgement, plans, and decisions. *Elementary School Journal*, 83, 392–413.

Shavelson, R. J. and Stern, P. (1981). Research on teachers' pedagogical thoughts, judgments, decisions, and behavior. *Review of Educational Research*, 51, 455–498.

Shen, J., Zhang, A., Zhang, C., Caldarella, P., Richardson, M. J. and Shatzer, R. H. (2009). Chinese elementary school teachers' perceptions of students' classroom behavior problems. *Educational Psychology*, 29(2), 187–202.

Shulman, L. (1986). Those who understand: knowledge growth in teaching. *Educational Researcher*, 15(2), 4–14.

Shulman, L. S. (1987). Knowledge and teaching: foundations of the new reform, *Harvard Educational Review*, 57(1), 1–22.

Sigel, I. E. (1985). A conceptual analysis of beliefs. In I. E. Sigel (Ed.) *Parental belief systems: the psychological consequences for children* (pp. 345-371). Hillsdale, NJ: Erlbaum.

Silvestri, L. (2001). Pre-service teachers' self-reported knowledge of classroom management. *Education*, 121(3), 575-580.

Sinclair, J. and Coulthard, M. (1975). *Towards an analysis of discourse*. Oxford: Oxford University Press.

Skott, J. (2001, June). Why belief research raises the right question but provides the wrong type of answer. Paper presented at the 3rd Nordic Conference on Mathematics Education, Kristianstad, Sweden.

Speer, N. M. (2005). Issues of methods and theory in the study of mathematics teachers' professed and attributed beliefs. *Educational Studies in Mathematics*, 58(3), 361-391.

Speer, N. M. (2008). Connecting beliefs and practices: a fine-grained analysis of a college mathematics teachers' collections of beliefs and their relationship to his instructional practices. *Cognition and Instruction*, 26(2), 218-267.

Stevick, E. (1982). *Teaching and learning languages*. New York: Cambridge University Press.

Sun, D. (2012). 'Everything goes smoothly': a case study of an immigrant Chinese language teacher's personal practical knowledge. *Teaching and Teacher Education*, 28(5), 760-767.

Svalberg, A. M. L. and Askham, J. (2014). Student teachers' collaborative construction of grammar awareness: the case of a highly competent learner. *Language Awareness*, 23(1-2), 123-137.

Taguchi, N. (2005). Japanese teachers' perceptions and practice of the communicative approach. *Language Teacher*, 29(3), 3-12.

te Molder, H. and Potter, J. (Eds) (2005). *Conversation and cognition*. Cambridge: Cambridge University Press.

Terasaki, A. (2005). Pre-announcement sequences in conversation. In G. Lerner (Ed.) *Conversation analysis: studies from the first generation* (pp. 171-224). Amsterdam, the Netherlands: John Benjamins.

Tharp, R. G. and Gallimore, R. (1988). *Rousing minds to life: teaching, learning and schooling in social context*. Cambridge: Cambridge University Press.

Thompson, A. G. (1992). Teachers' beliefs and conceptions: A synthesis of the research. In D. A. Grouws (Ed.) *Handbook of research on mathematics teaching and learning* (pp. 127-146). New York: Macmillan.

Thornbury, S. (2006). *An A-Z of ELT*. Oxford: Macmillan.

Tillema, H. H. (2000). Belief change towards self-directed learning in student teachers: immersion in practice or reflection on action. *Teaching and Teacher Education*, 16, 575-591.

Timperley, H. and Alton-Lee, A. (2008). Reframing teacher professional learning: an alternative policy approach to strengthening valued outcomes for diverse learners. *Review of Research in Education*, 32, 328-369.

Tochon, F. and Munby, H. (1993). Novice and expert teachers' time epistemology: a wave function from didactics to pedagogy. *Teacher and Teacher Education*, 9(2), 205-218.

Törner, G. (2002). Mathematical beliefs – a search for a common ground: some theoretical considerations on structuring beliefs, some research questions, and some phenomenological observations. In G. C. Leder, E. Pehkonen and G. Törner (Eds) *Beliefs: a hidden variable in mathematics education?* (pp. 73-94). Dordrecht: Kluwer Academic Publishers.

Toth, P. D. (2011). Social and cognitive factors in making teacher-led classroom discourse relevant for L2 grammatical development. *The Modern Language Journal*, 95(1), 1-25.

Tsang, W. K. (2004). Teachers' personal practical knowledge and interactive decisions. *Language Teaching Research*, 8(2), 163-198.

Tsui, A. (1995). *Introducing classroom interaction*. London: Penguin.

Tsui, A. B. M. (2003). *Understanding expertise in teaching*. New York: Cambridge University Press.
Tsui, A. B. M. (2005). Expertise in teaching: perspectives and issues. In K. Johnson (Ed.) *Expertise in second language learning and teaching* (pp. 167–189). Basingstoke: Palgrave Macmillan.
Tsui, A. B. M. (2007). Complexities of identity formation: a narrative inquiry of an EFL teacher. *TESOL Quarterly*, 41, 657–680.
Tsui, A. B. M. (2009). Teaching expertise: approaches, perspectives and characterizations. In A. Burns and J. Richards (Eds) *Second language teacher education* (pp. 190–198). Cambridge: Cambridge University Press.
Tudor, I. (2001). *The dynamics of the language classroom*. Cambridge: Cambridge University Press.
Uhlenbeck, A., Verloop, N. and Beijard, D. (2002). Requirements for an assessment procedure for beginning teachers: implications from recent theories on teaching and assessment. *Teachers College Record*, 104(2), 242–272.
Underwood, R. (2012). Teacher beliefs and intentions regarding the instruction of English grammar under national curriculum reforms: a theory of planned behaviour perspective. *Teaching and Teacher Education*, 12(6), 911–925.
Urzúa, A. and Vásquez, C. (2008). Reflection and professional identity in teachers' future-oriented discourse. *Teaching and Teacher Education*, 24(7), 1935–1946.
van Lier, L. (1988). *The classroom and the language learner. Ethnography and second-language classroom research*. Harlow, UK: Longman.
van Lier, L. (1996). *Interaction in the language curriculum: awareness, autonomy and authenticity*. New York: Longman.
van Lier, L. (2000). From input to affordance: social-interactive learning from an ecological perspective. In J. Lantolf (Ed.) *Sociocultural theory and second language learning* (pp. 245–260). Oxford: Oxford University Press.
van Lier, L. (2004). *The ecology and semiotics of language learning: a sociocultural perspective*. Dordrecht: Kluwer Academic.
Varghese, M., Morgan, B., Johnston, B. and Johnson, K. (2005). Theorizing language teacher identity: three perspectives and beyond. *Journal of Language, Identity, and Education*, 4(1), 21–44.
Vélez-Rendón, G. (2002). Second language teacher education: a review of the literature. *Foreign Language Annals*, 35(4), 457–467.
Verloop, N., Van Driel, J. and Meijer, P. C. (2001). Teacher knowledge and the knowledge base of teaching. *International Journal of Educational Research*, 35(5), 441–461.
Vygotsky, L. S. (1978). *Mind in society*. Cambridge, MA: Harvard University Press.
Vygotsky, L.S. (1981). The genesis of higher mental functions. In J. V. Wertsch (Ed.) *The concept of activity in Soviet psychology* (pp. 144–188). Armonk, NY: M.E. Sharpe.
Vygotsky, L. S. (1986). *Thought and language*. Cambridge, MA: The MIT Press.
Walsh, S. (2002). Construction or Obstruction: teacher talk and learner involvement in the EFL Classroom. *Language Teaching Research*, 6(1), 3–23.
Walsh, S. (2006). *Investigating classroom discourse*. London: Routledge.
Walsh, S. (2011). *Exploring classroom discourse: language in action*. London: Routledge.
Walsh, S. (2013). *Classroom discourse and teacher development*. Edinburgh: Edinburgh University Press.
Walsh, S. and Li, L. (2013). Conversation as space for learning. *International Journal of Applied Linguistics*, 23(2), 244–267.
Waring, H. Z. (2008). Using explicit positive assessment in the language classroom: IRF, feedback, and learning opportunities. *The Modern Language Journal*, 92(4), 577–594.

Waring, H. Z. (2011). Learner initiatives and learning opportunities. *Classroom Discourse*, 2(2), 201–218.

Wegerif, R. (2006). A dialogic understanding of the relationship between CSCL and teaching thinking skills. *International Journal of Computer-Supported Collaborative Learning*, 1(1), 143–157.

Weinstein, C. S. (1989). Teacher education students' perceptions of teaching. *Journal of Teacher Education*, 40(2), 53–60.

Wells, G. (1993). Reevaluating the IRF sequence: a proposal for the articulation of theories of activity and discourse for the analysis of teaching and learning in the classroom. *Linguistics and Education*, 5, 1–37.

Wenden, A. (1986). What do second language learners know about their language learning? A second look at retrospective accounts. *Applied Linguistics*, 7, 186–205.

Wenden, A. (1987). How to be a successful language learner: insights and prescriptions from L2 learners. In A. Wenden and J. Rubin (Eds) *Learner strategies in language learning* (pp. 103–117). London: Prentice Hall.

Wenden, A. (1998). Metacognitive knowledge and language learning. *Applied Linguistics*, 19, 515–537.

Wenden, A. (1999). An introduction to metacognitive knowledge and beliefs in language learning: beyond the basics [Special Issue]. *System*, 27, 435–441.

Wenden, A. (2001). Metacognitive knowledge. In Breen, M. P. (Ed.), *Learner contributions to language learning. New Directions in Research* (pp. 44–64). Harlow, UK: Pearson Education Limited.

Wenger, E. (1998). *Communities of practice: learning, meaning, and identity*. New York: Cambridge University Press.

Wenger, E. (2009). Learning capability in social systems. EQUAL Final Report.

Wertsch, J. (1991). *Voices of the mind: a sociocultural approach to mediated action*. Cambridge, MA: Harvard University Press.

Westerman, D. A. (1991). Expert and novice teacher decision making. *Journal of Teacher Education*, 42(4), 292–305.

Williams, M. and Burden, R. (1997). *Psychology for language teachers*. Cambridge: Cambridge University Press.

Willis, J. (1992). Inner and outer: spoken discourse in the language classroom. In M. Coulthard (Ed.) *Advances in spoken discourse analysis* (pp. 111–122). London: Routledge.

Willis, J. (1996). *A framework for task-based learning*. Harlow: Longman.

Wilson, M. S. and Cooney, T. J. (2002). Mathematics teacher change and development. The role of beliefs. In G. C. Leder, E. Pehkonen and G. Torner (Eds) *Beliefs: a hidden variable in mathematics education?* (pp. 127–148). Dordrecht/Boston/London: Kluwer Academic Publishers.

Wilson, S. M., Floden, R. E. and Ferrini-Mundy, J. (2002). Teacher preparation research: an insider's view from the outside. *Journal of Teacher Education*, 53(3), 190–204.

Wilson, N. and McLean, S. (1994). *Questionnaire design: a practical introduction*. Newtonabbey, Northern Ireland: University of Ulster Press.

Wittrock, M. C. (Ed.) (1986). *Handbook of research on teaching* (3rd edition). New York: Macmillan (pp. 255–296).

Wong, J. and Waring, H. Z. (2009). 'Very good' as a teacher response. *ELT Journal*, 63(3), 195–203.

Wong, J. and Waring, H. Z. (2010). *Conversation analysis and second language pedagogy: a guide for ESL/EFL teachers*. New York: Routledge.

Woods, D. (1991). Teachers' interpretations of second language teaching curricula. *RELC Journal*, 22, 1–19.

Woods, D. (1996). *Teacher cognition in language teaching*. Cambridge: Cambridge University Press.

Woods, D. (2003). The social construction of beliefs in the language classroom. In P. Kalaja and A. Barcelos (Eds), *Beliefs about SLA: new research approaches* (pp. 201–229). Dordrecht/Boston/London: Kluwer Academic Publishers.

Woodward, T. (1986). Loop input – a process idea. *The Teacher Trainer*, I, 6–7.

Woodward, T. (2003). Loop input. *ELT Journal*, 57(3), 301–304.

Wright, T. (2005). *Classroom management in language education*. Basingstoke: Palgrave Macmillan.

Wright, T. (2010). Second language teacher education: review of recent research on practice. *Language Teaching*, 43, 259–296.

Wyatt, M. (2009). Practical knowledge growth in communicative language teaching. *TESL-EJ*, 13(2). Accessed 22 September 2016 at http://www.tesl-ej.org/pdf/ej50/a2.pdf

Xu, S. and Connelly, F. M. (2009). Narrative inquiry for teacher education and development: focus on English as a foreign language in China. *Teaching and Teacher Education*, 25(2), 219–227.

Yang, N. (2000). Teachers' beliefs about language learning and teaching: a cross-cultural comparison. Paper presented at the Texas Foreign Language Education Conference 2000 (TexFLEC 2000), University of Texas at Austin, 31 March–1 April 2000. Accessed 22 September 2016 at http://eric.ed.gov/?id=ED468309

Yin, R. (2009). *Case study research: design and methods* (4th edition). London and Singapore: Sage.

Young, T. J. and Sachdev, I. (2011). Intercultural communicative competence: exploring English language teachers' beliefs and practices. *Language Awareness*, 20, 81–98.

Young, R. F. (2008). *Language and interaction: an advanced resource book*. London and New York: Routledge.

Zeichner, K. M., Tabachnik, B. R. and Densmore, K. (1987). Individual, institutional, and cultural influences on the development of teachers' craft knowledge. In J. Calderhead (Ed.) *Exploring teachers' thinking* (pp. 21–59). London: Cassell.

Zembylas, M. (2002). Constructing genealogies of teachers' emotions in science teaching. *Journal of Research in Science Teaching*, 39, 79–103.

Zembylas, M. (2003). Interrogating 'teacher identity': emotion, resistance and self-formation. *Educational Theory*, 53, 107–127.

Zembylas, M. (2005). Beyond teacher cognition and teacher beliefs: the value of the ethnography of emotions in teaching. *International Journal of Qualitative Studies in Education*, 18(4), 465–487.

Zembylas, M. (2007). Emotional ecology: the intersection of emotional knowledge and pedagogical content knowledge in teaching. *Teaching and Teacher Education*, 23(4), 355–367.

Zuengler, J. (2011). Many lessons from a school: what classroom discourse analysis reveals. *Language Teaching*, 44(1), 55–63.

INDEX

accuracy, 46, 68–9, 93, 107–8, 125, 163, 165, 172
affordances, 171
agency, 193
approaches
  cognitive, 35, 39
  communicative, 60, 70, 85, 102, 111, 162
  contextual, 35, 41, 44
  discovery-based, 162
  ecological, 171
  emic, 175
  function-based, 40
  grammar-oriented, 175
  grounded, 61, 175
  learner-centred, 181
  metacognitive, 35
  methodological, 34–5, 40
  normative, 35
  psychological, 70, 161, 181
  research-based, 183
  social, 60, 187
  student-centred, 110–11
  top-down, 105
assessment, 7, 14, 19, 44, 90, 108, 142, 178, 184
assumptions and knowledge, 17
attitudes, 6, 9, 15, 18–19, 24–5, 31–2, 38, 56, 58, 66, 77, 161
authoritative role, 2, 99, 156, 167
autonomy, 4, 14, 164
awareness
  cognitive, 150
  metacognitive, 127

BAK, 17–18
BALLI (Beliefs about Language Learning Inventory), 35–7, 76
behaviours, 3–4, 13–15, 24–5, 27, 29, 31, 39, 46, 48, 50, 126–7, 147, 157, 164, 179
belief construction, 60
belief development, 9, 70, 76
beliefs, 2, 5–7, 9, 13–15, 17–21, 23–46, 48–52, 54–6, 58–67, 69, 75–8, 80, 103, 161–5, 194–5
  articulated, 41, 45–6, 49
  attributed, 49
  change, 33
  enacted/attributed, 28
  espoused, 43
  established, 76
  individual's, 42–3
  nature of, 35, 44
  overarching, 32, 61
  personal, 52
  preconceived, 15
  pre-existing, 59, 76
  prior, 20
  rooted, 39, 135
  socio-cultural educational, 135
  stated/espoused, 39
  teacher's, 18, 28, 62
beliefs and knowledge, 25–6, 31, 54
beliefs and practice, 28–31, 41, 46, 49, 165
beliefs-in-action, 43
Beliefs Inventory, 36, 39–41
belief systems, 17, 27–8, 44, 184
  pre-existing, 76

CA (conversation analysis), 1, 4, 9, 32, 35, 44, 52, 57–8, 60, 161, 194
CDRP (Collaborative Dialogic Reflective Practice), 187–8
CIC (classroom interactional competence), 88, 96, 119–20, 134, 180–1
classroom discourse, 45, 90–1, 136, 167, 170
classroom interaction, 3, 43, 45–6, 56, 66–7, 94, 119–21, 137, 152, 166, 170, 181, 186
classroom interaction structures, 166, 169, 175
classroom management, 29, 42, 77, 102, 106, 125–6, 133–4, 179
classroom observation, 44–5, 105
classroom participation, 126, 166
classroom pedagogy, 27
CLT (communicative language teaching), 23, 26, 49, 85, 163–5, 175
cognition, 3, 9–10, 18–20, 30–4, 44–5, 48–50, 52–6, 58, 60–1, 70–1, 75, 77–8, 175–6, 192, 194–5
  distributed, 56–8, 157

218

cognition and conversation, 71
cognition development, 55, 183
cognition-in-interaction, 3, 32, 50, 56, 67, 78, 161, 169, 184, 194–5
cognitive apprenticeship, 183, 185
cognitive perspective, 30–1, 33, 35, 52, 58, 61
cognitive processes, 39, 171
collaboration, 20, 42, 168, 184, 187, 190
community
  professional, 20, 186
  social learning, 168
competence, intercultural, 13
complexity, 7, 31, 34, 39–41, 56, 63, 112, 136, 166, 172, 183, 186, 190
conceptions, 18–19, 24–6, 49, 53–4, 56, 58–9, 70, 75, 78, 106–9, 133, 135, 164–5, 177–8, 181
conceptualising, 3–4, 56, 75, 107, 176, 184, 191, 194–5
content knowledge, 76, 84, 107, 177
  disciplinary, 77
  insufficient, 80
content subject knowledge, 22
context approach, 166
contexts, 3–9, 17–24, 26–7, 29–31, 34–6, 40–2, 52–4, 67–8, 75–6, 106–8, 113–14, 163–7, 179–82, 186–7, 191–2
  cultural, 192
  educational, 20, 40, 77, 194
  historical, 20
  institutional, 7, 29
  mental, 7
  moment-by-moment, 194
  practical, 7
  pragmatic, 7
  psychological, 31, 54
  real-life, 43, 119
  socio-cultural, 38
  static, 6
contextual factors, 7, 18–20, 29, 41, 49, 65, 114, 180, 192, 194
contextual knowledge, 107–8, 111, 113–14, 116, 133, 180, 195
conversation and cognition, 52, 71
conversation space, 156
corrective feedback, 37, 91, 93, 123, 144, 154, 172
critical reflection, 182, 186–8
cultural knowledge, 99, 155, 157
  insufficient, 130–1
culture, 4–5, 8, 29, 36, 39, 42–4, 80, 99, 114, 116, 134, 178, 180
  institutional, 20
  local, 116
curriculum, 7, 20, 27–8, 30, 50, 67, 77, 107–9, 114, 121, 128, 135–6, 178, 180, 192–3
curriculum knowledge, 77

decision-making, 3, 8–9, 14–15, 17–19, 27–8, 59–60, 111–12, 114, 117, 135–7, 156–7, 172, 174, 189–90, 194–5
decision-making process, 136, 175
definition of beliefs, 24–5
deliberate choices, 183
deliberate practice, 105, 109, 182
developing disciplinary knowledge, 103
developing learning strategy, 134
developing pedagogical knowledge, 78, 85, 99
dialogic, 180, 187–90
dialogic interaction, 124, 152
dialogic spaces, 169
discourse analysis, 9, 32, 41, 45, 191
discourse marker, 63, 70, 82, 87, 89, 101, 145, 147–8, 150
discrepancies, 20, 28–31, 49
discursive, 9, 30, 32–3, 50, 52, 55–7, 59–60, 62, 70, 75, 102–3, 161, 166, 175–6, 181–2
discursive approaches, 53
discursive psychological perspective, 31, 55
display questions, 121, 168
divergence, 7, 20, 43
DP (discursive psychology), 8–9, 31–2, 35, 52–4, 56–8, 60, 70–1, 165–6, 172, 194–5
DP perspective, 35, 54, 66, 70, 167, 172
DP perspective beliefs, 32
DP perspective cognition, 52

effective learning, 179
effective pedagogy, 4, 13, 77, 166, 192
EFL (English as a Foreign Language), 4, 6
emotional knowledge, 108–9
emotions, 56, 90
engagement, 9, 67, 88, 105, 135, 150, 165, 170, 175, 179
evaluation, 26, 92, 120, 124, 170–1, 188
exchange, 48, 85, 90–1, 98–9, 102, 122, 128, 133, 140–1, 156, 167
experience, 19–20, 22–4, 26, 55–6, 63, 65, 82–4, 89–90, 105, 109–10, 112, 131–2, 178, 181–2, 185
expertise, 9, 104–6, 109, 111, 117, 119, 128, 131–2, 134, 152, 154, 172–5, 179, 181–2, 195
  developing, 104–5, 182
  distributed, 106
  multiple, 106, 128
experts, 71, 77, 104–7, 128, 130–1, 171, 174, 176, 182, 189
expert teachers, 9, 104–9, 111–14, 116–17, 119–24, 126–8, 130, 133–4, 136, 172, 174, 179, 182, 189–90

feedback, 68–9, 85, 89–91, 94, 101, 103, 112, 119–24, 141, 144, 162, 166–7, 170–1, 175, 188
  direct, 123, 172

feedback (cont.)
  dis-preferred, 90, 92
  embedded, 125
  giving, 85, 90, 97
  immediate, 125
  indirect, 2, 94
  lack of, 90–1, 139
  negative, 91, 124
feedback/evaluation, 45
feedback move, 92–4, 122, 171
feedback strategies, 94, 115, 124, 154
flexibility, 86, 108–9, 111, 119, 123, 128, 131–3, 149, 152, 154, 182
  lack of, 109–10
focus, pedagogical, 107, 138, 145–6, 157

glossing, 139–40, 142, 146, 157, 174
good interactive decisions, 24, 135
grammar, 2, 13, 27, 37–9, 42–3, 57, 62–3, 79–80, 82–3, 102, 163, 165, 177, 179
grammar learning, 149, 165
grammar rules, 27, 40, 98, 179
grammar teaching, 2, 38, 43
grammar work, explicit, 38, 165
gross categorisation, 54

hesitation marker, 79, 97, 140, 142

identity, 14, 23, 58, 82, 95, 103, 192–5
  collective, 98
  multiple, 192
  non-native speaker, 193
  professional, 102, 193–4
identity construction, 192
identity development, 97
identity formation, 192
identity-in-discourse, 193
identity shifts, 192
ideology, 4–6, 14, 24–5, 78, 80, 82, 126, 180
IDRF (Initiation-Dialogic space-Response-Feedback), 169
Initiation-Dialogic space-Response-Feedback (IDRF), 169
inquiry, 2, 4, 34, 40, 77, 176
instructional decisions, 13, 28, 100, 166, 178
instructional practices, 10, 39, 41, 166, 175, 190, 193
instructions, 8, 77, 86, 92, 94, 101–2, 108, 120, 126, 148, 162, 186, 189, 194
  knowledge of, 23, 48
insufficient knowledge, 85, 128, 130, 134, 137, 148, 155, 157, 178
insufficient subject knowledge, 99, 178
interaction, 2–3, 5–9, 17–20, 31–3, 42–8, 52–69, 75, 77–8, 80, 103–8, 119–21, 166–72, 180–1, 188, 191–4

interactional analysis, 4, 44, 46, 48, 71
interactional competence, 87, 119–20, 133, 154, 168, 181, 191, 193
interactional organisations, 58
interactional patterns, 14, 122–3
interactional strategies, 2, 75, 119–20, 125, 132–4, 141–2, 157, 170–1, 174–5, 181
interactional structure, 120, 122, 167
  language-focused, 162
interactional work, 53, 82, 89, 134, 142, 147, 154, 170, 172, 194
interactionist, 30–1, 33, 45, 48
interaction patterns, 8, 177
interactive decisions, 9, 17, 20, 23–4, 50, 95, 135–8, 145, 149–52, 155–8, 162, 172–4, 189, 195
  making, 87, 150, 157, 174
interactive process, 20
interactive work, 93–4, 144
intersubjectivity, 4, 57
inter-subjectivity, 9
IRF, spiral, 122, 169
IRF (Initiation-Response-Feedback), 43, 90, 121–2, 166, 168
ITRF, 168

knowing, 3–4, 54, 56, 59, 61, 75, 77, 85–6, 103, 108, 176, 178, 180, 189–92, 194–5
knowledge, 8–9, 17–23, 25–8, 40, 54–6, 59, 75–80, 90–1, 102–4, 106–12, 132–3, 174–7, 179–82, 184–6, 193–5
  acquiring, 55, 162
  articulated, 64
  background, 23
  cognitive, 36
  collective, 163
  contextualised, 108
  disciplinary, 78, 108
  explicit, 38
  fixed, 64
  formal, 23
  integrated, 108–9
  interrelated, 107
  legitimate, 182
  metacognitive, 35
  practical, 22–3, 48, 77, 109, 117, 182
  practical pedagogic, 111
  prior, 21, 108, 116
  procedural, 26, 77
  subject-content, 182
knowledge and beliefs, 9, 17–18, 25–6, 45, 50, 59, 80
knowledge base, 77–8, 80, 182
knowledge-base, 184
knowledge capacity, 178
knowledge co-construction, 168
knowledge construction, 22
knowledge domains, 98, 106–7

knowledge growth
  investigated practical, 23
  practical, 184
knowledge source, 7, 80, 99, 177
knowledge transmission, 162, 167, 193
Kolb's experiential learning, 20

language awareness, 177, 190–1
language knowledge, 107, 178, 190, 193
language learning beliefs, 37, 41
language teaching, 1, 4, 9, 36, 42, 50, 61, 75, 77, 82, 164, 166
learner contributions, unexpected, 138–9, 145, 156
learner identities, 165
learner-initiation, 146
learner involvement, 47
learner participation, 170–1, 181
learners, knowledge of, 48, 77
learning
  experiential, 21, 56
  knowledge-based, 179, 184
learning environment, 5, 170, 177, 185
learning experience, 18, 181
  personal, 55, 183
learning process, 102, 165, 169–71
learning strategy, 42, 127, 152, 157
learning styles, 7, 22, 29, 77, 111, 117, 179
linguistic knowledge, 40, 100, 113, 165, 175
long-term learning opportunities, 128, 174

macro-context, 7, 114, 131, 136, 163, 177
metacognitive strategies, 152, 157
meta-knowledge, 191
metalanguage, 102, 179
metaphors, 18, 22–3, 41, 135, 161
methodology, 7, 28, 34–5, 45, 53, 136, 165, 194
methods, instructional, 78
micro-analysis, 61
micro-contexts, 6–7, 50, 57, 84, 114, 117, 131, 136, 155–7, 162–3, 166, 192
  interrelated, 170
misbehaviour, 126–7, 179
misconceptions, 20, 35, 59–60
moment-by-moment thinking, 3, 182, 190

narrative inquiry, 22, 77
narratives, 22, 41
non-expert, 105, 182
novice and expert, 104, 120, 189
novice and expert teachers, 9, 104–6, 133, 182
novice teachers, 86, 88, 104–7, 109–11, 114–16, 119–21, 123, 126–8, 131–4, 179, 182, 189–90
  learning phase, 127
novice teacher's thinking, 111

observation, apprenticeship of, 37, 75

participation opportunity, immediate, 133
pedagogical awareness, 33
pedagogical beliefs, 25, 38
pedagogical content knowledge, 77, 107
pedagogical decisions, 111
  making, 86, 111
pedagogical effectiveness, 2
pedagogical goals, 58, 87, 92–5, 119–20, 135, 137–8, 146, 154, 156, 162–4, 170, 172, 174–5, 181, 183
pedagogical goals priority, 174
pedagogical knowledge, 10, 55, 77, 85–7, 98–9, 107–9, 111, 133, 175, 177, 179–80, 184–5, 190, 195
  practical, 117
pedagogical knowledge domains, 107
pedagogical practice, 28, 42
pedagogical principle, 164
pedagogical purposes, 121–2, 125
pedagogical reality, 7
pedagogical understanding, 166
pedagogy
  learner-centred, 109
  student-centred, 110
peer reflection, 81
perceptions, 6–7, 13–14, 23–5, 35, 38–9, 49, 53–6, 61, 126, 157, 164
personal experience, 23, 64, 89–90, 131, 183–4, 192, 195
personal knowledge, 55, 77, 177
  practical, 181
personal practical knowledge, 18, 22–3, 47–8, 77, 181, 189
perspectives, 5–6, 8, 22, 25–6, 28, 30–2, 45, 52, 54–6, 162–3, 166–7, 169–70, 175–6, 181, 183
  cognitive-based, 8, 30
  interactionist, 8, 30–1, 35, 44–5
  social interactional, 92
  socio-cultural, 20, 171, 183
positive assessment, 84, 92–3, 97–8, 142
positive feedback, 92, 113–14, 119, 123, 133, 154
preconceptions, 18–19, 25
pre-service teacher cognition development, 76
pre-service teachers, 9, 20, 37, 75–8, 81, 97, 100, 103, 137, 177–8, 184
process, 14–17, 19–21, 27, 29, 52–6, 58–9, 61, 68, 76–7, 97, 102–3, 168–9, 176–7, 181–2, 189–91
  experiential, 77, 176
professional contexts, 4–5, 8–10, 42, 52, 75, 90, 104, 117, 161, 163, 180, 191–2, 194–5
professional development, 10, 15, 18, 21, 27–8, 38, 56, 61, 67, 161, 184–6, 192, 195
professional knowledge, 23, 77, 95, 186–7
  formal, 22
professional knowledge landscapes, 22

professional learning, 20, 75, 91, 183–8, 191, 195
psychological perspective, 9, 32–3, 50, 52, 55–7, 59, 62, 64, 70, 75, 166, 175–6, 182, 186, 190

reflection-in-action, 20–1, 109, 117, 174–5
reflection-on-action, 21, 109
reflective approach, 187–8, 190
reflective practice, 20, 106, 176, 186–7
 data-led, 186–7
research methodologies, 22, 30, 35, 44
research strategy, 34, 43–4, 69

scaffolding, 120, 171–2, 183, 188–90
schemata, 17, 24, 103
school culture, 20, 29–30, 114–15, 192
SCT (sequence-closing third), 90–1
second language teacher education (SLTE), 15, 176–7, 183
self-reflection, 9, 78, 135
sequence-closing third *see* SCT
series of interactional events, 3, 66
shared understanding, 28, 32, 49, 56–7, 63–4, 69–70, 81–2, 140, 163, 169
SLA (second language acquisition), 34–5, 78
social interaction, 3–4, 9, 20, 31, 52–3, 78, 161, 192, 194
social practice, 54, 75, 78, 82–4, 112, 163, 168, 175, 178, 190–1, 193
socio-cultural space, 14
socio-cultural theory, 20
student knowledge, 87, 132, 149
student participation, 21, 92, 132, 152, 168, 171
student teacher cognition, 85, 184
student teachers, 9, 23, 26, 36–9, 47–8, 76, 78, 80–91, 93–6, 98–100, 102–3, 179, 181, 184, 189
subject content knowledge, 55, 184
subject knowledge, 8, 61, 80, 84, 98–100, 102–3, 107–9, 131, 133, 167, 177–9, 184, 190, 193, 195
subject matter knowledge, 23
symbiotic relationships, 29, 43

talk-in-interaction, 4, 60, 182
target knowledge, 95, 98, 149–50, 152, 157
task authenticity, 89
task-based language teaching (TBLT), 164
task design, 14
task performance, 105
TBLT (task-based language teaching), 164
teacher beliefs, 69, 166
teacher cognition, 3–4, 7–10, 13–16, 18–20, 29–35, 39–41, 47–61, 63–5, 69–71, 75–7, 161–6, 176–7, 180–1, 183–6, 190–5
 domains of, 15, 52

study of language, 8, 34
teacher cognition-in-interaction, 33, 176, 191, 195
teacher education
 in-service, 23, 188
 pre-service, 103, 190
teacher identity, 76, 103, 192–4
teacher knowledge, 4, 20–3, 25–6, 76–7, 176–7, 179, 183, 190–1
teacher learning, 3–4, 10, 13, 15, 18, 20–1, 77, 87, 103–4, 176–7, 183, 185, 188, 190–1, 195
teacher repetition, 90–2
teachers
 experienced, 37, 43, 105, 128, 155, 182
 interaction display, 3
 interactive choices, 24
teachers' beliefs, 24, 26, 28, 170
teacher's beliefs/thinking, 1
teachers' knowledge, 181
teachers' knowledge and beliefs, 20, 28, 45, 76, 98
teachers' thought processes, 16
teacher's understanding, 61, 162, 176
teachers' understanding and beliefs, 164–5, 194
teacher thinking, 21, 26, 55, 60
teaching approach, 28, 110–11
teaching behaviours, 44, 50, 75, 127, 134
teaching content, 108–10
teaching experience, 26, 29, 50, 109, 117, 181–2
teaching methodology, 7, 27, 163–5, 175, 179
teaching methods, 10, 27, 83, 85–6, 115, 163–4, 175, 179
teaching process, 13, 17
theories-in-use, 173–4
thinking
 contemporary, 18
 critical, 186
 reflective, 21, 168, 180
 theoretical, 177, 190
 traditional, 30
thinking-in-action, 59
thinking processes, 15, 55
thinking skills, 168–9
thinking space, 168

understandings and beliefs, 9, 52, 67, 162
understanding talk-in-interaction, 32, 57
unexpected contributions, 137–8, 141
unexpected learning contributions, 157

values, 1–4, 7, 24, 27, 29–30, 40, 42, 44, 52, 56, 76–7, 81, 115–16, 161, 165
video-based reflection, 60, 69, 91, 189
vocabulary, 6, 37, 39, 43, 62–3, 68–9, 82, 98, 103, 108–9, 111, 113, 125, 128, 163